MORE PRAISE FOR
MEASURING THE NETWORKED NONPROFIT

"Kanter and Paine use their wit and wisdom to make the process of measuring your impact and making change accessible, and even fun!"

—**Holly Ross,** executive director, NTEN

"Social change organizations just got a yard stick for measuring success and learning from failure."

—**Premal Shah,** president, Kiva—Loans That Change Lives

"The book is an invaluable roadmap for moving to data-informed decision-making and producing greater impact for those they serve."

—**Mario Morino,** chairman, Venture Philanthropy Partners

"Kanter and Paine share a wealth of insights and practical advice that will enable organizations to truly understand the real impact of their digital and social efforts."

—**Jean Case,** CEO and cofounder, Case Foundation

"This book is a gift for those facing the task of measuring nonprofit performance in our complex, interconnected age."

—**Jacob Harold,** program officer, William and Flora Hewlett Foundation

"This must-read book for the sector shows how simple yet powerful measurement can help a nonprofit effectively get actionable information to increase impact."

—**Dr. Akhtar Badshah,** senior director, Citizenship and Public Affairs, Microsoft

"As nonprofits devote increasing energy to social media, getting measurement right is critical to helping us learn and impact. This book unpacks this daunting subject in a practical and actionable way."

—**Stephen J. Downs,** Chief Technology and Information Officer, Robert Wood Johnson Foundation

"*Measuring the Networked Nonprofit* is more than a 'how-to,' it's a citizen's owners manual for making change happen."

—**Lucy Bernholz,** visiting scholar, Stanford University
Center on Philanthropy and Civil Society

"The need to understand how to leverage social networks for measurable impact has never been greater. This pioneering book on the critical topic of measurement will be essential for any nonprofit seeking to be truly effective."

—**Jennifer Aaker,** General Atlantic Professor of Marketing,
Winnick Family Faculty Fellow for 2011–2012, and
Vineet Singal, Stanford alumnus and leader, 100KCheeks campaign

"The combination of nonprofit social media savoire faire and superior measurement discipline in *Measuring the Networked Nonprofit* makes for an unparalleled discussion about organizational performance."

—**Geoff Livingston,** author and marketing strategist

"This book belongs on the shelf of every nonprofit leader. The authors do a great job of clearly laying out practical advice for social media measurement."

—**Ritu Sharma** and **Darian Rodriguez Heyman,**
cofounders, Social Media for Nonprofits

"Finally, a user-friendly guide to demystifying measurement, why it matters, and how nonprofits can take it on."

—**Laura L. Efurd,** Chief Strategy and Innovation
Officer, ZeroDivide

"Data is like fine food: you can enjoy eating it but do you know how to make it? The authors have written the ultimate cookbook!"

—**Nancy Lublin,** DoSomething.org

"Kanter and Paine present a comprehensive and welcome addition to the social network knowledge base that will serve to awaken the data geek in all of us, tempting us to explore both new tools and networks, while also inspiring us to assess the impact of how these networks are contributing toward our missions and the greater good."

—**Janet Camarena,** director, Foundation Center—San Francisco

"Attention everyone who is using social media to do good in the world: This book is your must-have survival guide to measuring what matters."

—**Katya Andresen,** COO, Network for Good and author,
Robin Hood Marketing

"Hi, I'm Daniel and I'm a recovering measurementaphobic. This book helped me break down walls I had built for forty years."
—**Daniel Ben-Horin,** founder and co-CEO, TechSoup Global

"Accelerating external change coupled with new tools for engagement challenges even the most networked nonprofits in making sense of feedback around complex issues. This book is as much about leadership as it is about measuring."
—**Jeff Clarke,** interim president and CEO, Council on Foundations

"A timely and valuable contribution to the evaluation, learning, and improvement movement in the social sector."
—**Johanna Morariu,** director, Innovation Network

"This book will be a catalyst for nonprofits to power social change because it explains clearly how to use measurement."
—**Wendy Harman,** American Red Cross

"*Measuring the Networked Nonprofit* teaches organizations of all sizes how to be obsessed with impact—for good."
—**Claire Díaz-Ortiz (née Williams),** Social Innovation

"If you want to unlock the power of data and measurement to dramatically scale your engagement, fundraising, and impact, this book is your *must buy, must read, must apply.*"
—**Simon Mainwaring,** founder, We First and *New York Times* bestselling author of *We First*

"If you work in any capacity in the nonprofit sector and think impact measurement is just another burdensome task, this book is for you. It is a guide to finding the joy and inspiration in evaluating the impact of our work."
—**Cheryl Francisconi,** director, Institute of International Education, Ethiopia

"Data driven improvements that deliver an emotional punch and improve the bottom-line? Absolutely! Let Katie and Beth show you how it's done."
—**Avinash Kaushik,** author, *Web Analytics 2.0* and *Web Analytics: An Hour A Day*

"Paine and Kanter have created a mind-blowingly useful, practical, valuable guide to making the most of social media for every non-profit interested in getting better at doing good."
—**Jim Sterne,** founder, eMetrics Marketing Optimization Summit and chairman, Digital Analytics Association

"This book is a must-read for all nonprofits who care about creating change."

—**Allyson Kapin,** partner at Rad Campaign

"This timely and practical book will help networked nonprofits untangle measurement and the big, hairy 'social media ROI' question."

—**Steve Bridger,** Builder of Bridges

"Nonprofit managers and philanthropists will find practical and insightful recipes and examples for measurement programs that will help their efforts rise above the noise and create real social change."

—**Kami Watson Huyse,** CEO, Zoetica

"One of the biggest challenges of leveraging networked approaches to social change is the challenge of measurement. Well, no longer. Thankfully Kanter— the smartest person on this topic—has come to our rescue with a thoughtful, well-informed approach to 'measuring the networked nonprofit' that can help us all assess our results, and continuously learn and adapt to increase our impact."

—**Heather McLeod Grant,** consultant,
The Monitor Institute and author, *Forces for Good:
The Six Practices of High-Impact Nonprofits*

"People always ask me what's next in social media for social change, and now the answer is simple: *Measuring the Networked Nonprofit!* This book is exactly what we need, a simple, clear, easy-to-use primer on measuring the use and effect of social media for nonprofits from the two most knowledgeable people on the topic. It's exactly what we needed when we needed it most."

—**Allison Fine,** coauthor, *The Networked Nonprofit*

"Beth Kanter is widely recognized in the nonprofit sector as the go-to person for understanding both how to use and the implications of social media. With this book, she answers the hardest of our burning questions: 'But how do I know if my social media strategy is working?' A must-read for leaders, practitioners, and strategists."

—**Deanna Zandt,** author of *Share This!
How You Will Change the World With Social Networking*

Measuring the
Networked Nonprofit

Measuring the Networked Nonprofit

USING DATA TO CHANGE THE WORLD

Beth Kanter and
Katie Delahaye
Paine

Edited by
William T. Paarlberg

Foreword by Laura
Arrillaga-Andreessen

JOSSEY-BASS
A Wiley Imprint
www.josseybass.com

Published by Jossey-Bass A Wiley Imprint One Montgomery Street, Suite 1200, San Francisco, CA 94104-4594–www.josseybass.com

Jossey-Bass books and products are available through most bookstores. To contact Jossey-Bass directly call our Customer Care Department within the U.S. at 800-956-7739, outside the U.S. at 317-572-3986, or fax 317-572-4002.

Wiley also publishes its books in a variety of electronic formats and by print-on-demand. Not all content that is available in standard print versions of this book may appear or be packaged in all book formats. If you have purchased a version of this book that did not include media that is referenced by or accompanies a standard print version, you may request this media by visiting http://booksupport.wiley.com. For more information about Wiley products, visit us www.wiley.com.

Library of Congress Cataloging-in-Publication Data

Kanter, Beth, 1957–
    Measuring the networked nonprofit : using data to change the world / by Beth Kanter and Katie Delahaye Paine ; edited by William T. Paarlberg.—First edition.
       pages cm
    Includes bibliographical references and index.
    ISBN 978-1-118-13760-4 (paper), ISBN 978-1-118-26347-1 (ebk.), ISBN 978-1-118-23881-3 (ebk.), ISBN 978-1-118-22541-7 (ebk.)
      1. Nonprofit organizations.   2. Social networks.   I. Delahaye Paine, Katie, 1952–   II. Paarlberg, William T.   III. Title.
    HD62.6.K358   2012
    658.5'036—dc23

                                  2012016809

Printed in the United States of America
FIRST EDITION
PB Printing   10 9 8 7 6 5 4 3 2 1

CONTENTS

Figures and Tables   xi

Foreword by Laura Arrillaga-Andreessen   xiii

Preface: The Queen of Nonprofits Meets the Goddess of Measurement   xvii

Acknowledgments   xxiii

The Authors   xxvii

PART ONE: Introduction of Concepts   1

ONE The Secret Sauce for Nonprofits: Networked
Strategies + Measurement = Amazing Success   3

TWO The Rise of the Networked Nonprofit: A New
Paradigm for Nonprofit Success   13

PART TWO: Basic Measurement Principles, How-Tos,
and Best Practices   27

THREE Creating a Data-Informed Culture: How Your Organization
Can Embrace the Data and Use What It Can Teach You   29

FOUR Measurement Is Power: How to Take Control
of Your Programs and Progress with the Art and
Science of Measurement   41

FIVE Don't Confuse Activity with Results: The Value of
Expressing Your Results in Terms of Organizational Goals   59

SIX The Ladder of Engagement: How to Measure Engagement and Use It to Improve Relationships with Your Stakeholders   77

SEVEN How to Turn Your Stakeholders into Fundraisers: Social Fundraising and How Measurement Can Make It More Effective   99

EIGHT Measurement Tools: How to Choose and Use the Right Tool for the Job   119

NINE Measurement and the Aha! Moment: Using Your Data to Tell Stories, Make Decisions, and Change the World   151

PART THREE: Advanced Measurement Concepts and Practices for Networked Nonprofits   171

TEN Measuring What Really Matters: The Importance and Measurement of Relationships   173

ELEVEN Understanding, Visualizing, and Improving Networks   187

TWELVE Influence Measurement: How to Determine Your Influence and That of Your Organization, Free Agents, and Nonprofit Champions   203

THIRTEEN How to Be Naked and Measure It: Transparency Is a Networked Nonprofit's Best Friend   221

FOURTEEN Measuring the Impact of the Crowd   235

Epilogue: With Measurement and Learning, Networked Nonprofits Can Change the World   245
Appendix A: Measuring Relationships and Relationship Research   247
Appendix B: Crawl, Walk, Run, Fly Assessment Tool for Networked Nonprofits   251
Appendix C: Social Media Measurement Checklist   255
Appendix D: A Checklist for Monitoring Services   261
Notes   269
Glossary   281
Resources for Tools, Tutorials, and Assistance   287
Index   289

FIGURES AND TABLES

FIGURES

1.1	Carie Lewis and Bella Celebrate	4
1.2	The HSUS's Million Fan Campaign Facebook Page	6
2.1	Wendy Harman Tweets About the American Red Cross	16
5.1	The Theory of Change of Grantmakers for Effective Organizations	73
6.1	Grist's Ladder of Engagement	80
6.2	Farming Is the New Hipster Occupation of Choice	83
6.3	Invisible Dogs Pledge Form	89
7.1	Autism Speaks' E-Mail Open Rates	106
8.1	NTEN Journal Survey	124
8.2	Feeding America's: Social Listening Dashboard	132
8.3	Feeding America's Facebook Tracking	141
9.1	A Hospital's Spider Chart	154
9.2	The Humane Society's Infographic to Report Results	165
9.3	Beth Kanter's Facebook Insights Dashboard	166
11.1	Social Network Analysis Map of Tech Soup	197
11.2	Using Sticky Notes to Map National Wildlife Foundation's Social Network	199
12.1	Keywords That the Blue Key Campaign Used to Identify Influencers in Traackr	210
12.2	Blue Key Campaign Metrics for Tracking Twitter Data	212
12.3	The Blue Key Team Uses Google Analytics to Analyze Web Traffic	213

TABLES

4.1	Matching Measurement Tools with Objectives	52
5.1	Planning the Value of Social Media	68
8.1	Selecting Measurement Tools to Measure Your Goals	122
8.2	Comparison of Survey Tools	127
8.3	Comparison of Manual and Automated Media Content Analysis	133
B.1	Crawl, Walk, Run, Fly Assessment Tool	251

FOREWORD

When I think of innovation, three things come to mind: the creation of something new, the renewal of something that already exists, and the emergence of new thinking around existing processes and systems. What's exciting is that I see all three at work in the nonprofit sector today. It's a thrilling time. A new culture of innovation is sweeping across the philanthropic landscape, bringing with it dramatically increased potential for social change. Yet the onus is on us—the individuals who work in and support nonprofits— to help that culture establish deep roots. This means building the kind of robust measurement metrics that will empower us to take a hard look at what works and what does not—and then to use that information as the basis for innovation.

As a philanthropist, social entrepreneur, and academic based in Palo Alto, California, I find myself sitting at the epicenter of innovation: Silicon Valley. I watch enthralled as every day, new technologies, apps, software, and platforms enter our lives, disrupting the old ways and transforming how we work, connect, interact, and give. I see innovation everywhere, and not only among Silicon Valley's new generation of tech entrepreneurs. It's also present in the brilliant young minds of the students I teach at Stanford University and its Graduate School of Business, in the approaches to problem solving taken by my partners at SV2 (Silicon Valley Social Venture Fund, the venture philanthropy partnership that I founded), and in the compelling research that informs practice at Stanford PACS (the Center on Philanthropy and Civil Society, which I created and of which I am now chair).

Yet in the world of philanthropy, we often fail to apply innovation to solving social problems. That's because we rarely find out how our money is being spent, where it's going to end up, or how it will move the needle on the problems we want to help solve. Innovation is all about finding a better way of doing things. But if you want to find a better way of traveling from where you are now to where you want to be, you need to start by analyzing your current route before you can think about how to improve on it.

The trouble is that our giving tends to be emotionally driven. A 2010 study found that about 65 percent of all individual giving (which makes up more than 80 percent of all American philanthropy) has no research behind it.[1] It's not that we're not generous—far from it. In 2010 Americans gave more than $290 billion and volunteered over 8 billion hours. More than 1.5 million nonprofits, from large, endowed institutions to small, grassroots organizations, worked tirelessly to make our communities and world a better place. The problem is that we are not maximizing the potential of this generosity.

When donors give without any proof of impact or trying to understand precisely how their gifts bring about change, we put drastic limits on our philanthropic potential. When we give purely based on emotion, we also leave the nonprofits we fund with no incentive to measure or understand that impact. That's a lose-lose-lose situation: as donors, we lose the chance to improve our giving by making informed decisions; as nonprofit leaders, we lose the chance to make the programs and services we provide more effective; and as citizens of this planet, we lose out on the chance to live in a better world.

There could hardly be a better moment for a book such as this. In her valuable book, *The Networked Nonprofit*, Beth Kanter and her cowriter, Allison Fine, showed nonprofit leaders across all generations how to use social media for social good.[2] Now, in *Measuring the Networked Nonprofit*, Beth Kanter and Katie Paine have given us a must-read guide for anyone using social media and other tools to improve their work and increase their accountability.

Social change is not about what we hope we achieve but how we are going to achieve it. What is so powerful about *Measuring the Networked Nonprofit* is that not only does it provide a set of tools for using measurement and data; it also explains how to measure the effectiveness of the different ways of achieving social change.

This book appears at a critical moment. Because of the rapid advance of technology, our world is changing at a pace that's faster than ever before, and this rate of change is constantly accelerating. Over the past decade, the philanthropic sector has undergone the most profound evolution since modern philanthropy's invention more than a century ago. And of all the changes we've witnessed, perhaps the most radical has emerged in the place where technology, innovation, and philanthropy intersect.

The way we engage in meaningful social change is being fundamentally altered by technology. Technology is increasing access to information and connecting us in ways never before possible. It's transforming the way we approach problem solving. It's making it possible to reach billions of people globally through online giving platforms. It's democratizing our ability to make the world a better place, and social media are among the most powerful technological forces behind this phenomenon.

When it comes to connecting with donors—particularly younger ones and those with modest means—social media can help nonprofits get their message out to hundreds of thousands of individuals, regardless of their location. Nonprofits can use technology not only to solicit thousands of small donations, which can combine to produce extremely large sums, or volunteers; they can also inform and inspire a whole new generation of supporters, who may in turn create social media campaigns among their own networks.

The beauty of social media is that they help us expand our philanthropic potential dramatically. But with it comes a whole new set of challenges, and one of the most pressing is measuring impact. How do we know how many people we are reaching? What types of messages are grabbing people's attention online and which are falling on deaf ears? How do we assess the effectiveness of a social media campaign?

Measurement entails qualitative and quantitative data, hard and soft metrics. It can be expensive and time-consuming, and it requires deep thought and analysis. Yet without this analysis, we cannot improve our performance. The ability to learn from every gift we give or receive and every program we fund or run is one of the social sector's greatest areas of untapped potential.

Meanwhile, one of its greatest failures is the incessant reinvention of the wheel. Despite our best intentions, we tend to duplicate efforts that are not successful. The only way to avoid this wasteful, vicious cycle is by learning how to measure our actions and apply our learning to the way we do it the next time. Those who want to make a difference—whether social entrepreneurs; nonprofit staff members, executives, or board members; volunteers; or donors—need to complete an assessment of what they are doing now to inform how they do it in the future.

Of course, many individual donors and nonprofit teams are already practicing data-driven, research-based work and using those data and research to improve their programs and services. These people can serve as inspirations and examples to us all.

And as these individuals would be the first to admit, taking generosity and shared purpose and turning it into social change is far from easy. What I have found, however, is that every time I generate data around a gift I've made or understand the impact of a social program I've initiated, this measurement shows me that it leads to greater and more meaningful change. The upfront costs of time, intellect, and money are paid back many times over in my increased ability to improve lives and help tackle big problems.

We all need to give in a way that matters more—to shift our giving from reactive to proactive, sympathetic to strategic, isolated to collaborative. We need to become better partners to the organizations that we support, working with them to learn from experience and innovate for the future. Whether we support nonprofits through financial donations, gifts of time or intellectual capital, or the sharing of our networks, we need to give in a way that is far more accountable and measured. Individual lives depend on it, communities depend on it—our world depends on it.

Laura Arrillaga-Andreessen
Stanford Graduate School of Business

Beth used to think measurement was the business equivalent of Darth Vader running after her with a radioactive light saber. She had almost flunked math back in eighth grade, and she never lost the sense that anything with data and numbers in it was beyond her ability to learn. She didn't know her way around a spreadsheet and figured that whatever measurement involved, it was going to be a lot of extra work in any case.

But Beth kept hearing from nonprofits that they wanted a way to be more effective with social media. She knew that people and organizations needed to learn from experience, and she had the suspicion that there must be some way to do this in an organized fashion using measurement.

Then she discovered Katie Delahaye Paine. Katie has decades of experience helping organizations of all shapes and sizes define success and measure it, so she knows how to make measurement simple and relevant. Beth started reading KDPaine's Measurement Blog. She even boldly submitted a panel to SXSW's Social Media, Nonprofit, ROI Poetry Slam in 2009 and asked Katie to participate. That's when she discovered that measurement is really powerful—we'll tell you more about that later in this book—and that Katie could dispense clear, practical measurement advice—in iambic pentameter, no less. Today Beth has left her fear far behind and has embraced measurement as a vital tool of the networked nonprofit.

HOW THIS BOOK HELPS NONPROFITS BECOME MORE SUCCESSFUL

This book takes the ideas that were just germinating in that poetry slam and builds them into solid advice illustrated with dozens of examples of nonprofits that have also made the leap from measurement-phobes to measurement mavens. Beth's first book, *The Networked Nonprofit*, coauthored with Allison Fine, provided frameworks and recommendations for nonprofits to transform their organizational culture to embrace a new way of working. *Measuring the Networked Nonprofit* aims at helping nonprofit leaders take those first steps to measure the effectiveness of that transformation.[1]

These transformed nonprofits are using social media metrics and data intelligently to improve their decision making and quantify success. This book covers the many ways that networked nonprofits make the most of measurement:

- They don't just add up numbers; they measure their impact on the mission and organizational goals.

- They value progress and measure results using insight, relationships, organizational results, and social change outcomes.

- They use key performance indicators to make decisions, effect continuous process improvement, and understand what works and what doesn't.

- They measure failure first. Learning from failure is like compost: although it might stink at first, it gets more valuable over time. It is also important to understand the cause of success because it may have happened by accident.

- They are experts at setting up and measuring low-risk experiments to test their strategy and tactics and learn from them.

- They join the "spreadsheet appreciation society," filling their rows and columns with meaningful data and avoiding bogus metrics like the plague.

- They use data to set priorities and better juggle workloads.

We understand that not all nonprofits are starting from the same place in becoming networked nonprofits or in measurement. This book will help nonprofits that are just starting to embrace a networked way of working and aren't measuring at all, as well as those that are already networked and want to improve the measurement they're already doing.

WHY ALL NONPROFITS NEED TO EMBRACE MEASUREMENT

Affecting social change is, of course, the ultimate goal for nonprofit organizations. But you can't get to any destination without a road map and some signposts along the way. Measurement is your map, and metrics are your signposts. Connecting with people, deepening engagement, and inspiring donations are important building blocks for change, and they are relatively easy to measure. There are metrics for measuring conversions from conversation to checks, e-mail list sign-ups, petition signatures, or e-mails to an elected official.

As a networked nonprofit, you know how to leverage your social networks online to make change offline. This book teaches you how to use measurement to better understand your networks, measure outcomes offline, and understand cause and effect. It will guide you through the process of setting up measurement systems that will provide actionable information so you can quickly become more successful.

MEASUREMENT IS NOTHING TO FEAR

Back in 2009, when Beth finally put her measurement fears behind her, she started to notice something at her workshops and presentations: she would do an interactive icebreaker exercise, asking anyone to stand up if their organization was on Facebook, to keep standing if their organization was on Twitter, and so on. In recent years, after she ticked off the names of social media platforms, most people in the room have been standing. She'd then asked them to remain standing if they were using measurement to improve what they were doing. Usually 70 percent of those in the room sat down. Then she asked the folks who were sitting down why they didn't use measurement. What she heard were four key reasons.

Fear of Consequences

No one wants to take risks if the results aren't worth it or, even worse, learn that precious time was wasted. It is only natural to worry that the data might show that one's apparently brilliant idea didn't work. Many of the nonprofit measurement mavens profiled in this book admit to having felt this way. But as they used measurement to understand and improve their programs, they found they had more control over their outcomes, and they did better work. When you apply the measurement techniques in this book, your nonprofit will be rewarded, not punished.

Fear of Setting Measurable Objectives

People often fear that by setting objectives, they will be held accountable for someone else's unreasonable expectations, be it the board, senior management, or their funders. But measurement helps set correct expectations. Creative types worry that taking the time to clarify what you're measuring might kill the freshness of an idea. But creativity only gets you so far. To get to real results, you need a game plan for analyzing your data and applying what you learn. This book is all about how to do that.

Fear of the Data Dump

Unfortunately, some nonprofits have become addicted to collecting data just to say they are. They default to the "measure everything" approach based on the mistaken belief that more data (or even bogus data) are better than none. These misguided tactics result in bloated spreadsheets to which no one pays attention. Part of the purpose of this book is to provide simple guidelines for picking the right tools to collect the right data. We teach you how to gain insight from your measurement data and use them to make decisions without getting overwhelmed.

Fear That Measurement Is Too Much Work or Too Expensive

Far too many organizations see measurement as something that they are paying for in addition to a program, especially if they need to bring in outside expertise or invest in training. But for most of those organizations, the data already exist. Some nonprofits don't measure because they consider it to be too time-consuming—just one more chore on a seemingly endless list. But measurement is actually one way to reduce the number of chores on that endless list, because it gives your organization the data to say, "No," or, "Hell yeah!"

MEASUREMENT IS THE SECRET SAUCE; WE PROVIDE THE RECIPE

This book is organized into three parts; think of it as a three-course meal. The first course is an introduction to measurement and networked nonprofit practices. It's the gastronomical equivalent of setting the table and serving the soup. Then come several chapters on the meat and potatoes of basic measurement techniques. Finally, for a special dessert, there are chapters on advanced measurement techniques for networked nonprofit practices.

If you are new to measurement, the best way to get started is by doing simple pilot studies using the guidelines and examples provided in the early chapters. If you are already experienced at measurement, you'll be tempted to jump right to the chapters on advanced measurement techniques. Before you do so, however, keep in mind that the measurement of practices like crowdsourcing, transparency, and networks is still in an embryonic stage and quickly evolving. We hope that this book will inspire networked nonprofits to continue to contribute to the development of these important areas.

Of course, the last thing a busy nonprofit needs is another difficult-to-master procedure. That's why every chapter in this book leads you through simple steps to measure what matters. There are checklists, tips, resources, and advice to get you started quickly. After reading this book, you'll realize that measurement gets results, gives you greater control, makes you more powerful, and will help you change the world. And it can be fun!

We look forward to hearing your stories of success and what you have learned from and about measurement at http://www.measurenetworkednonprofit.org.

To my husband, Walter, and our children, Harry and Sara, whose patience I needed to write this book and whose love helps me live a life filled with generosity, learning, and wisdom.—B.K.

To my families, both Paine and White, and all the parents, aunts, uncles, and cousins who have instilled in me both the obligation to do the right thing and be accountable. This odd mixture of soft heart and hard nose enabled me to write this book with Beth that I hope will help to both change the world and improve accountability—K.D.P.

ACKNOWLEDGMENTS

We are blessed with networks of people with amazing energy, creativity, and generosity of spirit who assisted in the development of this book. We are particularly grateful for the assistance of the wonderful people who work in the trenches of nonprofits, social media, measurement, and social change every day. They are our muses. We have learned from them as they work to make the world a better place to live.

This book would not have been possible without our editor, William Paarlberg. Whether it was help in winnowing down all the stories to those that were most relevant, or structuring our ideas so they made sense to other people, Bill was an amazing writing coach and editor. We both came out on the other side of this book process much better writers. We are eternally grateful to Bill for his patience, questions, suggestions, and editing skills.

We thank the team at Jossey-Bass for their assistance and support throughout this process. Alison Hankey and Dani Scoville have supported our writing process with great care and vision. Rob Cottingham, our glorious cartoonist, made us laugh so hard we snorted our coffee through our noses.

We are enormously indebted to our expert content reviewers—Kathy Reich, Mario Marino, Wendy Harman, Diana Scearce, Holly Ross, Jason Falls, Shonali Burke, and Lucy Bernholz—for their time and thoughtful suggestions.

Beth offers special thanks to Allison Fine, her coauthor on her first book, *The Networked Nonprofit*, for sharing her ideas about measurement and being an awesome colleague and friend. Beth also thanks The Sharing Foundation, and particularly Dr. Nancy Hendrie, who has been her role model for working on social change and caring for children in Cambodia. She thanks Laura Arrillaga-Andreessen for her support and encouragement while writing and for writing the Foreword to the book.

Beth thanks the David and Lucile Packard Foundation and the Organizational Effectiveness Program, which supported her work with three "Measuring the Networked Nonprofit" peer learning exchanges (http://measure-netnon .wikispaces.com/) with more than fifty grantees. These grantees bravely tested out ideas and concepts in the chapters that follow, and many are quoted or contributed case studies to this book. Many others also tested these ideas including Friending the Finish Line grantees (http://friending-finish-line.wikispaces.com/) and family planning grantees from Pakistan and India (http://networked-ngo .wikispaces.com)

In particular, Beth thanks current and former foundation staff members who were especially generous with their time and support, including Stephanie McAuliffe, Chris DeCardy, Carol Larson, Kathy Reich, Irene Wong, Linda Baker, Liane Wong, Gene Lewit, Jenny Calixto Quigley, Musimbi Kanyoro, Kai Lee, Jamie Dean, Lisa Monzón, Cheryl Chang, Lester Coutinho, Jessica Lopatka, and Sandra Bass. She also acknowledges the consultants and experts who work closely with Packard Foundation staff and grantees: Dan Cohen, Holly Minch, Kristin Grimm, Katherine Fulton and Gabriel Kasper, Heather McLeod-Grant, Noah Flowers, Eugene Eric Kim, June Holley, and Michael Quinn Patton.

Katie thanks her colleagues on the Institute for Public Relations Measurement Commission and the academic community who did so much of the early research that formed her perspectives on measurement. Jim and Larissa Grunig, Brad Rawlins, and, especially, Don Stacks have brought hundreds of academics and their research to the International Public Relations and Research Conference, where she learned pretty much everything she knows about measurement. She also thanks her measurement mavens and clients, especially James Fetig, from the Corporation for National and Community Service, who have a passion for data and have continually raised the bar and pushed measurement to the next level.

Finally, Katie thanks her staff at KDPaine & Partners, who have put up with her "writing holidays" and ensured that the company ran smoothly in her absence. In particular, this book would never have been finished without the help of Doug Chapin.

We offer special thanks to our nonprofit, measurement, and social media gurus, who generously shared their knowledge, stories, and experiences to help shape this book. They include Jennifer Aaker and the student-run 100K Cheeks, Lucy Bernholz, Daniel Ben-Horin, Kristin Rowe-Finkbeiner, Anita Jackson, Ashley Boyd, Shonali Burke, Teddy Witherington, James Nickerson, Clay Lord, Wendy Harman, Zan McColloch-Lussier, Meg Garlinghouse, Jonathon Colman, Laura Lee Dooley, Jon Dunn, David J. Neff, Sarah Granger, Heather Ramsey, June Holley, Deborah Meehan, Nelson Layag, Susan Nesbitt, Wendy Harman, Danielle Brigida, Frank Barry, Melanie Mathos, John Kenyon, Humberto Kam, Vickie McMurchie, Debbie Ford-Scriba, Meg Biallas, the team at GlobalGiving, Carie Lewis, James Leventhal, Perla Ni, HollyRoss, Amy Sample Ward, Debra Askanase, Ash Shepherd, Marnie Webb, Rachel Weidinger, Stephanie Rudat, Geoff Livingston, Kami Huyse, Ted Fickes, Mark Horvath, Shawn Ahmed, George Weiner, Nancy Lublin, Akhtar Badash, Craig Newmark, Allyson Kapin, Guillaume Decugis, Laura Efurd, Merle Lawrence, Howard Rheingold, Robin Good, Jan Gordon, Roberto Cremonini, Tom Kelly, Susan Kistler, Mario Marino, Cheryl Collins, Eric Peterson, John Lovett, Soren Gordhamer, the e-Mediat teams in Jordan, Lebanon, Tunisia, and Morocco, and the many others who helped make this book a reality.

Finally, we both thank our blog readers and online friends who are participating in the ongoing conversation about measurement and learning for social change. Thanks for sharing your experiences and ideas and allowing us to experiment and learn together with you. And thanks for sharing this learning journey as we all look at how networked nonprofits can change the world with measurement.

THE AUTHORS

Beth Kanter (sometimes known as "The Queen of Nonprofits") has worked in the nonprofit sector for over thirty-three years. She started *Beth's Blog* in 2003 when many people were asking her, "What's a blog?" Today it is one of the most popular and influential blogs for nonprofits. While writing this book, she was a visiting scholar at the David and Lucile Packard Foundation, where she facilitated peer exchanges with Packard grantees on measuring the networked nonprofit. Over her time at the Packard Foundation, she has coached thousands of nonprofits on how to become networked nonprofits and how to use measurement.

Over the ten years she has written her blog, she has modeled public learning and helped shine a light on social media measurement mavens and network weavers working in nonprofit trenches. She earned recognition from *BusinessWeek* magazine as one of the social media innovators of 2009.

Beth has designed capacity-building and training programs so that nonprofits around the world can learn how to embrace the principles of social media practice. From the Middle East to India to Australia to Africa, scores of nonprofits have benefited from her wisdom.

In addition, in her capacity as a board member, Beth has volunteered her time to use social networks to support the work of The Sharing Foundation, an organization that takes care of children in Cambodia by providing health care, education, and empowerment programs. Her accomplishments include being the first person ever to use Twitter for fundraising in 2007, winning the first Giving Challenge sponsored by the Case Foundation, and raising money to underwrite the college education of Leng Sopharath, an orphan from Kampong

Speu orphanage, who started her senior year at Norton University in Cambodia as an accounting major. Beth also helped sponsor the first blogging conference in Cambodia for three hundred Cambodian young people. Beth will donate her share of the royalties from the sales of the book to support The Sharing Foundation's work in Cambodia.

Katie Delahaye Paine (sometimes known as "The Goddess of Measurement") launched her first measurement company, The Delahaye Group, in 1987. It was dedicated to measuring results for public affairs, communications, and marketing professionals. Since then, Paine and her staff have read and analyzed millions of articles, interviewed thousands of people, and analyzed hundreds of programs in her endless pursuit of good metrics that help organizations achieve their goals. In 2002, she launched KDPaine & Partners, LLC, a company dedicated to providing affordable metrics to nonprofits, government agencies, and small businesses.

In 1996 she pioneered measurement of consumer-generated media when a consumer electronics company asked her to design a research program "to measure this Internet thing," including forums, news groups, and Web sites. In 2003, when social media began to spread in the form of blogs, someone suggested she write a paper on how to measure blogs. She started her own—*KDPaine's Measurement Blog* (http://kdpaine.blogs.com/)—and in the process learned how to measure them. She's been measuring social media in its various forms ever since.

Her first two books, *Measuring Public Relationships* and *Measure What Matters*, educated organizations on how to decide what really matters to their companies and how to measure it. Now, in *Measuring the Networked Nonprofit*, Paine applies her measurement expertise to networked nonprofits, so they can more quickly learn what is working and what is not in their social media programs.

Measuring the
Networked Nonprofit

PART ONE

Introduction of Concepts

The Secret Sauce for Nonprofits

Networked Strategies +
Measurement = Amazing Success

Our data analysis has uncovered a surprising correlation...

Carie Lewis positioned the party hat on her dog Bella's head, leaned down from her desk, and said, "Say cheeseburger!" Carie's boss snapped a photo with a mobile phone and shared it on the nonprofit organization's Facebook page (Figure 1.1).[1]

You may be wondering why Carie's dog was in her office wearing a party hat. Perhaps you're even more curious as to why the photo was posted on Facebook. Carie Lewis is the director of emerging media for The Humane Society of the

Figure 1.1
Carie Lewis and Bella Celebrate

United States (HSUS), the nation's largest animal protection organization, where she has been responsible for social media for more than five years. The HSUS has a pet-friendly office policy because its staff, like its constituents, are animal lovers. The party hats? They were celebrating because The HSUS Facebook page had just broken the 1 million fan mark.

Says Lewis, "Although we prefer not to focus on numbers of fans as a measure of ultimate success, 1 million fans is a huge landmark that we celebrated with our online community of animal lovers." According to a 2011 nonprofit social media benchmark study sponsored by Craig Newmark, animal charities are among the most active on social networks, perhaps because people love photos of cute animals.[2] But there was more to it than that.

The HSUS fans are more than just fans; they love to talk about how much they love their pets and care for animals. They share photos online, donate to The HSUS (and tell their friends to do so), and take action on animal rights issues when they receive a call to action. In answer to the question of how The HSUS built a fan base on Facebook that is not only large but is always ready get involved in supporting animals, Lewis responds, "We would not be successful if we were not using measurement to track and learn and constantly improve."[3]

Lewis is a curator of social media metrics. She and her colleagues in other departments build their integrated advocacy or fundraising campaigns around outcomes, key performance indicators, and associated metrics. "We look at three things," Lewis noted: "actions taken, donations made, and customer service wins. That's also how our department has been able to obtain more resources to handle the volume we have." They use measurable objectives for specific campaigns, and Lewis tracks everything they do on social networks in order to improve and get better results.

For its campaign to reach 1 million fans, depicted in the screen capture in Figure 1.2, The HSUS wanted to create a celebration so that fans could engage and participate in the fun. They wanted to create a personalized experience that makes the fans feel that they are a part of something really great. Carie noted, "Because we've been using measurement to improve our social media use for years, we know that we need to make these participatory campaigns as easy and simple as possible for stakeholders."

Lewis found that getting everyone in her organization on the same page about evaluating results is crucial: "Before launching any campaign, I present

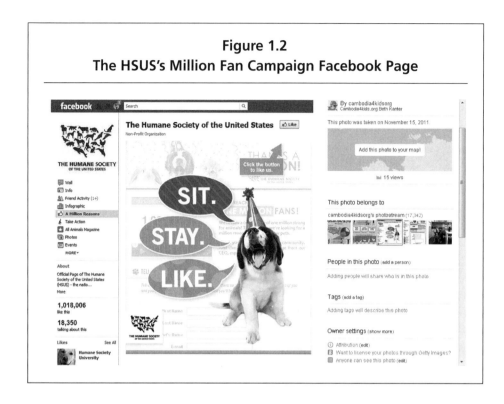

Figure 1.2
The HSUS's Million Fan Campaign Facebook Page

the measurable objectives and strategies at a cross-department meeting. We spend a lot of time clarifying what success looks like and what metrics we will collect to measure it." These sessions also generate many great ideas for strategy, including the idea to create an infographic describing the organization's fans on Facebook.

Lewis is often called in to consult with different departments or affiliates: "We've codified our best practices on measurement and offer a menu of social media tactics that we review with them, letting them know the options, and use cases for each. Most important is a report template that helps them collect the right metrics and to do a content analysis. We even have a section that asks, 'What did you learn?'"

Carie writes out "the objectives and metrics and measurement plan before we launch. That way we know what it will take to reach the goals, but also we get an opportunity to continuously improve what we're doing. In the long run, we know it is helping the animals we all love. Working as a networked nonprofit without a measurement plan is a waste of resources and does a disservice to our mission."

THE KEYS TO NONPROFIT SUCCESS: NETWORKING AND MEASUREMENT

Two key processes lead to tremendous success for nonprofits: becoming networked and using measurement. This book, through numerous examples and practical techniques, explores the many ways in which these two concepts dramatically improve the efficiency and success of nonprofits.

A *networked nonprofit* is an organization that uses social networks and the technology of social media to greatly extend its reach, capabilities, and effectiveness. *Measurement* is the process of collecting data on your communications results and using the data to learn and improve your programs. An organization with a *data-informed culture* uses data to help make decisions and uses measurement to continuously improve and refine its systems. Each chapter of this book provides examples of organizations that are using these techniques to achieve success.

Most nonprofit organizations use at least some sort of informal measurement and some form of social media–enabled networking. Many nonprofits are striving to build a data-informed culture and networked mind-set. But few organizations use these powerful techniques to their greatest potential. One of these is MomsRising.org, a poster child for networked nonprofits and nonprofit measurement mavens.

MOMSRISING: A SUPERSTAR OF NETWORKED NONPROFITS KNOWS THE JOYS OF MEASUREMENT

Kristin Rowe-Finkbeiner and Joan Blades founded MomsRising in 2006. To design this nonprofit, they combined their experience in grassroots organizing and social media with successful ideas from organizations like MoveOn, ColorOfChange, League of Conservation Voters, and others. The result was an organization that embraces constant learning from experience and embeds this powerful concept in its organizational culture and processes. It has fueled the organization's growth from zero members in May 2006 to over a million active members—moms, dads, grandparents, aunts, and uncles—today.

MomsRising uses measurement to achieve tremendous success. As you read this book, you will find several themes concerning the value of measurement and many examples of how it is used. Here are nine of them.

Theme 1: "Likes" on Facebook Is Not a Victory—Social Change Is

Proper measurement keeps organizations focused on results rather than the tools they use, a theme we explore in greater detail in Chapter Four. MomsRising, for instance, does not simply count "likes" on Facebook. Instead, it uses social change to define its successes and develops metrics accordingly. Its most important goals generally include these:

- Getting policies passed on family-related issues
- Increasing capacity
- Increasing the movement size by increasing membership
- Working with aligned partner organizations
- Garnering attention from all media through creative engagement

For MomsRising, the holy grail of results is getting legislatures to pass family-friendly policies. This requires grabbing the attention of policymakers. As one indicator of progress toward that goal, it counted an invitation to bring mothers to the White House to talk with policymakers about their experience with Medicaid. The White House blogged about the power of people's stories, and MomsRising members blogged about their White House experience, resulting in even greater exposure for their messages. Says Rowe-Finkbeiner, "The after-story is just as important because it will often get picked up by mainstream media outlets like NPR or the *Huffington Post*."

Theme 2: Measurement Helps Nonprofits Understand and Improve Their Social Networks

Another theme of this book is that measurement helps nonprofits listen to and engage with their constituents. Measurement enables organizations to assess and improve their relationships with their members and stakeholders. This powerful technique will help you understand how your stakeholders perceive you, what they do with the information you send to them, and how it bears on their behavior. This theme is explored in more detail in Chapter Five.

An important part of MomsRising's decision making is the use of member feedback in the form of stories or comments on social channels or e-mail and in more structured ways such as surveys. Says Rowe-Finkbeiner, "We are in constant dialogue with our members to figure out what works and what doesn't. The data keeps us focused on our mission of building a movement for family economic security, while listening and engaging with our members breathes life into our movement."

Theme 3: Measurement Means Data for Decisions, Not for Data's Sake

Unfortunately, many organizations see measurement as collecting data to dump on the boardroom table or the executive director's desk. But measurement isn't about justifying one's existence or budget, and it isn't about it filling spreadsheets with lots of "just-in-case" data to throw over the fence.

Measurement is about using data to learn to become more effective and more efficient. It's about doing your job better, and helping your organization achieve its mission with fewer resources. It's about reaching more people, and becoming better at saving the world.

Theme 4: Measurement Makes You Plan for Success

More and more nonprofits are making larger investments in social media: hiring dedicated staff, upgrading Web sites to incorporate social features, and using more powerful professional tools to do the work. Measurement helps you make smarter investments and helps you use those investments in a smarter way. Having a social media measurement plan and approach is no longer an afterthought. It's the smart way to run an organization.

Theme 5: Good Measurement Is Good Governance

As networked nonprofits become more skilled in their social media practice, their boards and senior management are becoming more knowledgeable about this area. They expect reports showing social media results, and they expect results expressed in the kind of language that measurement provides. In addition, foundations and other funders want credible evaluation reports and demonstrations of impact. Today boards and foundations increasingly include executives from the for-profit world who have come to expect actionable data and standardized measurement systems.

Theme 6: Data Without Insight Is Just Trivia

The key to MomsRising's success is that it uses data to refine its strategies and tactics. It has achieved its success not by luck or gut instinct but by using measurement to make decisions.

MomsRising holds a weekly staff meeting, nicknamed "Metrics Monday." Prior to this meeting each program and campaign staff person reviews his or her results as part of an explicit process of preparation. The meeting is actually a group conversation about what actions to reinforce, how to refine messages, and what other improvements need to be made. Says Rowe-Finkbeiner, "Our dashboards have multiple views: a high-level view and the ability to drill down into specific campaigns. This informs our discussion."

Theme 7: Measuring Failure Is Part of the Path to Success

Some experiments bomb. Some projects or ideas seem brilliant at first, but when the results come in the data shows that they simply didn't work. The staff at MomsRising give themselves permission to kill these. To remove the stigma of failure, they do this with humor, calling it a "joyful funeral." To learn from the experience, they reflect on why it didn't work.

Theme 8: Incremental Success Is Not Failure

Many organizations experiment with social media. Networked nonprofits are expert at setting up and measuring low-risk experiments and pilots. What sets MomsRising apart is that the staff don't do aimless experiments; they set realistic expectations for success and measure along the way. What they have learned is that many times victories happen in baby steps. They know from experience that many of their campaigns that incorporate social media lead to incremental successes.

Yet some experiments, actions, or issues provide dramatic results. For example, a MomsRising interactive educational video garnered over 12 million views, hundreds of comments, and thousands of new members who signed up or took action. Rowe-Finkbeiner says, "That type of success does not happen every day, but we need to try for that kind of success every day. We can do it only if we decide not to pursue things that don't work." They analyze these game-changing successes to understand how they can be replicated and to make sure they weren't accidents.

Theme 9: Measurement Is Valuable at Every Level of Functioning

Any nonprofit can learn to use measurement to make its social media more effective. It is not hard to get started and doesn't require expensive software, a graduate degree, or even an aptitude for mathematics. The trick is to start simple and grow from there. This book shows you how to do that.

Networked nonprofits and measurement programs exist at all levels of functioning, from just beginning to fully functioning. These are not one-time add-on upgrades. They are journeys—step-by-step processes of learning by doing. You can't measure any nonprofit just by clicking a button, or hiring someone, or doing a single project. You can't become a networked nonprofit that way either. But you can take the first step to get started.

CONCLUSION

This book is filled with remarkable social media and nonprofit success stories, stories of organizations that have embraced the core principles of being a networked nonprofit and measurement. Measurement is the key to improving social media practice and how to work in a networked way, and this book shows you how to do just that.

Any nonprofit can become a networked nonprofit and learn how to apply the measurement techniques in this book. From improving your networks, to planning strategy, to communicating with your membership and boardroom alike, measurement is the tool that will help you become more efficient, more effective, and better at saving the world.

The Rise of the Networked Nonprofit

A New Paradigm for Nonprofit Success

I love your work! Can we commission you to do our networked
non-profit's org chart?

Wendy Harman is director of social strategy at the American Red Cross. She met Beth Kanter in 2005, and Beth has been following the Red Cross's progress ever since. Over the years, the American Red Cross has gradually been embracing social media and a networked way of working. Beth has incorporated Harman's experience and wisdom in many of her presentations and blog posts. And Beth and Allison Fine profiled the American Red Cross in their book *The Networked Nonprofit*.[1]

On January 11, 2010, Harman received a chat message from Beth. It was Beth's birthday, and she was doing what she had done on her birthday for the previous five years, working as a free agent to fundraise for The Sharing Foundation, an organization that supports an orphanage in Cambodia by providing education and health care for children there. Beth's children, Harry and Sara, lived in that orphanage, so putting her social media skills to use like this is something much more personal than just another way for her to give back.

When Harman made a donation, Beth immediately replied with a thank-you message, and asked, "How's it going?" Harman answered, "Change is slow, but we're making good progress. Our social media policy is in place, and I just taught two hundred disaster relief workers how to Tweet!" Beth e-mailed back, "You rock!" Harman, who seemed to be in a pensive mood, responded, "You know, sometimes I ask myself: 'To what end?'"[2]

Harman got her answer the very next day. On January 12, 2010, the Haiti earthquake struck, killing 300,000 people outright and leaving roughly a million and a half homeless. What better example of the mission of the Red Cross?

As the mainstream news flooded the airwaves with human suffering, the Red Cross hit the ground in Haiti with hundreds of disaster relief workers. It also swung into action raising money to help the earthquake victims, including initiating a text-to-give campaign of exceptional vigor and ambition. Over the next few months, Americans used their cell phones to text pledges totaling more than $41 million, the largest amount to date for a text-message giving program.[3]

This unprecedented fundraising power of the cell phone caught everyone's attention. But what was even more dramatic was to watch the Red Cross grow and change as a result of this tragedy. Here was an institution that had been adopting social media only slowly, and suddenly it blossomed into a full-fledged networked nonprofit. Social media at the Red Cross had burst from the communications silo to other departments, including on-the-ground disaster relief.

It was clear from the Twitter stream that social media had proved to be a valuable channel for communications during a natural disaster. Harman's Twitter lessons were paying off faster than she ever could have imagined (Figure 2.1).

Fast-forward six months. At the 2010 Nonprofit 2.0 Unconference in Washington, D.C., Beth and Allison Fine discussed their book in the opening keynote address. Following them at the podium was Wendy Harman, who shared some insights about the Red Cross's social media work leading up to the Haiti relief efforts. She drove home two vital points about organizations and their progress in becoming networked nonprofits:

- *Don't give up in the middle.* Many nonprofits begin using social media and set out on the path to becoming a networked nonprofit with over-inflated expectations. Midway through an experiment, they hit a bump in the road, view it as a failure, and give up. Everything looks like a failure in the middle. Don't give up!

- *Networks ebb and flow like the ocean.* Networks have different stages of development and functioning, and they wax and wane according to need. If you've built your network, it will someday prove its value. Like the Red Cross, it will be there for you.

WHAT IS A NETWORKED NONPROFIT?

The Networked Nonprofit introduced the concept of a new kind of nonprofit organization—one that leverages the power of social media to expand its network of supporters and thereby greatly increase its capacity and success. It then profiled two types of these networked nonprofits: those born as networked nonprofits, like MomsRising.org which introduced in Chapter One, and traditional nonprofits that are on their way to becoming networked

Figure 2.1
Wendy Harman Tweets About the American Red Cross

Good morning. Can see next big sm job at ARC is coordinating w other orgs to act on data that comes in via sm, crisis mapping.

4:38 AM Jan 18th from UberTwitter   Reply   Retweet

wharman
Wendy Harman

© 2009 Twitter   About Us   Contact   Blog   Status   Goodies   API   Business   Help   Jobs   Terms   Privacy

Home   Profile   Find People   Settings   Help   Sign out

@redcross volunteer @winnie_romeril (flight EMT by day) tweeting in Haiti. Proud bc @clairesale and I taught her how in a training.

5:20 PM Jan 16th from web
Retweeted by you and 1 other   Reply   Retweeted (Undo)

wharman
Wendy Harman

nonprofits, like the Red Cross. *The Networked Nonprofit* walked nonprofit leaders through the process of changing their orientation from managing organizations to participating in and managing social networks. It was aimed at helping nonprofit leaders take the first steps to becoming successful managers of social media.

MomsRising.org exhibits most of the qualities that distinguish networked nonprofits. It understands how to build relationships and engage with people and organizations while leveraging its network to get results.

SEVEN VITAL CHARACTERISTICS OF NETWORKED NONPROFITS

Knowing how to use social media well is not just about knowing which button to push or what technological wizardry to employ. The power of a networked approach is its ability to connect people to one another and help build strong, resilient, trusting relationships that lead to real on-the-ground social change. We see seven characteristics as vital in this approach:

1. *Networked nonprofits know their organizations are part of a much larger ecosystem of organizations and individuals that provides valuable resources.* They understand that they don't need to own the to-do list, only the results.

2. *Networked nonprofits know that relationships are the result of all the interactions and conversations they have with their networks.* They are comfortable doing their work transparently. It makes them open to serendipity and new ideas.

3. *Networked nonprofits experiment and learn from experience.* They are masters at experimenting their way into dramatic wins. They don't shy away from failure because it leads them to innovation and success.

4. *Networked nonprofits have data-informed cultures.* They use data to develop strategy, measure success, assess their experiments, and then make decisions on how best to move forward with new strategies.

5. *Networked nonprofits know how to inspire people.* They motivate their networks of support to help shape the organization's programs, share stories in order to raise awareness of social issues, change attitudes and behavior, and organize communities to provide services or advocate for legislation.

BEING AND DOING: THE TAO OF THE NETWORKED NONPROFIT

The conceptual framework introduced in *The Networked Nonprofit* divides the qualities of networked nonprofits into two categories: being and doing. "Being" refers to the different ways of working in a connected world and "doing" to the tactical implementation—for example:

Being	Doing
Understands networks, network weaving, social capital	Works with free agent fundraisers
Creates social culture	Uses crowdsourcing to design and implement programs
Listens, engages, builds relationships	Uses learning loops and real feedback for experimenting and learning
Builds trust through transparency	Leverages friending to fundraising
Embraces simplicity	Governs through networks

Becoming a networked nonprofit framework is not about just knowing which button to push or what technological wizardry to employ, but about embracing a whole new way of working, as expressed in the "being" column.

6. *Networked nonprofits work differently from other organizations.* They enjoy a social culture that encourages everyone in and outside the organization to participate and spread their mission. They challenge deeply held assumptions about leadership, roles, and structures. They have broken down departmental silos. They are comfortable sharing control or cocreating

with their networks—whether that means allowing people to retell the organization's story in their own words or scaling programs.

7. *Networked nonprofits are masters at using social media.* They are adept at using tools that encourage conversations and building relationships between people and between people and organizations. They are able to scale their efforts quickly, easily, and inexpensively. They are adept at blending tried-and-true methods with new digital tools.

HOW MOMSRISING GENERATED 100,000 LETTERS TO CONGRESS

MomsRising is an example of how one networked nonprofit achieved amazing and measurable success: it generated 100,000 letters to Congress using its network of supporters, data-informed decision making, and multiple communications channels.

MomsRising has become very good at organizing support for legislation and related projects by quickly developing citizen engagement campaigns. These campaigns, called *rapid response*, use a variety of communications channels to contact supporters, develop materials, and then distribute those materials to the media and concerned parties.

To build its rapid-response campaigns, MomsRising leverages the experience of its membership by encouraging members to share personal stories and ideas. It then uses the most moving of these as the basis for designing and implementing communications materials, which are typically tested and retested to determine which are the most effective. These are then distributed over several different communications channels to ensure maximum exposure for their messages.

Statistics Put People to Sleep; Stories Get Attention In July 2011, Congress threatened to make tens of billions of dollars in cuts to Medicaid and Medicare. MomsRising knew that its constituency very much depended on Medicaid. The nonprofit also knew that a widely held myth in Washington was that although Medicare has a strong constituency, Medicaid does not. MomsRising wanted to dispel this misperception by demonstrating to Congress that there was a vigorous grassroots constituency that supported Medicaid.

Years of message testing and research had taught MomsRising that when you're trying to change minds, wonky stats fall flat but people's stories resonate.[4]

So its leaders decided on a strategy of getting in front of the media with stories of moms who benefit from Medicaid.

Using a story collection landing page on their Web site, they urged their members to share stories of how Medicaid was helping families. This tactic collected over five hundred stories from forty-three states. After cherry-picking the best ones to illustrate their message, they used them to craft effective calls for action that encouraged their members and the public to write letters. To reach the widest possible audience, these action alerts were sent out over multiple social media and traditional media channels. The result was over 100,000 letters to Congress about the importance of Medicaid.

MomsRising used those stories in other ways too, including hard-copy "storybook" compilations hand-delivered to Congress and the White House, and letters to the editors in traditional newspapers. Notes Kristin Rowe-Finkbeiner, executive director of MomsRising.org:

> Social media channels like Twitter and Facebook are important to us because we can share our stories directly with targeted members of Congress. We post specific stories on legislators' Facebook walls or we @reply them on Twitter. We've found that there are fewer filters between us and Congress when we use social media channels. While they can easily ignore our emails and phone calls, they can't avoid it when we share the story directly with them through social media channels: They have to respond.[5]

BECOMING A NETWORKED NONPROFIT: THE CRAWL, WALK, RUN, FLY MODEL

Learning to use social media and other emerging technologies and putting the ideas from *The Networked Nonprofit* into practice will be successful only if nonprofits take small, incremental, and strategic steps. Our model incorporates four levels of social media practice: crawl, walk, run, and fly. Each level indicates where the organization is with respect to becoming a networked nonprofit.

It is important to note that reaching the highest level of networked nonprofit practice takes months, if not years. Even an organization like MomsRising, which was born as a networked nonprofit and has several years of social media experience, has not won its dramatic victories over night.

BETH KANTER ON HOW "CRAWL, WALK, RUN, FLY" WAS CREATED AND USED

After coaching and facilitating workshops for hundreds, if not thousands, of nonprofit organizations, I started to notice differences in their practices and what types of capacity building were needed at different stages to get them to the next level. If there is one thing I've learned from working with many nonprofits in their quests to become networked nonprofits, it's that slow, small steps work best. I call this approach "slow social media" to encourage nonprofits to slow down and be mindful of their practice.

In February 2011, I was invited to Microsoft headquarters in Seattle to provide the keynote address at the Washington Technology for Good Conference for three hundred local nonprofits.[6] Several weeks earlier, as I was preparing my presentation, I came across Martin Luther King, Jr.'s "fly, run, walk, crawl" quote, and it inspired my practice model.

Microsoft had given me seventy-five minutes on the morning agenda. I decided to use the crawl, walk, run, fly (CWRF) framework to make the session interactive and test it as a self-assessment approach. So I walked participants through a simple explanation of the model. Then I had people discuss it with their peers, and we had a full group discussion about where people were and what was needed to get to the next step. Participants shared success stories, challenges, and current social media usage. What struck me was that many of these stories had some element of measurement.

The Foundation for Early Learning, for example, shared a story about how it used social media to spread awareness of a funding program. In doing so, the organization reached a wider audience and saw a 33 percent increase in traffic and downloads of information. When asked to share how they had achieved that success, foundation representatives spoke of the importance of listening and setting realistic expectations for results.

The Museum of History and Industry (MOHAI) in Seattle uses social media to engage Seattle residents with whom they might not otherwise connect. One MOHAI employee told the story of how she began to create a series of YouTube videos, one of them featuring herself in the mouth of an alligator, a familiar icon in a local park. When the videos started to catch on, she used the viewing data to convince her boss to add resources for such videos to the budget. Her work is now part of the MOHAI Minute video series, and through their responses to the videos, Seattle residents now can weigh in on how history is being interpreted.

Since Seattle, I have refined CWRF and used it in my workshops. As a visiting scholar at the David and Lucile Packard Foundation, I have used the framework to coach hundreds of grantees around the world. I have brought it to the Middle East, where I used it in a capacity-building curriculum for the "E-Mediat program," which provides training and capacity for nongovernmental organizations in the Middle East to use social media for civil society goals. Trainers in five Arab countries are now using it to train over three hundred nongovernmental organizations.[7]

The most important lesson I've learned is that going slow, with small incremental steps, leads to success in becoming a networked nonprofit.

The crawl, walk, run, fly hierarchy is designed to help organizations understand that becoming a networked nonprofit is typically a complex and lengthy process. Its purpose is to encourage and motivate organizations to succeed by helping them understand the nature of the process they are going through. This model is simply a method for organizations to figure out what type of measurement they are ready for.

Not every nonprofit will go through the levels at the same pace because different organizations have different cultures, capacities, communication objectives, program designs, and target audiences. Moreover, the reality will be messy; an organization might not precisely fit the profile in any specific category. But every organization can take pride in its success at whatever level it has achieved.

Appendix B sets out a crawl, walk, run, fly self-assessment checklist that any organization can use to evaluate where it is in its development as a networked nonprofit. This will help you figure out where you need to improve your current practice and where measurement can be of help as you make progress.

Crawl

Organizations in the crawl stage of becoming networked nonprofits are not using social media or emerging technology at all or, if they are using it, are not using it consistently. These organizations lack a robust communications strategy or program plan that can be scaled using a networked approach. Crawlers are not just smaller nonprofits; they include larger institutions that have all the basics in place but lack a social culture or are resisting transforming from a command-and-control style to a more networked mind-set. These nonprofits need to develop a basic communications strategy or program plan. They will learn and benefit from the inspiring stories we share in this book.

Perhaps your organization has a robust program plan or communications strategy in place but is facing challenges to adopting a networked way of working. If so, you should start with a discussion of the issues, followed by codifying the rules in a social media policy. The first measurement step at this level is setting up a listening process and integrating listening on social channels into planning research.

Walk

Nonprofits at the walk stage (dubbed "the walkers") are using one or more social media tools consistently, but this use isn't linked to a communications strategy, campaign, or program plan. They have in place best practices on tools and techniques as part of the organizational skill set but may need assistance in developing a social media strategy to support short- and long-term SMART (specific, measurable, achievable, realistic, and time) objectives. They may also need help to correctly identify the audiences they need to target.

Walkers have internalized listening and are able to use the data they collect to improve engagement and content best practices. At this stage, leaders may not fully understand social media and networked ways of working. Often the question, "What's the value?" surfaces. The organization should implement a small, low-risk pilot that can collect stories and numbers to help leaders better understand the value and benefit and costs (we discuss how to do this in Chapter Five). Nonprofits in the walk stage need to avoid spreading the organization's resources too thin. They should instead focus on one or two social media tools, going deep on tactics, and generating tangible results to demonstrate value.

Walkers must identify low-cost ways to build capacity internally, for example, by using interns or volunteers effectively and integrating social media tasks into existing job descriptions. Staff members should evaluate their job tasks and identify what they don't need to do in order to make time for social media and other emerging technologies, all with support from leaders. They must also enlist the help of their social networks outside their organization.

A nonprofit's social media policy in the walk stage formalizes the value and vision for social media use and networked approach and encourages free agent outsiders to help with implementation. The organization integrates simple measurement techniques and learning as an organizational habit that helps improve practice.

Run

Nonprofits at the run stage use one or more social media tools and are strategic, identifying key result areas and key performance metrics that drive everything they do. They also have a formal ladder of engagement and know how to measure it. They understand the importance of visualizing their networks and measuring their relationships. (At this level, an organization is religiously practicing the basic measurement steps we set out in Chapter Four.)

In these organizations, social media are not in a silo or guarded by one person or department. With a social media policy in place and a more social culture, the organization is comfortable with working transparently and working with people outside its organization like the free agents we discuss in Chapter Twelve. They know how to use measurement to identify these influencers. The board is also using social media as part of its governance role.

The main problem at this stage is scaling. To build internal capacity, organizations may need to bring on a half- or full-time staff person who serves as a community manager, building relationships with people on social media or new technology platforms. This social media point person also works internally as a network weaver or trainer to help departments and individuals use social media to support the organization's programs.

These runners effectively integrate social media and emerging technologies such as mobile messaging across all communications channels and know the right combination of measurement tools to evaluate their performance. They have strong capacity in content creation as well as repurposing or remixing across channels and use crowdsourcing to create and spread content. Runners also incorporate social fundraising, knowing that community engagement is as important to measure as dollars raised.

For program strategy, runners use crowdsourcing to help design pilots, generate feedback on an evaluation, or rethink programs. They know how to measure the impact of the crowd, as we discuss later in the book. The organization has adequately engaged and built relationships with key influencers—both organizations and individuals. The organization has codified and shared its program work flow and has made all program tools and materials available so its network can assist with implementation.

Fly

Organizations at the fly stage have mastered everything at the running stage and internalized it. These "flyers" create a culture of public learning for both individuals and the entire organization. They embrace failure and success alike and learn from both. The organization uses data to make decisions, but leaders understand how to lead from the heart as well as the head. The organization has documented and shared dramatic results with its stakeholders and peer organizations. Flyers are part of a vibrant network of people and organizations focused on social change.

Organizations in this category have adopted sophisticated measurement techniques, tools, and processes. This may include benchmarking, testing, shared organizational dashboards, and linking results to job compensation for larger institutions. Above all, measurement is not viewed as an afterthought. It is part of an ongoing decision-making process that helps the organization continuously improve its programs.

CONCLUSION

A networked nonprofit leverages the power of social media and working in a networked fashion to expand its network of supporters and thereby greatly increase its capacity and success. Becoming a networked nonprofit can be a slow process, but with patience, your organization will realize the powerful benefits of this profound transformation. Appendix B offers a checklist to help your organization work through how to improve networked nonprofit practices. Measurement techniques that you'll learn in the next few chapters will help you achieve better results.

PART TWO

Basic Measurement Principles, How-Tos, and Best Practices

Creating a Data-Informed Culture

How Your Organization Can Embrace the Data and Use What It Can Teach You

You know this chart we've based the past three years of strategy on?
Call me crazy, but I think it's sideways.

DoSomething.org is a fully functioning data-informed culture founded by Andrew Shue and Michael Sanchez to convince young people that community service is as popular, cool, and, most important, normal, as watching TV or playing sports. Their idea was that if community service became ingrained in young people, then they wouldn't think twice about helping others or volunteering. Back in 1993, Shue approached the prolific television producer Aaron Spelling and asked for thirty seconds of airtime on his popular show *Melrose Place* to tell the world about DoSomething.org. Spelling agreed, and DoSomething.org was officially launched.

DoSomething.org, a midsized nonprofit with about forty staff members, including two full-time data analysts, focuses on social change makers under twenty-five years of age and delivers most of its programs through the Web, mobile messaging, and social networks. They don't collect data for data's sake. They use their data to shape programs and drive social change, making decisions based on a balance of data and experience.

DATA INFORMED, NOT DATA DRIVEN

DoSomething.org is an example of a nonprofit with a *data-informed* culture, something very different from a *data-driven* culture. The term *data driven* has been used to describe organizations that rely solely on cold hard data to make decisions. Being data driven sounds great—in theory. But, because it doesn't acknowledge the importance of basing decisions on multiple information sources, it can doom an organization to epic failures.

Eric Peterson, founder of the Analysis Exchange, an effort that matches analytics volunteers with nonprofits, suggests that the phrase *data informed* is a far more useful label than *data driven* because it describes agile, responsive, and intelligent businesses that are better able to succeed in a rapidly changing environment.[1] Alex Howard, Government 2.0 Washington Correspondent for O'Reilly Media, describes the subtle distinction: "You can be informed by data but not driven by it. The inverse is probably not as true, however, though I can imagine someone being driven by bad data and therefore not being well informed."[2]

The concept of being data informed resonates with nonprofit and public sector practitioners as well. Data-informed cultures are not slaves to their data. Mario Morino uses the phrase "information-based introspection" to refer to using and applying data in context to excel.[3]

Says Ian Thorpe, senior information and knowledge manager at UNICEF, "In the world of development aid there is an obsession with being 'evidence-based,' but, realistically, everything we do depends a lot on context and on people (and on politics and personal preferences)."[4] Thorpe goes on to say that multiple sources for decision making are critical: "Data is an important part of the story, but not all of it. Nonprofits have to balance an overreliance on passion or belief in one's mission with over-fetishization of data and analysis."

"DATA INFORMED" MEANS MORE THAN KPIs AND MEASUREMENT

Data-informed cultures have the conscious use of assessment, revision, and learning built into the way they plan, manage, and operate. From leadership, to strategy, to decision making, to meetings, to job descriptions, a data-informed culture has continuous improvement embedded in the way it functions.

Key performance indicators (KPIs) are the specific quantifiable metrics that an organization agrees are necessary to achieve success. They are the mileposts that tell a data-informed organization whether it is making progress toward its goals. Too often, however, organizations choose KPIs that simply reflect activity.

Measurement is a tool that data-informed cultures use to improve their programs; they observe the results of their programs and then learn from those results to improve and refine their next programs. These cultures design measurement into their projects not just so they have measurable outcomes but so they have the data necessary to guide how to improve them.

Measurement can be used for many things, and some of them are undesirable, like justifying your existence, getting someone fired, or proving a point. But data-informed cultures use measurement to continuously improve.

These cultures exist at various levels, from barely there to fully developed. This chapter discusses a fully functioning data-informed culture and sets out how to change your organization to become data informed.

CREATING DOSOMETHING.ORG'S DATA-INFORMED CULTURE

According to CEO Nancy Lublin, several key elements contribute to DoSomething.org's data-informed culture.[5]

It Starts at the Top

Creating a data-informed culture comes down to leadership. At DoSomething.org, it starts with the board, which is dominated by leaders in the tech field, including Reid Hoffman, cofounder of LinkedIn, and Raj Kapoor, cofounder of Snapfish. Hoffman has famously said, "The future of the Web is data." Lublin purposefully developed a data-informed culture, building her team with staff members who share her passion, like chief technology officer George Weiner.[6]

Weiner manages the Internet, computer, and online communication strategy for DoSomething.org. He says, "One of the biggest challenges to nonprofits becoming more data-informed is the HiPPO in the room that no one wants to talk about. 'HiPPO' stands for 'Highest Paid Person in the Organization,' and it's usually your CEO. The HiPPO has to buy into data-informed decisions; otherwise it doesn't happen."

Don't Just Count; Understand Why

The DoSomething.org staff mine their program data for actionable insights that they share with Lublin at regular meetings. "I think one of the reasons our organizational culture has evolved is that our nonprofit is 90 percent funded by corporate sponsorships," she explains. "They look at us as a media purchase. As a result, we've always collected key performance metrics—not just traffic, but engagement metrics and, of course, actions taken. But we don't just count; we try to understand why."

Lublin has brought in leading thinkers from the corporate sector to mentor her and her staff on how to think about their data. She was fortunate, she says, "to spend some time with John Lilly from Mozilla. He encouraged us to have a more open philosophy for sharing and analyzing our data. If we're transparent about sharing our dashboards, it generates feedback and discussion from our stakeholders that leads to improvement."

Don't Be a Slave to Data; Think

Lublin advises nonprofits to listen to the data but stay focused on their mission: "I don't mean that we don't have a spine. If the data told us to focus on senior citizens, we'd package it up and send it to another organization because it doesn't support our goal of activating young people to take action."

Lublin also talks about the importance of constant experimentation: "And it isn't just saying, 'Okay, we'll try this.' We state a specific hypothesis with a number and measure against that." DoSomething.org integrates critical metrics from social media, e-mail, short message service, and the Web. They don't just count their data; they use sophisticated methods like A/B testing. (A/B testing is an advertising and marketing practice in which different versions of an ad, e-mail, or strategy are deployed and their results compared to determine which is the most effective.)

Fail Fest and Pink Boas: Don't Be Afraid to Fail

DoSomething.org doesn't use its data to pat itself on the back or make the staff feel good. Lublin notes that they're not afraid of failure. They hold regular "fail-fest" meetings, where each person on staff has to present a campaign or program failure and share three things they learned about themselves and three things the organization learned. To remove the stigma from failure, Lublin says, "We wear pink boas when we present."

Spend More Time Thinking About the Data, Less on Collecting It

DoSomething.org uses its data to continuously improve programs, develop content, and shape campaign strategies. So DoSomething.org wants its staff to spend more of its brainpower thinking about the data, rather than collecting it. To ensure that this happens, DoSomething.org's data analyst, Bob Filbin, does more than program formulas in Excel spreadsheets: "One of the biggest barriers in nonprofits is finding the time to collect data, the time to analyze, and the time to act on it. Unless someone is put in charge of data, and it's a key part of their job description, accelerating along the path toward empowered data-informed culture is going to be hard, if not impossible."[7]

Tear Down Those Silos

Lublin says that it is important not to silo data analysts: "You can't treat them like accountants who sit quietly in the background and assign categories to expenses. I've made sure that our data analyst shares an office and works interactively with staff." Filbin is responsible for ensuring sure that departmental and overall organizational goals are aligned and that social media data is seamlessly integrated into achieving key organizational results. His goal, he says, "is to make sure that every person and department has access to the data they need in order to create actionable changes in their work. Each person has an automated dashboard that has different levels of detail and relates to organizational results."

Make It Personal, and Make It Relevant

Filbin also knows how to overcome staff resistance: "Reports should be presented in a way that seeks to avoid bruised egos. Rather than bringing a number to a meeting, people should be reviewing their own statistics and data. This is part of what I am doing at DoSomething.org—closing the data loop; making sure each department can access its data to answer their questions."

Even the Smallest Victory Is a Win

Filbin says it is important to start with sharing small wins. "For example, I shared an analysis of A/B testing for Facebook ads for an event sign-up. We discovered the conversion rate was very low because we directed people to an external site [our own Web site] rather than a sign-up page on Facebook. This insight helped us use Facebook ads more effectively to bring people to the event."

THE STAGES OF BECOMING DATA INFORMED: CRAWL, WALK, RUN, FLY

Obviously not all nonprofits are born with the data-informed gene. And it's not a culture you can acquire along with your analytics software. It's an evolutionary process that happens in the four stages of crawl, walk, run, and fly.

Crawl

At this stage, the organization does not know where to start. It collects data from time to time but does no formal reporting. What data is collected does not relate to decision making. There are no systems in place, no dashboards, and no collection methods. Staff members are often overwhelmed by the thought of measurement, and the task falls to the bottom of their to-do lists. There is no process for analyzing success or failure. Decisions are all passion driven.

Walk

Organizations in the walking stage are regularly collecting data but not in a consistent manner. For example, different people and departments may be collecting but not sharing data. Data is focused on the metrics specific to social media channels but not linked to high-level organizational results or mission-driven goals across programs and could even be the wrong data. Discussions on how to improve results are rarely part of staff meetings, and there are no linkages to organizational experience. The organization does not understand the fine distinction between being data driven and the intelligent use of data.

Run

At this stage, the nonprofit has an organization-wide system and dashboard for collecting measurement data that is shared among departments. Decisions are based on multiple sources rather than on a single piece of data or intuition. Managers hold weekly check-ins to evaluate what's working and what's not across communications channels, as well as any specific social media feedback received that could help shape future campaigns or social media use.

The nonprofit now monitors feedback from target audiences in real time and supplements that information with trend or survey data. The organization may work with measurement consultants or specialists to improve skills and capacity, and it provides training and professional development for staff to learn how to use measurement tools.

Fly

At this phase, the nonprofit has established key performance indicators that it uses across programs. It has a staff person responsible for managing the organization's data, but staff are empowered to check and apply their own data. In addition to providing weekly check-ins, the organizational dashboard includes key performance metrics related to goals. The organizational dashboard is shared across departments, and a process is in place for analyzing, discussing, and applying results. Staff members use data visualization techniques to report the data analysis but also to reflect on best practices culled from the data. There is no shame or blame game because of "failures"; instead, these are embraced as learning opportunities. A regular report to senior leadership provided by staff details high-level successes, challenges, and recommendations for moving forward. Staff performance reviews incorporate how well the organization is doing on its KPIs. Leadership celebrates successes by sharing measurement data across the organization.

BECOMING DATA INFORMED: CHANGE IS EASY WITH BABY STEPS

Changing an organization's culture to a more data-informed approach must begin with baby steps. Although it does not have to be difficult to orchestrate, it does need to start from the top. Unless senior management can agree on the definitions of success and how they will be measured, you can waste a tremendous amount of time accumulating data but not using it. (Chapter Four describes the basic steps of any measurement program and discusses how to set up a measurement pilot program, and Chapter Five examines how to identify the value of success.)

Getting started on the path to becoming a data-informed nonprofit is a matter of having some important internal conversations. It is not just about having new inspiration about measurement or working with new tools; it means thinking differently about the organization and how it works.

Begin at the End: Discuss and Identify Results

If your organization doesn't know exactly what you're going to measure, you can't become data informed. Unless you have a discussion upfront of what success looks like, you'll end up collecting data, but the information won't help you make decisions, and you will waste everyone's time. So begin at the end by carefully identifying desired outcomes.

Don't be afraid of a bit of healthy disagreement. The best measurement programs are born of and benefit from lively conversations about what really matters to the organization. You need to keep your "mission" hat on and keep the conversation focused on the ultimate goals of the organization. Just keep repeating: it's not about "credit," it's about achieving the mission.

You will also want to manage expectations. What is realistic to expect given your current investment in social media or compared to peer organizations? What do short-term, medium-term, and longer-term results look like?

You might need to bring in a consultant to facilitate a meeting to help get consensus. Or you may need to bring in a measurement expert to help you clarify what you want to measure and why. This doesn't have to be expensive.

For example, as we discuss in Chapter Eight, the Analysis Exchange helped the American Leadership Forum by supplying an analytics volunteer to create a framework and system for gathering data.

Become a Curator of Metrics

If you are the person responsible for implementing social media for your organization, either part time or as your whole job, you need to become what John Lovett defines as a "curator of metrics" in his book *Social Media Metrics Secrets*.[8] This is someone, like Carie Lewis from the Humane Society in Chapter One, who understands the different types of metrics and ensures that the organization is using data in an intelligent way. A curator of metrics knows how to help guide the organization into choosing the right metrics and report insights in a way that connects them to organizational goals.

Use Experiments to Make the Case to Evolve

One way to evolve into a data-informed organization is through implementing a series of social media measurement experiments, as described below and in Chapter Four. Each needs to have solid metrics and should be designed to provide results that will help you make the case to evolve. Keep the end in mind when agreeing on how experiments will be structured, run, and measured. The experiments should not be willy-nilly, but help you develop and test your strategies and tactics and lead the way to best practices.

Take a Baby Step: A Data Collection Project To get started, select a project, event, small campaign, or program that is a high priority on your organization's work plan for the year, incorporates social media, and you can apply a couple of good metrics to. Be mindful of other organizational deadlines that may divert energy and focus from this important first step. You might find it difficult to set aside quality time to focus on it.

Don't try to measure every objective or collect all potentially relevant data. Make this project easy to manage. You should also have a very clear idea about what you want to learn. Keep in mind that you are going to use your report to make the case for a more comprehensive measurement program.

It's important to make sure that anyone who is going to use the data, or sit in a meeting and review the data, buys into your metrics. That could be the executive director, a program manager, the board of trustees, or other people in your department. If there are many different decision makers, you may need to do a formal survey to make sure that everyone ends up on the same page. Sara Thomas, who handles social media for Ocean Conservancy, says, "It was really useful to bring in my entire department on the effort rather than working solo on the project. This helped with buy-in."[9]

Learn from Your Results Analyze your data, and understand how it can help inform decisions. Make sure you educate through examples. Show how adding a data-informed approach can avoid ineffective campaigns and increase audience satisfaction.

More important, you need to do more than just develop discipline around collecting data; what you want is the discipline to look at what you've collected and generate insights. That requires reflection, not just counting.

Doing a measurement pilot will help you wrestle with larger questions about how social media fits into an organization's overall efforts—for example:

- Which vehicles and channels gain us the most traction?

- How should we adjust our workload internally to reflect those results?

- How are our social media activities helping us meet our overall strategic goals?

- How are our efforts using social media supporting our programs?

Reflecting does not have to be a private activity. It can be done in connected, transparent ways. The organization's blog or Web site can be a place to share lessons learned with readers and ask them for their feedback and suggestions as well. The result is a powerful way to learn and improve over time.

CONCLUSION

To start the shift to a data-informed culture, begin with small incremental steps with the full support of leadership. It's important to think big, looking at key results, but since many outcomes deal with long-term changes, you can't get there overnight nor can your organization transform its culture overnight.

Measurement Is Power

How to Take Control of Your Programs and Progress with the Art and Science of Measurement

Who's mommy's little snugglebunny? You are! Who increased revenue 22.7% when we put his picture on the donation page? You did!

Lisa Leong, program manager at Kearny Street Workshop (KSW), pored over her social media metrics spreadsheet every month, analyzing all the comments on KSW's Facebook page and categorizing them by topic. She compared those results to her Facebook Insights metrics to figure out what content resonated with their audience. One day, as she went over the results, the connection between adding personality to Facebook posts and an increase in exhibit attendance jumped out at her. "Who knew," she asked, "we could inspire all those online conversations just by adding a bit of our own personality to our posts?"[1]

Leong explained, "Doing this tracking over several months, we discovered that our previous approach of posting promotional content about events with an impersonal organizational voice simply fell flat with our audience on Facebook. As we started to give it more personality, we discovered that this not only initiated conversations about the art and artists, but our survey data showed us that new people were coming through the doors because they heard about us on Facebook."

KSW's mission is to produce, present, and promote art that empowers Asian American artists and communities. Founded in 1972 in San Francisco's Chinatown/Manilatown, its artistic programs both honor the community's cultural heritage and nurture emerging artists and contemporary practices. The organization offers educational workshops, performances, and exhibitions that showcase stories of diverse individuals and communities in the Bay Area. It uses its Web site, e-mail, print, local, and ethnic media channels to promote its programs.

When KSW started to experiment with social media, Leong, like any other good measurement maven, started out with clear objectives:

> Our goal was to increase awareness, engagement, and participation in our programs both for audiences and artists. But we are a small nonprofit, with a two-person staff. I am the social media manager, but it isn't 100 percent of my job. We started with identifying our objectives and metrics that would help us improve our content and engagement strategy. We tracked results by collecting several metrics

from Facebook Insights, tracking participation in our events, and by adding some questions to our event surveys.

Their goals and metrics were:

1. *Increase exposure* as measured by the number of likes on Facebook.

Tool: Facebook Insights

Result: Increased fan base by 72 percent

2. *Increase engagement* by doubling comments/likes per post.

Tool: Facebook Insights

Result: Post feedback went up 269 percent

3. *Increase participation* of new people in classes and events.

Tool: Event survey

Result: Ten percent of new students or attendees say they learned about KSW through Facebook

"We had to think carefully about the work flow," Leong adds. "I spend an hour a month planning our editorial calendar with my executive director. It's a simple spreadsheet that lists the different types of content, topics, and, of course, our success metrics. We look at that data to help us make more effective decisions the next month. In addition, I spend two hours per week on social media. I gather my data weekly so it isn't overwhelming."

MEASUREMENT MAKES YOUR ORGANIZATION POWERFUL

Leong has discovered what many measurement mavens already know: measurement is powerful, and it makes you and your organization powerful. Measurement is powerful because it provides insight and knowledge you never knew you had access to. With a good measurement program, your path toward improvement becomes clear. Dilemmas and power struggles disappear and are replaced with smarter, more supportable decisions. New data gives birth to new ideas, and—voilà!—your organization is improving.

Lisa has this to say about KSW's efforts:

> Using what we have learned, our online community is growing and interacting more with us. We are excited to try out new content ideas

like historical photos, congratulatory videos from artists who got their start at KSW, stories and poetry from artists past and present, and engaging questions that invite response. The sexy part is measuring the results and seeing how we're giving our audience what they want.

Social media measurement is a not a form of voodoo black magic; it is an art and a science. The art part is how you articulate your organization's measures of success and formulate strategies to realize that success. To do this clearly and effectively requires careful thought and a thorough knowledge of your organization and its audiences, and, yes, a little creativity doesn't hurt. (Defining success is discussed in more detail in the next chapter.)

The science part of the equation is starting with a solid methodology and making sure that the tools you use line up with your goals. It's having clean, complete, and accurate data. In fact, the science of measurement is not just about data collection; it is having the diligence to make sense of the data and use what you learn to improve your organization. It's the learning that makes measurement so powerful, because learning leads to improvement that leads to social change.

Says Allison Fine, coauthor with Beth Kanter of *The Networked Nonprofit*, "The lure of measurement in the context of social media is a full-circle seduction. Networked nonprofits understand how to bring meaning to their metrics. These organizations don't just count their metrics, they focus on learning and improving."[2]

Teddy Witherington, executive director of the San Francisco Gay Men's Chorus, knows what it is like to learn the power of measuring social media: "When we started using social media, we just counted the number of followers and fans. Every time our numbers went up, we patted ourselves on the back and thought we were being successful." But as Witherington's organization embraced setting measurable social media objectives and collecting data to measure progress, they discovered why successful nonprofits fall in love with measurement: "Finding out what other people find fascinating is fascinating. It helps us to refine our content in ways that are consistent with shared beliefs and values to increase engagement and become an attractive network."[3]

Measurement is a process: you go through it, you get results, you make decisions and changes, you measure again, and you get better and more efficient at what you do. Measurement, in other words, isn't just about metrics or measurement tools. It is about having a system in place that can assure your nonprofit's stakeholders that their financial and moral support isn't being wasted. Measurement is connecting the dots between goals, strategies, tactics, and metrics. It helps you decide what works and what does not. It is about doing your job better, faster, and more efficiently. It's about getting better at changing the world.

A DOZEN REASONS THAT MEASUREMENT IS POWERFUL

1. It gives you feedback so you know you are headed in the right direction.

2. It stimulates ideas on what to do next.

3. It helps you document results, so, for instance, you can show your boss that you're not "just wasting time on Facebook."

4. It gives you a credible way to report back to funders and stakeholders.

5. It helps you learn what tools and techniques work best.

6. It saves you time, because you're not wasting it on efforts that don't get results.

7. It attracts success by helping you plan for it. And it tells you when you achieve it.

8. It helps you raise more money.

9. It helps you work smarter.

10. It fuels your passion for your work.

11. It generates excitement for your mission.

12. It helps you change the world.

formal discipline, governed by rules and processes established and researchers. Certainly you do not need a Ph.D. from MIT in your pocket to measure your networked nonprofit accurately. But fuzzy, unproven, or sloppy approaches to the formal discipline of measurement are a waste of time. Moreover, they are not necessary. To do measurement, you just have to follow the basic steps.

No matter what your program or campaign—be it an event, a Facebook page, a messaging campaign, or a donor outreach program—there are seven basic steps for doing good measurement and getting valid and actionable results.[4] These steps are discussed more completely, and with emphasis on for-profit businesses, in Katie Paine's book *Measure What Matters:*

Step 1: Define your goals. What do you want to change? What outcomes is this strategy or tactic going to achieve? What are your measurable objectives?

Step 2: Define your audiences. Who are you trying to reach? How do your efforts connect with those audiences to achieve your goals?

Step 3: Define your benchmarks. Who or what are you going to compare your results to?

Step 4: Define your metrics. What are the key performance indicators that you will use to judge your progress toward your goals?

Step 5: Define your time and costs. What is your investment?

Step 6: Select your data collection tools. What applications or systems are you going to use to collect your data?

Step 7: Collect your data, analyze the data, turn what you have learned into action, and start to measure again.

Let's discuss each of these steps, one at a time. We give an example of putting this framework into action in the next chapter.

Step 1: Define Your Goals

The biggest mistake that many nonprofits make is taking a "fire, ready, aim" approach to social media. In fact, the first thing you need to do is ask, "To what end?" What is the desired return? What's the goal? What problem will this program solve?

Without clearly defined outcomes, you won't know what success looks like and whether social media are bringing you value. Defining goals is not necessarily an easy task. Measurement requires measurable goals, and measurable goals require clearly defined time frames, audiences, and outcomes. It may take a while to achieve consensus on these objectives in your organization. Later in this chapter, you will learn about this process for a social media pilot, and Chapter Five is devoted to a discussion of measures of success.

While your specific results will vary depending on your organization's mission, programs, intent for social media, and maturity of practice, the outcomes that you will be measuring will probably include one or more of the following:

Brand or mission	Changes in perceptions or awareness of your brand or mission
	Changes in positioning of your brand or mission
Relationships	Improvement in or establishment of relationships
	Changes in the health and strength of your relationships with stakeholders
Behaviors	Increases in specific actions, such as attendance, donations, volunteerism, or memberships

Once you've identified your outcomes or intent, the next step is to translate these into SMART objectives. A SMART objective is specific, measurable, attainable, realistic, and timely. SMART objectives include the answers to the questions: By when? and How many?[5] For instance, a good SMART objective would be: "Increase by 10 percent the number of volunteers we convert into donors by the end of our fiscal year."

Many times organizations have difficulty making the link from results and outcomes to social media use. This is where using a theory of change methodology might come in handy. With such a framework you define your organization's progress as a series of step-by-step efforts and results. (This technique is discussed in more depth in Chapter Five.)

Step 2: Define Your Audiences

Now it is time to understand the audiences you are trying to reach and how your efforts connect with those audiences to achieve your goals. There's never been a nonprofit with enough resources to measure everything it wants to measure.

This is why this second step involves setting priorities about what you want to measure. You do this by listing all the various stakeholders that influence the success or failure of your mission or your organization. There are probably at least a dozen, but that's okay; write them all down. Then write down how having a good relationship with each of those groups contributes to the success of the organization. For example, a good relationship with local elected officials helps get bills passed or defeated that affect the policies you want to change.

Here's a fun and easy way to prioritize those stakeholder groups. First, raid your old board games for a pile of play money, or you can use colored dots. Then get all your decision makers in a room and give them money or dots representing $1 million to spend on communicating however they like to your stakeholders. They can spend it all on one group, evenly divide it, or allocate it in some other way, but they have to spend it all. Then add up the totals. Whichever stakeholder group ends up with the biggest budget is the first one you should measure. The second biggest budget is the second group to measure, and so on.

Step 3: Define Your Benchmarks

One of the most common questions that nonprofits ask when crafting SMART objectives is, "How do we know that we've identified the right number?" If you determine that 20 percent of the social media conversations contain your key messages for an advocacy campaign, you have no way of knowing if that 20 percent is a good number or a bad one. If the opposition is at 80 percent, then it's bad. If the opposition is at 5 percent, then it's great.

This is why measurement is a comparative tool; you always want to know not just the number for the month or the quarter, but whether that number is bigger or smaller than something else. For instance, the number of likes compared to last month or last quarter or the number of comments on your blog compared to the number on a peer's blog.

So the next step in measurement is to decide who or what you are going to compare yourself to. The most effective comparisons are to peer organizations or to your organization's past performance over time. Sometimes the latter is difficult because social media is relatively new for many nonprofits. Most organizations begin by measuring over time, and then add in peer institutions or organizations with which they might compete for share of volunteer hours or share of wallet. Again, what is important is to benchmark against what matters to your organization, and often that is whatever keeps your board and the executive director up at night.

Doing a benchmark study of similar organizations doesn't have to be an elaborate or time-consuming burden. Pang Houa Moua is the first communications director hired for SEARAC, a national organization that advances the interests of Cambodian, Laotian, and Vietnamese Americans by empowering communities to create a just and equitable society. Their communications strategy included working with twenty organizational partners, and they wanted to improve their Twitter results. Says Houa Moua, "I didn't want to pick a number out of the air: one that was too high and created unrealistic expectations, or one that was so low that we easily made it."[6] So to help plan strategy, staff did a quick and dirty benchmark study by interviewing their partners to learn the size of their audiences and what Twitter techniques were working for them.

Sometimes, for whatever reason, your organization may not have history to identify the right number. Sometimes you need to acknowledge this, take an educated guess as your baseline, and dive in. By measuring and learning from your first phase or first effort, you will be able to set a more realistic number for the next phase.

Arts Council Silicon Valley did just that in its first study of the effectiveness of social media as part of the outreach for its Artist Laureate Awards. Says Anna Weldon, director of communications, "We were tracking downloads of the application, as well as applications received. Because it was a new program, we didn't have a benchmark. We looked at other grant programs and established our numbers based on an educated guess. Now, having measured the results, we have established a baseline moving forward."[7]

Step 4: Define Your Metrics

The fourth step in the process is to define and get broad agreement on what metrics you will use. Key performance indicators (KPIs) are the metrics that are most important for charting progress toward your SMART objectives. There are hundreds, if not thousands, of metrics you could collect, so you have to decide on a small handful that will be most informative. Although the formal term is *key performance indicator*, a more colorfully accurate term is *kick butt index*. In other words, if the boss comes in and says, "Damn it, we're getting our butt kicked out there!" what does that mean? And if he or she says, "Congratulations, you're really kicking butt!" what does that mean?

Vickie McMurchie, the community manager for Surfrider Foundation, an environmental advocacy organization for oceans and beaches, is responsible for social media at her organization and has seen the value in connecting the dots between its goals and KPIs. According to McMurchie, "We devoted a staff meeting, which included senior staff and department heads, to discussing and identifying our key performance indicators. Getting everyone on the same page for the goals helped us avoid collecting useless data."[8]

The important thing to remember about KPIs is that you become what you measure, so they have to be meaningful, actionable, and relevant. If you've completed steps 1 through 3 already, your KPIs should fall naturally out of your earlier conversations about goals and stakeholder groups. It is just a matter of translating your priorities and goals into a number you can calculate—for instance:

- Percentage increase in donations
- Percentage increase in new donors or members
- Percentage reduction in cost per member acquired

For social media, typical KPIs are:

- Percentage increase in share of desirable coverage ("desirable" can mean positive tone or favorable positioning)
- Percentage increase in share of conversation
- Percentage increase in number of conversations expressing support for the cause
- Percentage increase in conversations that contain your key messages

Step 5: Define Your Time and Costs

If you are trying to calculate return on investment (ROI) using the method we describe in Chapter Five, you need to be very clear about defining the return. But you need to be equally accurate in defining the investment portion. Nothing is free—in life or in social media—so it is important to identify the true costs of your social media programs. Since most of the cost is going to be in staff time, you'll need to find out how much time social media requires, and determine how much time you're going to invest.

Most important, given the amount of time you plan to invest, are your expected results reasonable? You may need to revise your time investment upward or reduce your expectations. Think about the opportunity cost of not investing time and whether you're shifting resources.

Also, you will want to be able to compare the costs of alternative ways of achieving your goals. For instance, if your plan is to use social media to get your key messages out, and possible alternative media are billboards and print ads, then you will need to find the cost per message communicated for all three media so you can compare them. If the goal is raising dollars, you may need to be able to compare social media costs to the costs of a direct mail campaign. Be honest and transparent about what your real costs are.

Step 6: Select Your Data Collection Tools

Your measurement tools are the techniques you use to collect data or KPIs. These include Google or other Web analytics, surveys, and content analysis. (Measurement tools are covered in more depth in Chapter Eight.) For now, remember that any tool is useless unless it measures what you have defined as a goal. The tools you use have to be able to connect your activities, their impact on the audiences, and your goals.

For example, if your nonprofit's goal is to improve children's health, then let's say you decide that lawmakers and policy advocates are your most important stakeholders, because a good relationship with them will mean that better child health policies are adopted. Your activity would be deploying a Twitter strategy to reach out directly to lawmakers and advocacy groups. You would measure the engagement in your Twitter stream via links and retweets, and then you would tie that activity to the impact of your Twitter strategy as measured by returned phone calls and meetings scheduled. If you have enough time, you'd do a preprogram relationship study before you started the Twitter campaign to see how those lawmakers and advocacy groups perceived your organization. And then you'd follow it up with a postprogram relationship survey six months or a year later. If you don't have that much time, you might want to track the retweets, responses, use of a hashtag, and message contents of tweets around the campaign.

The tools you choose need to deliver the sort of data that will help you evaluate progress toward your objectives. Don't allow yourself to get sidetracked. It is very easy to become seduced by the latest social media analytics tool or suffer from what blogger Alexandra Samuel calls "analytophilia"—obsessing over raw data without a clear idea of what you're looking for.[9]

There are three general types of measurement tools:

- Content analysis of social or traditional media
- Primary audience surveys via online, mail, or phone
- Web and social media analytics

Which one you use depends on the goals you established in step 1 and the KPIs you've established in step 4. You start with the object, then the KPI, then figure out what tool you need, as we've outlined in Table 4.1.

Table 4.1

Matching Measurement Tools with Objectives

Objective	KPIs	Tools
More efficient member acquisition	Percentage decrease in cost per member acquisition Change in ratio of traffic to completed registrations	Web Analytics and customer relationship management (CRM)
Reduction in churn	Percentage renewal rate by activity	Web Analytics and customer relationship management (CRM)
Engage marketplace	Percentage repeat traffic Percentage increase in retweets Percentage increase in use of hashtags Percentage increase in engagement	Web analytics or content analysis: Omniture, Google Analytics Facebook analytics Twitalyzer or Excel Twit Stats
Communicate messages	Percentage of social media items containing key messages Total opportunities to see key messages Cost per opportunity to see key messages	Media content analysis Survey
Change positioning	Percentage shift in perceptions Percentage change in nature of conversation	Survey Content analysis
Improved relationships	Percentage improvement in relationship score Percentage improvement in trust score	Survey

Step 7: Collect Data, Analyze Results, Take Action, and Measure Again

For any measurement to work, you need to assess results, make changes, see if those changes had impact, make more changes, and so on. That's how you continuously improve your program.

Do a postmortem and ask what went right and what went wrong. Remember that there are no failures, just unrealized opportunities. And if you don't use your results to learn, you'll never be able to take advantage of those opportunities. *Warning:* Focusing on only the best, most exciting results is tempting, and typical, but it gets you nowhere. If you are going to improve, you need to *stop* doing what *doesn't* work, so look for the weakest links. Move resources from what's not working to what is working.

Report regularly. Your data should be used for resource planning, so about a month before budgets are due, make sure you have all the data in hand. Then establish a regular reporting schedule so you don't just do a data dump at the end of a program. (See Chapter Nine for more on reporting and learning from success and failure.)

GETTING ALIGNMENT: THE HARDEST PART OF MEASUREMENT

Deciding what to measure is 90 percent of the process. Getting alignment, that is, getting everyone involved to agree on a project and its measures of success, is the hardest thing your organization will do. To avoid bruised egos and potential obstruction from coworkers, take sufficient time to get buy-in from everyone who will use or make decisions based on your results. Step 2 above describes a decision-making process of getting everyone important into a room and then voting with play money that can be quite effective in getting everyone to agree on audiences, goals, measures of success, or priorities in general. ("Begin at the End: Discuss and Identify Results" in Chapter Three offers more on healthy disagreements and managing expectations.)

Here is a case study about how one organization, Community Catalyst, achieved consensus on a measurement pilot program.[10]

Community Catalyst is a grass-tops advocacy organization that ensures that consumers have a voice in the health care system, primarily working with state-level consumer policy advocate organizations across the United States. They provide these organizations with policy analysis, strategy, organizing, and communications support so they in turn can reach state and federal legislators.

Like many other nonprofits, Community Catalyst dipped its toes in the social media waters not too long ago, beginning with a project blog about prescription drugs that encouraged discussion and engaged with thought leaders. This modest foray into the blogosphere paved the way for an organizational blog that covers a broad array of topics related to their different projects. It wasn't until 2009 that the organization added Facebook and Twitter to its communications toolbox.

Says Christine Lindberg, communications associate, "When we first added Facebook and Twitter there was a lot of skepticism. We kept hearing from coworkers, 'We don't work directly with consumers, so Twitter isn't relevant to our work.' Policy specialists felt that it was impossible to boil down complex policy points to 140 characters, and if they did, the audience wasn't there to read them."

Community Catalyst had run a couple of tests after talking with several partners that were using Twitter successfully, and, says Lindberg, "We just jumped in. A few months later, when the Affordable Care Act came around, we incorporated Twitter into our communications plans and became more intentional about using Tweets to directly connect with policymakers."

Community Catalyst understood that it needed a measurement plan. But taking on a full-blown measurement program, along with an aggressive integrated social media strategy for all programs and campaigns, seemed overwhelming. Lindberg says, "Social media measurement has to be manageable. It can't be overly time-consuming, as I don't work full time on social media." Community Catalyst realized it needed to start its measurement with one issue or campaign area and perhaps even one channel.

Community Catalyst's communications director, Kathy Melley, called for a meeting with Lindberg and other staff members to discuss designing a social media measurement pilot. They asked questions like these: What does success look like? What does failure look like? How can social media enhance success for a program or campaign that is high on our organizational priority list?

The team used a voting process to whittle down the choices to two very different ideas. Says Lindberg,

> The first was to measure an integrated campaign to promote a new microsite that explains how health insurance works. The project had a clear engagement ladder and direct outcomes to measure. Success would mean more traffic to the microsite and more people joining our mailing list.

The second idea was to measure a communications strategy for model legislation on health care payment reform. It also had a fairly clear engagement ladder, but the outcomes would be getting legislation introduced and ultimately passed in key states, which is, of course, a much longer-term process.

The first idea was appealing to the team because it was easy to measure. But the organization frequently worked on campaigns similar to the second idea and had struggled to find ways to integrate social media into its calls to action to collaborate with their state advocate organizations. As Lindberg explains, "Our role is often that of the middleman or coach, and it's important to explore and document how social media has value in campaigns where we are supporting our state partners. So to measure this project would be particularly useful for our program and policy staff."

Community Catalyst decided to go with the second idea but to measure shorter-term outcomes. The decision makers agreed that their key result would be "to empower their state advocate partners to more effectively work with state legislators, mayors, and policy makers on the issue of payment reform." They also agreed on their KPIs:

- Number of state advocates who take on the issue
- Number of state advocates who implement an integrated campaign
- Number of relevant bills introduced
- Number of relevant legislative bills passed

The next step was to use this pilot as an opportunity to improve their practice on Twitter and use it to engage with partners for this specific campaign. They identified several capacity-building results:

- To understand how to best use Twitter to share and provide resources and policy information with partners
- To identify best practices on Twitter and replicate them in future campaigns
- To track the specific conversations that state advocates are having about specific bills and see if those conversations grow over time
- To track where bills are in the legislative process

As of the writing of this book, it is too soon to know the results of this pilot. What is clear so far is that Community Catalyst has carefully designed a social media measurement pilot that is a small but significant incremental step, is manageable, and will help improve their results. The organization is no longer ignoring social media measurement, and it's confidently developing the measurement habit.

HOW TO GET YOUR ORGANIZATION STARTED IN MEASUREMENT

You may be wondering how to get started. Our advice is to begin with a simple pilot study. Make it easy and manageable. The idea is to successfully measure a program and thereby ease your organization into the measurement habit, so don't try to take on too much.

Chapter Three provided a list of important points for organizations that are changing their culture to become data informed. Once an organization has made that decision, it can use the following guidelines to get a measurement pilot off the ground:

Five Tips to Get Started in Measurement

1. *Start small.* Start with a small and manageable measurement pilot. Success will help your organization create a habit of collecting, analyzing, and applying data.

2. *Keep asking, "To what end?" to decide what is important.* Spend plenty of time identifying what you want to measure. Have your team think through what success looks like, and be sure to get past saying that it is "a thousand followers on Twitter." This is another application of the "To what end?" question: Keep asking why a thousand followers is important until you discover a reason directly related to your organization's mission. Also, do a "premortem" to understand what failure might look like: What are the worst results you can expect? Why would they happen?

3. *Plan to measure, and then follow your plan.* Don't collect data unless you have built measurement in from the start with SMART objectives and a benchmark to measure your results against. Don't wait until the end of the pilot to gather and analyze your data. Collect data in regular weekly or monthly increments.

4. *Find the wisdom in the data, and use it.* Don't ever just shovel data onto your executive director's desk. Share high-level insights, and make recommendations that can spark ideas on improvement

5. *Less is more; keep it simple.* Discipline yourself to measure only one objective or one channel, and don't collect more than seven data points.

CONCLUSION

Measurement is a powerful process that proceeds by simple steps to help you learn from your experience and become a more efficient organization. Use a small, manageable, and focused pilot to help you learn the basic steps of measurement. Keep incorporating additional measurement pilots, and before you know it, you'll have created an organizational habit.

REFLECTION QUESTIONS

Use these questions to help you design a measurement pilot:

1. What is keeping your executive director or the board up at night that social media can provide a solution to?

2. Is there a specific event, campaign, program, benchmarking study, or other small, manageable project within a discrete time period that would make the ideal social media project?

3. Is the project high up on your organization's to-do list?

4. Where can measurement improve your social media practice?

5. Who within your organization needs to help define results or give input on what to measure and why it is important?

6. Are there potential office politics? How can you mitigate them? Do you need to bring in an outside facilitator for a team meeting?

Don't Confuse Activity with Results

The Value of Expressing Your Results in Terms of Organizational Goals

Seriously? **Nobody** remembers the theory of change behind our launching a 24-7 live hamster webcam?!

*S*uccess comes in many forms. In business, return on investment (ROI) is perhaps the most common measure of success, but it is by no means the only one. Nonprofits use various definitions of success, usually based on their social change goals. Sometimes they measure success in terms of ROI, sometimes in terms of long-term goals, and other times in shorter-term results along a path to the long-term goals. We discuss all of these options in this chapter. In addition, shorter-term results often include increasing engagement (discussed in Chapter Six) and strengthening relationships (discussed in Chapter Ten).

As we have noted in previous chapters, measurement is a repetitive learning process of setting goals for a program, executing the program, evaluating its results to see what was most and least effective, revising procedures, setting new goals, executing the program again, and so on. Central to this iterative measurement process is goal setting and defining value: What does success look like? What results are important to measure? How do you translate results into value when the board or executive director asks why the organization is investing time in social media?

Not everything your organization does in social media will have a direct causal relationship to donations or earned revenue. Much of social media's value lies in its ability to help you learn and improve, understand the attitudes and opinions of your stakeholders, and ultimately build relationships. These intangible benefits may be difficult to express in dollars and cents, but their value is nonetheless considerable.

And before you say, "You can't measure that!" remember that corporations do it every day. They measure intellectual property, the value of their brands, and the value of their reputations. These intangibles are valuable business assets.

Social media is a vital tool for networked nonprofits, and it is critical that they invest heavily in it. Yet nonprofits often have difficulty expressing the true value of networked approaches and social media in a way that organizational leaders can readily understand. This chapter will help you with that by showing you how to understand various measures of success and then by showing you how to measure social media efforts in terms of progress toward that success.

We begin with an example of how nonprofits can communicate the value of social media to their boards and senior management by relating it to organizational measures of success.

OUR DAILY BREAD GETS A RISE OUT OF FACEBOOK

Our Daily Bread (ODB) is a small social service agency in Fairfax, Virginia. Its mission is to identify and address the unmet basic needs of area residents and empower the community to help its neighbors achieve self-sufficiency. According to ODB development manager Diane Hill, ODB staff (all of them part time) devote as a team a modest five to ten hours a week to social media, with the objective of engaging stakeholders and cultivating potential donors.[1]

After setting up a Facebook page, staff began to engage with their fans on a regular basis. When they set up an Amazon Wish List for their food pantry, they posted an announcement and link first on the Facebook page. Within minutes, a Facebook fan commented that she had just placed an order for ODB. Surprised and pleased at the quick response, the food manager immediately thanked the donor in the Facebook comments.

The next day, an anonymous donation arrived from Amazon: a big box filled with cases of diapers. Hill thought to herself, *This must be from the individual on Facebook.* So she checked the person's Facebook profile and smiled: it was a young mother, their target demographic for new financial donations. Hill searched for her name in ODB's donor database and discovered she had attended the organization's big fundraiser earlier that year as a first-time donor.

Curious, and since she had the donor's address, Hill sent a thank-you e-mail and asked the donor if she had donated the diapers. The donor responded with a very engaging e-mail to say that no, she had donated a different item. She also shared that she had learned about ODB at a local paint-your-own-pottery studio that partnered with ODB for its annual Empty Bowls fundraiser. ODB's mission to help families in need resonated with her, so she and her young son attended with her friends and enjoyed the event. Since that e-mail exchange, ODB has continued to cultivate the donor, who has subsequently gotten her friends involved and has continued to make in-kind and cash donations.

Clearly ODB's Facebook investment paid off. Yet if Hill had simply calculated the success of her Facebook efforts based on the dollar amount of donations to ODB's food pantry, the full value would have been greatly underestimated. Even more important, when the board asked, "Why are staff spending time on Facebook?" the staff could confidently answer that these efforts are helping the organization achieve its mission by cultivating valuable donors who also volunteer and get their friends involved and who will continue to do so. Thus, Facebook helps provide resources to serve ODB's clients.

CONNECTING YOUR SOCIAL MEDIA PROGRAM TO WHAT MATTERS TO YOUR ORGANIZATION

Affecting social change is, of course, the ultimate goal for nonprofit organizations. Learning best practices on how to use social media and a networked approach to connect with people, deepen relationships, and get donations are just steps along the path to social change. Social change happens when the people in your organization's network take action—whether that is to call their elected representatives, volunteer for your nonprofit or refrain from purchasing bottled water.

For social media and other aspects of a networked strategy to be effective, they must be aligned with an organization's program and communications goals. These goals may or may not be revenue related. A nonprofit's ultimate measure of success—achieving its mission—is not necessarily a financial goal. Thus, if you measure only revenue, you will not be able to adequately measure the success of your social media or even of your organization as a whole.

The American Red Cross understands this. Says Wendy Harman, social media director, "We do not view success solely as dollar amounts raised. We see success as empowering stakeholders to make our mission more efficient when a disaster strikes."

The essential question that networked nonprofits must answer is: "Of all the ways we could be investing our resources, is our networked strategy being implemented effectively to produce the social change that is our mission?" The way to answer this question is to align social media to organizational objectives, identify success, define value, and then use measurement for continuous improvement.

UNDERSTANDING HOW TO USE ROI

Return on investment (ROI) is a commonly used, and misused, expression of the effectiveness of programs. Of particular relevance to networked nonprofits is the continuing search for "the ROI of social media." First, we need to be specific about the definition of ROI. In recent years there have been a number of pseudo-redefinitions of ROI, from "return on influence," to "return on intimacy," to "return on ignorance."

So let's be very clear: ROI is the abbreviation for a business term, *return on investment*. DuPont created it in the 1920s as a financial measure, and Alfred Sloan used it to make General Motors manageable. ROI is calculated by subtracting the cost of an investment from the gain of an investment and dividing that by the cost of the investment. ROI is commonly expressed as a percentage. The equation looks like this:

$$ROI = (R - I)/I,$$

where R = return and I = investment.

The calculated ROI takes into account not only whether the effort generated a profit but what that profit was relative to the assets it took to generate it. A major advantage of using ROI to express the success of a project is that it allows direct comparison to the financial success of other projects.

Using ROI to Compare the Return on Social Media Efforts

The Seacoast Concert for a Cure is an annual New Hampshire seacoast concert with the sole goal of raising money for three local nonprofits that support breast cancer survivors. The three nonprofits split the net proceeds from the concert each year. Since 2008, those proceeds have totaled ten thousand dollars, so each charity gets about $3,300. Organizing the event falls to a small committee made up of the executive directors, board members of the charities. Each year, the individual charities must ask themselves: Do we do the concert again? Is it worth it?

Let's use hypothetical ROI projections to compare the results of possible alternative investments for two of the charities.

Consider charity A:

Net concert return for charity A = $3,300

Net concert investment = 80 hours of executive director's time @$40 per hour = $3,200

$$\text{Concert ROI} = (R - I)/I = 3{,}300 - 3{,}200/3{,}200 = 100/3{,}200 = 3\% .$$

Now let's suppose that instead of working on the concert, the executive director of charity A devoted some of her time to social media networking. We might suggest that she do two things:

- Identify four or five topics for a Google Alert, and add a few columns to her Hootsuite window—say, one hour a day for two weeks, or fourteen hours.
- Identify active social media influencers in the local area—say, two solid days, or sixteen hours.

That's a total investment in social media of thirty hours, or $1,200 of the director's time.

Now let's suppose that those social media efforts resulted in her connecting with the local Social Media Breakfast Club and recruiting ten new volunteers. Suppose that those new volunteers reach out to their employers and friends and identify two new local organizations as sponsors and donors, who donate a total of $2,000 worth of in-kind goods to the charity. These new volunteers and new partners may bring in more revenue in the long term, but for now, we can count that $2,000 in the "Return" column. So the ROI equation is:

$$(R - I)/I = (2,000 - 1,200)/1,200 = 800/1,200 = 66\% \, .$$

This hypothetical social media investment would result in a considerably better return than does the concert.

Now let's take charity B. Charity B has a part-time executive director who sends out e-mails, manages the budget and Web site, and finds and applies for grants. He did not work on the concert. All work on the concert for charity B was made by volunteer board members, except for $800 in materials. This is how the math works:

Total return for charity B from the concert = $3,300

Investment = $800

$$\text{ROI} = (R - I)/I = (3,300 - 800)/800 = 2,500/800 = 313\% \, .$$

In other words, charity B made back over three times its original investment of $800. It seems like a great return, but the question still is: Is that the best use of the director's and board members' time?

Let's suppose that charity B, instead of investing in the concert, pays the executive director for an additional ten hours per week for two months, to be spent on social media. That adds $400 a week, or $3,200, to the budget. Suppose the director spends his first month (forty hours) setting up Twitter, Facebook, and TweetDeck accounts. He also helps a few interested board members join Twitter and Facebook. The next month, using his new network, he connects with a number of prominent bloggers who run a charitable foundation and discovers that charity B is eligible for a $5,000 grant. In addition, a board member connects with the Twitter account of a high-profile sports team and develops that relationship into a $4,000 grant. Another board member connects with a local entrepreneur on Facebook who immediately writes a check for $1,000 and promises to sponsor the next charity B golf tournament at the $5,000 level. These are the calculations for ROI:

Total return for charity B from social media = $15,000

Investment: $3,200

$$ROI = (R - I)/I = (15,000 - 3,200)/3,200 = 11,800/3,200 = 369\% \,.$$

So social media would be a somewhat better investment.

Now suppose the board considers this situation and asks an important question: "Is the short-term infusion of cash from the concert a bigger help to the organization than the long-term relationships forged in social media?" That is not a quick or easy question to answer.

Clearly the lifetime value of the new contacts could be significant, but to realize that long-term return requires a long-term commitment to social media. And to estimate that return requires enough experience with social media and enough data on the value of relationships to back up an educated guess. This issue is not unique to small nonprofits; larger institutions with aging donor bases that are struggling to replace tried-and-true fundraising methods also face it.

Don't Use the Lingo of Accountants to Articulate Social Change

In the ninety years since it was developed, ROI has become so deeply embedded in business thinking that Wall Street views it as one of the major metrics for measuring business performance. Unfortunately, many people in the nonprofit and social media world use the term *ROI* as if they have actually been able to calculate the return on an investment. Chances are pretty good they haven't and instead are using *ROI* as a synonym for "results."

Let us be very clear: unless you've done the actual math, borrowing the lingo of accountants will not help you articulate value to your senior management or board. Quite the opposite is true. If you use the term *ROI* improperly, you are very likely to confuse and frustrate your organizational leadership.

HOW TO GET PAST THE "WHAT'S THE ROI?" ROADBLOCK

Many nonprofit directors and boards use, "What's the ROI?" as an argument to resist new initiatives involving social media or networked approaches. They often doubt the true value of these programs and seek a convenient way to reject them. One easy way to do this is to demand to know ROI:

"How much will it cost?"

"How much time will it take?"

"What's the dollar return we can expect?"

If you are feeling cocky, you might reply by asking them if they know the ROI of their mother or of the potted plants in the lobby. Do they demand precise ROI analysis for their lunches with potential big donors?

The point is that there are many investments for which ROI cannot be easily calculated, but that doesn't mean they are bad investments. From sending staff for training on a new system to an executive director's speech at a national conference, numerous programs show no obvious dollar returns, but they nonetheless provide significant benefits for an organization.

So don't automatically accept, "What's the ROI?" as a legitimate critique of a program that you propose. Our advice is to be prepared for this tactic by presenting the value of your proposal in terms that are closely aligned with the social change and financial goals of the organization.

Express the Value of Your Results in Terms of Organizational Goals

The good news is that there *is* a way to express your results in a clear and powerful fashion that your board will understand and appreciate: state your progress or results in terms of your organization's measures of success. How did your results help your organization achieve its mission? And, just as important, what programs did the least to help achieve the mission?

What you want to communicate is how your organization has received value from your efforts, that is, the impact that your effort has had on the mission. These are your results expressed in terms of measurable goals. For instance, to express the results of your social media campaign so that leadership will have a clearer picture of your success, say, "Our latest social media outreach program supported our goal to change policy because it generated increased Web traffic and greater exposure of our messages." Or, conversely, "We found that podcasts generated 50 percent less engagement among our target donors than we achieved with video, so we are shifting resources accordingly."

HOW TO THINK STRATEGICALLY ABOUT THE VALUE OF SOCIAL MEDIA FOR YOUR ORGANIZATION

The best way to ensure that your social media efforts help your organization achieve its mission is to plan to measure them that way from the start. Use Table 5.1 as a planning tool when your team meets to discuss what you're going to measure. One exercise would be to have your SMART objectives posted and have your team brainstorm the ultimate value and work backward.

If you are presenting a social media strategy or plan to your board or executive director, don't just discuss tactics. Be sure to explain how your plan translates into value for your nonprofit, what your success metrics are, and how you plan to measure it along the way. Also be clear about what is a short-term result and what is a long-term result.

NETWORKED NONPROFITS ASK, "WHAT'S THE SOCIAL IMPACT?"

In the nonprofit world, the goal of an organization is usually to achieve some sort of social impact, for example, save lives, preserve natural habitat, support

Table 5.1
Planning the Value of Social Media

SMART Objectives for Social Media	Ultimate Value	Success Metric	Data Needed	Tools Needed
Increase donations	More efficient fundraising	Percentage reduction in cost per dollar raised	At least one year of development data, for example, dollars raised	Excel
			Minimum monthly data on social media presence	Google News Alerts or other monitoring
Increase the donor base	More revenue from a more diverse base	Percentage increase in new donors	Development data on new versus existing donors	Donor relationship database
Increase the number of volunteers	More gets done Less burden on existing volunteers or staff	Percentage increase in volunteers	Two-year history of volunteer activity	Volunteer relationship database
Increase awareness	Increase donors and volunteers	Percentage increase in awareness	Awareness survey data	Analysis of social media presence
	Change in behavior	Percentage increase in visibility and prominence	Social media visibility data	Social media monitoring tool
		Positive correlation between increase in donors versus visibility		

Objective	Benefit	Measure	Data source	Tool
Improve relationships with existing donors and volunteers	Better management, more stable finances	Percentage improvement in relationship scores Percentage increase in donations from existing donors	Relationship survey data Development data on existing donors	Donor and volunteer relationship survey Customer relationship management (CRM) system
Improve engagement with stakeholders	Better feedback and ideas for innovation Better understanding of attitudes and perceptions of stakeholders	Percentage increase in engagement (for example, comments on YouTube, shares on Facebook, comments on blog)	Data on shares, likes, repeat visits, subscribes, and so on	Facebook Insights Google Analytics
Change in behavior of target audiences	Achieve the mission	Percentage decrease in bad behavior Percentage increase in good behavior	Data on the subject behavior	Society change data
Change in attitude about your organization	Percentage likely to volunteer or donate increases	Percentage increase in trust score or relationship score	Survey data on stakeholder attitudes	SurveyMonkey or other survey tool
Increase in skills and knowledge of staff	Improved results from intangible to tangible Using best practices, saving time	Increase in revenue per employee Percentage of employees who understand their roles and organizational mission	Accounting data Internal survey	Debriefing of data

arts events, or change government policy. But the value of behavioral change or social impact is often difficult to quantify. Typically a nonprofit wishes to raise money in the service of social change, so donation income is an indicator of its movement toward fulfilling its mission.

However, not everything your organization does in social media will have a direct causal relationship to donations or earned revenue or other hard results. "Much of the value is measured in intangibles that help you learn and improve, understand the attitudes and opinions of your stakeholders, improve engagement, and ultimately build relationships with the stakeholders who will determine the success or failure of your organization in reaching social impact," says Kathy Reich, director of the organizational effectiveness program at the David and Lucile Packard Foundation.[2] Therefore, it is important to measure both intangible and tangible results because they both are important in supporting the impact of the organization.

Getting a Handle on Tangible and Intangible Results

Tangibles, sometimes called "hard results," are typically required for organizational operations, are readily visible, are frequently short term, and are frequently presented as line items in a budget. These results are measured with transactional metrics and include donations, revenue raised, costs avoided, time saved, greater efficiency in use of resources, or waste avoided. They can also include the number of people served by a program, such as the "heads in beds" (the number of patients in beds at any given time) metric that hospitals use. Tangible results are:

- Objective
- Easy to quantify
- Easy to assign money or time values
- Common measures
- Credible with executive directors, funders, and boards

Intangibles, sometimes called "soft results," are vital for organizational effectiveness but may be difficult to quantify and are not tracked through budgeting or accounting procedures. Sometimes these are referred to as *process outcomes* because they are steps toward social impact and measured with transformational metrics. Intangible results include building awareness, increasing trust, generating new ideas, and deepening relationships. They:

- Usually describe attitudes, learning, or behavior
- Are usually more difficult to measure and quantify than tangible results, but they can be measured nevertheless
- Are usually difficult to assign a direct monetary value to
- Are often less credible as performance measures for executive directors, funders, and boards

Don't Be Hard on Soft Results: Show a Logical Path

Many organizations tend to ignore soft results like learning or engagement, often because management, boards, and funders have difficulty understanding the value. Soft results are often presented out of context and easily dismissed. Furthermore, many nonprofits are not able to show a logical path of results or what is called a "theory of change," discussed later in this chapter.

Here's an example of how the use of Facebook returned both tangible and intangible benefits.

Facebook and Donated Bras Provide Tangible Support for N Street Village

N Street Village is an empowerment and recovery community for homeless and low-income women in Washington, D.C. Recently the agency was offered a large donation of bras (a huge need), but to actually obtain them, the staff would have to drive almost two hours to pick them up. Given the size of the agency, this would have been extremely difficult to arrange and not an efficient use of time.

So the agency posted the need for a volunteer on its Facebook page, which had been set up several months previously. Within five minutes, someone responded with the offer to pick up the bras. This use of Facebook provided several benefits: an opportunity to volunteer, savings of staff time, costs avoided, and, of course, the direct benefit that the clothing provided for clients.

The lesson here is that the investment of time to build the network on Facebook was repaid, but not immediately. Unfortunately, management too frequently wants to see tangible results immediately. The solution is to provide interim tangible data on, say, a monthly basis—like growth in the size of the Facebook community, number of comments, or level of engagement. Then once a year, calculate the bottom line increase in efficiency by summarizing time spent as compared to time saved.

A THEORY OF CHANGE CAN DEMONSTRATE THE VALUE OF SOCIAL MEDIA

Many nonprofits struggle with how to chart an incremental path from the intangible to the tangible results in their strategies. What do they need to do and measure to make progress along their path to success?

This is where a theory-of-change method is valuable. A theory of change is a specific and measurable description of a social change initiative that forms the basis for a communications strategy or program plan and for ongoing decision making, measurement, and learning. Think of it as a ladder that defines all the rung-by-rung results required to climb up to a given long-term goal. A theory of change lays out the results and preconditions on a visual map that identifies the step-by-step pathway for social change.

In its simplest form, a theory of change consists of a series of, "So what?" statements that guide the design and management of an organization and its programs so that it can understand how to achieve socially meaningful outcomes. It requires stakeholders to articulate underlying assumptions that can be tested and measured, and it also charts an incremental path toward results.

Development of your own theory-of-change method begins with a "To what end?" discussion with your team. Your goal is to articulate SMART objectives with a clear chain of "so that" statements: "We will do such-and-such a thing *so that* we will achieve such-and-such an end." The intent is to get past simply saying, "We're going to get a thousand fans on Facebook," although that might be one early step along the journey.

Grantmakers for Effective Organizations is a coalition of more than two thousand individual members representing 350 grant-making organizations committed to building strong and effective nonprofit organizations. It developed its theory of change, which it calls a logic model, long before it started incorporating social media strategies. Staff worked with an internal group and consultants to develop it and then got feedback from members to get their buy-in. Its theory of change (Figure 5.1) serves as a foundation for its work because it defines the desired results. Based on the theory of change, staff develop an annual business plan and logic model, which includes how they measure results. Each year, to help them formulate their strategy and measurable goals, they reflect on measures of success and incorporate audience surveys.

According to Danielle Yates, manager of marketing, "Our logic model tells the story of how our programs impact the field and how to measure shorter-term

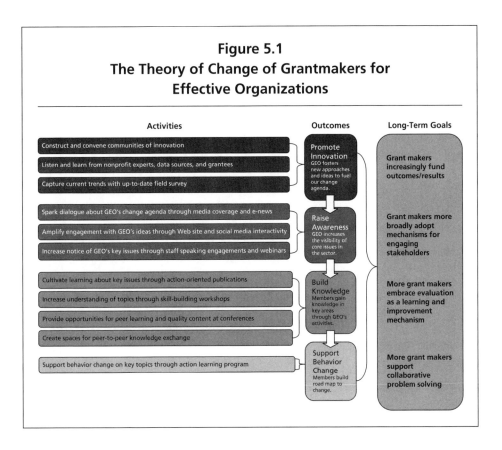

Figure 5.1
The Theory of Change of Grantmakers for Effective Organizations

Activities	Outcomes	Long-Term Goals
Construct and convene communities of innovation	**Promote Innovation** GEO fosters new approaches and ideas to fuel our change agenda.	**Grant makers increasingly fund outcomes/results**
Listen and learn from nonprofit experts, data sources, and grantees		
Capture current trends with up-to-date field survey		
Spark dialogue about GEO's change agenda through media coverage and e-news	**Raise Awareness** GEO increases the visibility of core issues in the sector.	**Grant makers more broadly adopt mechanisms for engaging stakeholders**
Amplify engagement with GEO's ideas through Web site and social media interactivity		
Increase notice of GEO's key issues through staff speaking engagements and webinars		
Cultivate learning about key issues through action-oriented publications	**Build Knowledge** Members gain knowledge in key areas through GEO's activities.	**More grant makers embrace evaluation as a learning and improvement mechanism**
Increase understanding of topics through skill-building workshops		
Provide opportunities for peer learning and quality content at conferences		
Create spaces for peer-to-peer knowledge exchange		
Support behavior change on key topics through action learning program	**Support Behavior Change** Members build road map to change.	**More grant makers support collaborative problem solving**

results that help get to longer-term outcomes. We look at greater awareness and engagement and the practice change that we're leading people toward."[3] "At first," she says, "we focused on measuring awareness, and we've made great progress. For 2012 we are focusing on measuring the next step along the path to longer-term outcomes, which is engagement. It is very much about scaffolding and a tiered approach. We annually update our logic model and strategy based on audience surveys and what we've learned from measuring progress."

Yates says, "It is really important to pick the right indicators or metrics. You must keep asking, 'Will this tell us if we're making progress?' If the answer is, 'not exactly,' then you need to clarify."

The process is about defining results and answering the "So what?" question. Says Yates, "If a thousand people follow us on Twitter, then so what? What do we want to get out of that? Do we want to move them to the next level of action? Download a publication? Attend a conference?"

HOW TO DEVELOP YOUR OWN THEORY OF CHANGE

According to Tom Kelly, associate director for evaluation at the Annie E. Casey Foundation, there are four basic steps to start building a theory of change[4]:

Step 1: Start at the end, and clarify your final goals.

Step 2: Identify the main strategies that you will implement to achieve those goals.

Step 3: Determine the length of time between strategy implementation and longer-term outcomes.

Step 4: Fill in the middle by identifying interim outcomes to occur on the way to the goals.

The last step is done by creating a "So that" chain based on the following question: "We do [strategy X] *so that* [Y results] occur for our audience." The Y results should be the direct change, result, or outcome of strategy X. Repeat this question until you have linked each strategy to your goals.

As an example, consider a fictional statewide children's welfare advocacy organization that wants to develop a theory of change to help it incorporate the use of social media. Their end result is that kids in their state are healthy and thrive.

Let's look at their series of "so that" statements:

"Our organization shares compelling content on social media channels that resonates with our audience of legislators *so that* we get more attention from policymakers."

"We want to get more attention from policymakers *so that* more kid-friendly policies will be adopted."

"We want more kid-friendly policies adopted *so that* kids get health care coverage."

"We want kids to have more health care coverage *so that* they are healthier."

Kelly goes on to say, "It is helpful to create visual representations of the 'so that' chains, like using sticky notes on the wall. You can use notes of different colors to write your strategies and outcomes, and these sheets can be easily rearranged. You also need to look at the typical types of outcomes likely to be associated with the type of work you are doing: advocacy, policy change, or behavior change."

CONCLUSION

Nonprofits use various definitions of success, usually based on their social change goals. Sometimes they measure success in terms of ROI, sometimes in terms of long-term goals, and other times in shorter-term results along a path to the long-term goals. Nonprofits must identify what success looks like based on their mission and then measure intangible and tangible results on the path toward social impact.

REFLECTION QUESTIONS

1. What are the short-term, midterm, and long-term results that we want to see as a result of integrating social media into our communications strategy?

2. How do we translate those into value for our organization? How does it translate into increased revenue, time savings, greater effectiveness, or on-the-ground social change?

3. What is the connection between our activities and our mission?

4. Are our goals primarily revenue related or relationship focused?

5. Are our goals in line with our activities and metrics? Can we see the connection between what we do and organizational success?

6. What is a realistic benchmark against which to measure success?

The Ladder of Engagement

How to Measure Engagement and Use It to Improve Relationships with Your Stakeholders

I know it's hard to measure engagement,
but there **has** to be a better way.

Engagement is the first step in building the relationship between your stakeholders and your brand. And in this era of overwhelming inundation of data and messages, an organization's relationships may be what most strongly distinguishes it from every other organization on a mission to change the world and get into hearts, minds, and wallets. That's the reason that engagement is so important to networked nonprofits and why everyone is trying to figure out how to measure it.

Measuring engagement is a way to determine whether you are making progress toward building a relationship. In other words, are you really having a dialogue that leads somewhere, or are you just yelling ever more loudly?

Because nonprofit organizations don't have resources to waste and their needs are generally too many, they can't ignore anyone interested in helping. Thus, most organizations have a diverse spectrum of supporters, from the lightly touched to the superenergized. To be successful, they need to create bite-size steps to engage all these supporters in their cause and to help them become more active doers, cheerleaders, and donors if they so choose. Thinking about engagement in this incremental way helps organizations understand and assess their efforts to move more people to deeper levels of involvement.

THE NONPROFIT WORLD'S LADDER OF ENGAGEMENT

The ladder of engagement is the nonprofit version of the for-profit world's marketing funnel, a time-honored concept with many variations. The marketing funnel is elegantly simple. It illustrates the different stages that people go through to become stakeholders. Most marketing funnels are based on the 1898 AIDA (awareness, interest, desire, action) concept promoted by E. St. Elmo Lewis.[1]

The AIDA marketing funnel has four basic stages:

Awareness	When someone becomes aware of your product or service
Interest	When someone becomes interested in learning more about your product or service
Desire	When someone wants to buy from you
Action	When someone buys something from you

The nonprofit version of the marketing funnel is essentially the same, but it is usually called a ladder of engagement or a pyramid. Every nonprofit needs to move people in stages from awareness to action. The difference for nonprofits is that the desired action is not necessarily purchasing a product, but making a donation or doing something that directly supports the organization's mission.

The ladder of engagement can be used as a tool to help analyze, strategize, and measure every campaign the organization does. But there is no one ladder or pyramid that works for every nonprofit. Nonprofits discover and create these based on their audience research and specific objectives, as in the following examples from Grist and Surfrider Foundation.

FROM TWEET HUGGERS TO EMBRACING THE HABIT OF SUSTAINABLE LIVING

Grist is a Seattle-based nonprofit that supports a destination news Web site for environmental news, reports, and opinion with a wry sense of humor. Chip Giller launched Grist in 1999 to counter the stereotype that all environmentalists were either dour doomsayers or holier-than-thou tree huggers. Says Giller, "Environmentalists often fall into a few stereotypes—you know the ones: they are descendants of John Muir who could care less about people and want to marry a tree, are self-righteous scolds, or wear Birkenstocks and hemp underwear and bicycle everywhere, uphill both ways. Trust me—I know these stereotypes well because I used to be one."[2]

Grist's editorial mission is to publish a new, positive form of green journalism with a comical twist. The vision is to spread independent environmental online content free of charge to a young and growing readership. Grist reports on everything from climate change to the organic food movement, demonstrating how the environment intersects with critical issues like poverty, health care, and economic growth. What started as a quirky Web site with a hundred readers has grown to a leading news source that engages millions who might otherwise be turned off by the bummer-of-the-day environmental news.

How Grist Uses Measurement to Learn How to Deepen Relationships

Grist has succeeded in connecting with a younger audience that not only reads its content but is also inspired to take action. It has accomplished this by using measurement to learn what it takes to move readers from being passive consumers of content to taking offline action. Says Giller, "We avoid the sign-the-petition type of actions. What we're after is getting people to change their behavior and thus creating a more environmentally just society." Grist's combination of entertaining content and clever integration of social media channels has inspired a new generation of environmentalists who don't take themselves so seriously.

Grist Builds Its Own Ladder of Engagement

Grist is a data-informed organization that uses a ladder of engagement not only to guide its content and social media integration strategy, but uses measurement at each rung of the ladder to ensure that it gets results. Says Giller, "Our theory of change is engaging users around content that empowers personal behavior change and ultimately impacts society at large. We're getting results because 87 percent of readers from our surveys have told us that they have taken action based on reading Grist."

Grist's ladder of engagement in Figure 6.1 is elegantly simple and illustrates how its audience makes the journey from passive consumers of information to

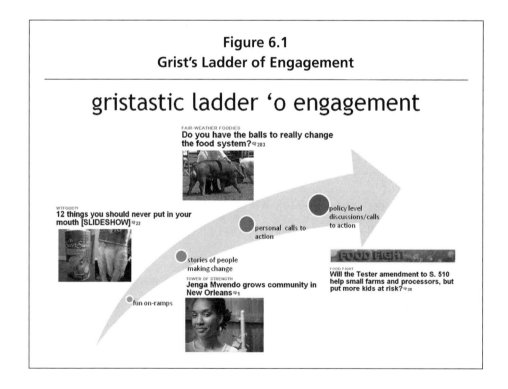

Figure 6.1
Grist's Ladder of Engagement

champions for sustainable living. The steps are fun on-ramps, sharing stories of personal behavior change, personal calls to action, and calls to action on policy change. Grist does not consider page views or other Web traffic statistics the end point, only an indicator of success at the bottom rung of the ladder. The real goal is higher up the ladder: societal change. If Grist isn't successful, the consequences are dire. Or as Giller says, "The planet will get it."

Grist's key measures are:

- *Footprint:* The reach of its activities, both online and offline
- *Engagement:* How readers engage with content by commenting, contributing content, and sharing the content with other people
- *Individual behavior change:* Impact on users' behaviors, including purchase decisions and daily routines that advance sustainable practices
- *Societal change:* Influence on society, policy discussions, and conversations that advance sustainable practices

Giller says that regardless of the topic, they are always thinking in incremental steps of engagement. They start with a simple question, "How can we inspire people to take action and change, and use social media as part of this strategy?" Consider Grist's coverage on food. It is devoured by a devoted flock of foodies, and the numbers show that it's some of the site's most popular content. For Grist, it's the bait that lures visitors to the first rung of the ladder. Organic food, sustainable agriculture practices, and climate change are all related, but most people don't associate them. Readers may come to the site looking for recipes for eggplant, but Grist's strategy is to lead them from how to prepare a tasty meal to a broader conversation on policy about nitrogen pollution or sustainable agricultural practices.

How Grist Moves from Social Media to the Real World: From Hashtags to Climate Hawks

To help make the leap from retweeting Twitter hashtags to real-world action, Erika Croxton, Grist's development director, says, "We view our social media channels as a fun on-ramp to our ladder of engagement. Once we've hooked them, we engage with our community until they own the idea and run with it. It means we have to be nimble and responsive measurement mavens."[3]

For example, Grist staff know from their survey research and analysis of comments on their posts that a lot of people care deeply about environmental issues but don't self-identify as environmentalists. As part of a recent engagement tactic, they crowd-sourced new terms for those who care about these issues but don't call themselves environmentalists, bringing in over 250 suggestions. The one that most resonated was *climate hawk.* Says Croxton, "This term eventually became the hashtag #climatehawk. What's happened now is that we have at least a hundred people a week using this hashtag without us pushing it. The mainstream media have adopted it, and it's attracting many new readers to our site. Someone is even selling bumper stickers with the phrase."

Another example comes from Grist's food and sustainable agriculture coverage.[4] It started with the Grist article, "Farming Is the New Hipster Occupation of Choice," a commentary on a *New York Times* article that reported that younger farmers are more likely to shun industrial farming techniques and embrace more sustainable practices. The problem is that the average age of farmers is rising, not dropping, and to encourage a sustainable food system, more policy support and programs need to be directed at younger farmers.

After Grist brought the discussion onto Twitter, a reader suggested the fun hashtag #hipsterfarmerbands. Readers then suggested humorous names for these bands, like "Radicchiohead" and "Lady Bah Bah" (Figure 6.2). Meanwhile, Grist continually seeded this conversation with links back to the original article. The tag trended on Twitter, capturing the attention of many and encouraging new visitors to the site to read and take action on changing federal policy. "Once something like this gets started," Croxton noted, "it takes on a life of its own."

Says Giller, "We've discovered that integrating social media, and properly tending to it and measuring and learning from it, is effective for attracting new readers, getting readers to engage with our content, and inspiring action—whether policy change or behavior change."

Grist's Measurement: Engagement, Indexes, and Surveys

Grist uses a combination of tools to measure along the ladder of engagement, including Google Analytics, surveys, real-time monitoring tools, and collecting anecdotal stories. Giller explains that "our whole team reviews reports from Google Analytics at staff meetings. It is like sipping fine wine. We analyze the content that users spend the most time on, referral traffic, and other key metrics over time." This helps inform decisions about content topics.

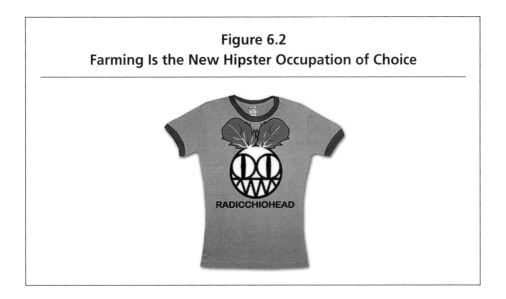

Figure 6.2
Farming Is the New Hipster Occupation of Choice

RADICCHIOHEAD

The editorial team, particularly the writers, uses real-time monitoring, which they describe as "crack." The team is careful not to do "drive-by" analysis, but balance this monitoring with other data sources to make editorial decisions. Says Giller, "Our content often plays off of breaking news, so real-time analysis can be really valuable in editorial choices."

For example, in August 2011, when a freak earthquake hit the east coast, Grist shared photos of some lawn chairs being turned over with the headline, "Photo of Devastation from the East Coast Earthquake."[5] Not only was the photo shared and liked by thousands of people through e-mails, on Twitter, and on Facebook, but it generated mainstream media attention and even got a chuckle out of prominent climate scientists. Because Grist staff had real-time data available, they knew they should quickly follow up with a series of articles highlighting scientific information about how extreme weather instances are tied to climate change.

To understand what people are doing with their content, Grist staff have created an engagement index based on commenting, sharing, likes, follows, and even donations. They use this index to guide decisions about engagement tactics, particularly through social media channels. Perhaps more important is how they measure behavioral change using regular surveys on the site, as well as an in-depth annual reader survey. They ask questions such as, "What actions have you taken based on something you read on Grist?" and, "Have you changed your eating behavior?" and, "Are you buying better?" They also ask whether a story has inspired them to participate in policy discussions or pursue an issue by contacting a company or local official.

To better understand the numbers, they draw insights from anecdotal stories, interviews, and comments. For example, they know from survey responses that readers who have not taken an action based on Grist content include people who say, "I'm already so green, I can't get any greener."

Giller acknowledges the huge challenge of measuring societal influence:

> We can rarely prove cause and effect and, to be honest, it is mostly based on qualitative data. We look at the company we keep, who is asking to be interviewed, and if we've broken stories or inserted new ideas into the conversation. Then we use those insights to help drive the conversation about sustainable practices and climate change to people who are not yet aware of the policy issues . . .
>
> We have embraced intelligent decision making, not excessive data collection. There's so much data we could collect, but it's potentially a morass. We pay attention to only a half-dozen key indicators related to our results around footprint, engagement, behavior change, and policy action.

With its approach of measuring along the ladder of engagement, Giller notes that Grist has garnered considerable insight about what works and what doesn't: "Our content has to meet people where they're at, so some is introductory level. We also know that facts alone do not drive behavior change. It is more important to see those changes modeled in your peer community, whatever that is. We shine a light on people who do make changes, and that inspires others."

THE LADDER OF ENGAGEMENT, ONE STEP AT A TIME

The strategy behind using a ladder of engagement is that an organization employs tactics—messaging, content, and channels—targeted to audiences at each rung of the ladder. These tactics strengthen their relationships with the organization or program and encourage them to step up to the next level. Combining this framework with measurement helps nonprofits understand which are the most effective tactics for each rung of the ladder. The ladder of engagement also provides a framework for envisioning the types of participation and involvement from stakeholders that organizations need to be successful.

But movement up the ladder doesn't just happen. As with Grist, most effective organizations make careful efforts to understand what decisions their audiences need to make to boost them to the next step. They carefully craft their asks or calls to action so as to influence those decisions.

It is important to note that not all organizations, and certainly not all audiences, will have the same ladders of engagement. Not every audience will move in an orderly step-by-step fashion from bystanders to committed movement leaders. It is not realistic, for instance, to assume that all donors will become further engaged with an organization just because they donated once to their friend's charity walkathon or to the latest international disaster relief effort.

In fact, the vast majority of fans, friends, and followers never go past that initial point of engagement. In most online communities, 90 percent of users are lurkers who never contribute, 9 percent of users contribute a little, and 1 percent of users account for almost all the activity.[6] Thus, you can't define success as getting everyone to the top.

Although everyone is probably capable of deepening their engagement with a cause, not everyone does it in the same way or at the same rate. This is why it is important to develop your own ladder of engagement based on careful observation of your own audiences and with reference to your own measures of success.

By defining a meaningful framework for understanding what motivates your audiences to progress up your ladder of engagement, your organization can better identify what data is important to collect and analyze. Here's an example.

Surfrider Creates Its Own Ladder of Engagement: More Thrilling Than Catching That Big Wave

Founded in the mid-1980s, Surfrider Foundation's mission is the protection and enjoyment of oceans, waves, and beaches through a powerful activist network.[7] It created and uses a ladder of engagement to map activism for online and offline actions, measuring success with one key metric, the coastal victory. Its ladder of engagement weaves online and offline actions together to illustrate how its activists progress—for instance, from awareness of Surfrider's campaigns, to downloading a fun iPhone app called "Beach Tetris," to showing up at the ocean shore to pick up trash.

Vickie McMurchie, community manager for Surfrider Foundation, has this to say:

> We care about people's initial engagement with us. That could be signing up for our weekly digital newsletter or commenting on a Facebook post. Since our goal is ocean activism, we measure if and when people take a deeper step. This could be coming to a beach cleanup or signing a digital petition . . .
>
> Social media has helped us build a large feeder system of people who are connected to us in a lightweight way, but that's not the ultimate definition of success. It's moving them into deeper ways to engage with our mission. This is no longer abstract, as we're measuring six different ways we can plug people into our mission.

McMurchie does regular analysis of the content that resonates with the people in the network: "We know that our audiences respond well to posts about celebrities engaging with our mission, but they *really* step it up when it comes to signing petitions or posts that ask them to vote for us to win money, or for them to watch videos or look at media."

It took McMurchie only a couple of meetings for her relatively small nonprofit to develop its own ladder of engagement: "We used our strategic plan as a starting point. Staff discussed and identified each rung of the ladder—degrees of engagement and the different actions." Once they got a description on paper, they asked for feedback from their chapter leaders. After they made the final decision about what to measure, they had different staff contribute data to the shared dashboard.

McMurchie noted that this customized ladder of engagement has helped get better results: "We've seen a steady increase of visitors and interactions on our social networks. We've learned that promoting events on our social networks has directly resulted in people attending events. In addition to the increase in attendance, we've also observed that as they become more involved, they're sharing that information with their friends and family who are then becoming more engaged online." And, she continues, measuring along a ladder of engagement is more thrilling than catching a big wave: "Before we started measuring each rung, we were really flying blind. We were just throwing Hail Marys and hoping that something would work and resonate with our audience."

Measurement has helped Surfrider staff fine-tune their engagement strategy and tactics. "We're working on a social media strategy that makes it easier for people to share Surfrider content with their network," McMurchie says. They used to post the same content to Twitter and Facebook, usually at the same time throughout the day, but they found that approach did not move people up the ladder of engagement.

McMurchie emphasizes the importance of tracking how well content resonates:

> The ladder of engagement has helped us to tailor our voice and content on different channels. For example, on Facebook I aim to be a friendly yet informative voice who will share information about our staff and offices. Mostly I'm there to educate and share pressing news stories that I think they will find informative and shocking. We mix Surfrider news and ocean-related news stories, as well as PSAs [public service announcements]. On Twitter, we're way more laid back and try to be "your friend"—a buddy you can complain to and ask questions of. Who's going to be a little more gruff and tell it like it is. We're still sharing news stories and promoting Surfrider Foundation, but we're engaging in conversations."

BEST FRIENDS MOVES PEOPLE FROM AWARENESS OF INVISIBLE DOGS TO ADOPTING REAL ONES

The use of measurement and testing has helped Best Friends Animal Society develop accurate messaging to encourage those in their network to take simple online and offline actions to save shelter dogs' lives. Here is how they used a ladder of engagement to improve the effectiveness of their Invisible Dogs campaign.

Best Friends launched the Invisible Dogs campaign in October 2011 to spotlight the plight of shelter dogs and encourage dog adoptions from shelters. Claudia M. Perrone, marketing manager for Best Friends, explained that they hoped "to call attention to the hundreds of thousands of very real but unseen dogs in U.S. animal shelters. Our goal is to capture the public's attention with the iconic invisible dog leash, which represents a homeless dog, in hopes of putting the odds in favor of invisible dogs getting adopted."[8]

The key metric is clear: dog adoption rates. And they know that the steps to dog adoption are awareness, engagement, education, visiting a shelter, and finally, adoption. The Invisible Dogs campaign is designed to move people up this ladder of engagement.

The initial push was to get people to the campaign microsite to educate them about the issue and pledge an action. David J. Neff, a consultant working with Best Friends, says, "They can adopt, which is the highest point of the ladder. But if they are not ready for that, they can volunteer at a shelter, attend a shelter event, or take a photo of a dog and spread it on their social media networks" (See Figure 6.3). The microsite makes it easy for the organization to track conversions and refine strategies.

"From the start," Perrone notes, "we wanted to have a very simple, clear message about the thousands of dogs in America's shelters waiting to be seen. Our approach was to capture people's attention in a fun, positive way and tap into their curiosity—wouldn't you look twice if you saw a bunch of people walking invisible dog leashes in your community?—and then provide easy, fun ways for them to get involved."

Neff says they used

> the #InvisibleDogs hashtag as part of a strategy to get them to visit the campaign site. We were able to track referrals from Twitter to see if they visited the site and if they pledged. We had over 40,000 visit the site, and 2,200 have taken the pledge to adopt a dog, walk a dog, or participate in an invisible leash walking event. We are also tracking dog adoptions. By doing a content analysis of the Tweets and conversations, we discovered that people understand the sad implications for dogs left in shelters. The hashtag also makes it very easy for our social media manager to reply to people on Twitter.

Neff notes that once people pledge at the site, their e-mail address is in the organization's database so they can send a thank-you and follow-up messages: "This allows us to test different e-mail messaging geared to get people to take the next action—visiting a shelter or adopting a dog. One thing we've learned from analyzing the chatter on Twitter and other channels is that it is important to get people to visit the shelter. So we did a National Shelter Check-in Day project, where we encouraged people to visit a local shelter and check-in on Facebook or Foursquare."

Another rung on the ladder of engagement was for supporters to create Invisible Dog events across the country. For those who pledged to attend or host

Figure 6.3
Invisible Dogs Pledge Form

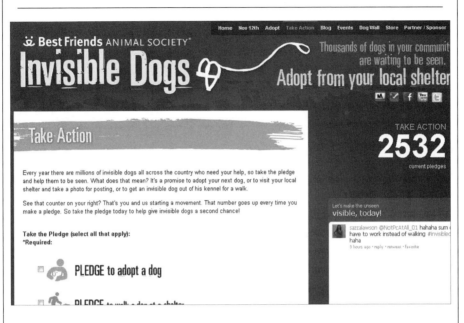

an event, staff sent a follow-up e-mail directing them to the MeetUp page. Says Neff, "Within the first six weeks of the campaign, fifty-two people in twenty cities created their own local meet-ups at shelters to walk 'invisible dogs' with the invisible dog leashes."

Neff says that their online Dog Wall has been valuable because, Neff says, it provides a lot of fantastic content: "We share great photos on our Facebook page and our fans love it—based on the likes and comments we get."

DEVELOPING YOUR OWN LADDER: LOW, MEDIUM, AND HIGH ENGAGEMENT

The rungs of your own ladder of engagement will depend on your organization's goals, communications strategies, and audiences, as will the metrics you use to measure each rung. What is most important to begin developing your ladder is to define the extremes. What do *unengaged* and *disengaged* mean for your organization? What does *high engagement* mean?

Let's consider, as a simplified example, a ladder with three rungs, or levels of engagement: low, medium, and high.

Typical Examples of Low-Level Engagement Behaviors

- Facebook likes

- Twitter follows

- Unique visits to your blog

- People who spend less than thirty seconds on your page

- People who land only on the home page

- Views on YouTube or Flickr

- Click on "Read More" or "Tell Me More" links

Typical Examples of Midlevel Engagement Behaviors

- Bookmarking or Digging content

- Twitter retweets or use of hashtags

- Posting ratings or reviews

- People who spend more than a minute on your site or visit more than two pages per visit

- Ratio of comments to posts on your blog or Facebook page
- Ratio of ratings to views on YouTube
- Number of links or track backs
- Frequency of checking in on Foursquare

Typical Examples of High-Level Engagement Behaviors:
- Request for membership in a LinkedIn group or online community
- Subscribes to a blog, YouTube channel, or Hulu channel, for example
- Facebook shares (including e-mail)
- Twitter direct messages
- Creating their own content
- Creating their own video
- Downloads of video, documents, and podcasts
- Conversions
- Donations
- Volunteering

SIX STEPS TO BUILDING YOUR LADDER OF ENGAGEMENT

To explain how to build a ladder of engagement, we use a hypothetical example told from the point of view of Katie, the executive director of Katie's Kat Shelter, a local animal shelter. (We will be continuing this example in the chapters that follow.)

Katie's grandmother started Katie's Kat Shelter (KKS) back in the 1960s. She began by taking in strays, turned it into a business, and named it after her grand-daughter. After several decades of steady growth, Katie's grandmother's health failed, and so did the fortunes of the shelter. It was up to Katie to bring the operation into the twenty-first century. The board had approved a new strategic plan, and now it was up to Katie to measure whether it was working.

To help her understand her organization and its audiences and to form a framework for measurement, Katie decided to build a ladder of engagement for KKS. The six steps that Katie used can be followed by any organization to develop its own ladder of engagement.

Step 1: Define the Goal

Katie knew that the first step in turning her ideas into practice was to be clear about the organization's goal. How would she ultimately define success? Was it organizational growth, social change, revenue, or something else? She knew that this critical decision would determine both the strategy and the structure of the engagement ladder.

Katie also knew that the demographics of the shelter's local area had changed from the 1960s; younger people had moved in, and the older population that was most familiar with KKS had either died or moved away.

Katie set as her SMART objective: Increase the percentage of members, volunteers, and supporters who are under the age of thirty-five by 5 percent by the end of the fiscal year.

Step 2: Define the Audiences

The KKS audience is anyone who cares about, has owned, and can own a pet within the KKS service area—about a fifty-mile radius. This includes anyone who has used the services in the past, including family members of people in the service area who may have moved away but still have family in the area.

KKS's target audience is personified by Veronica, a thirty-year-old volunteer who lives in the next town. She's been passionate about animals since she was a child, starting with two kittens that showed up on her doorstep when she was seven years old. So when a friend posted pictures of a kitten that he'd just adopted from KKS, she took notice. Since then she has moved steadily up the ladder of engagement to become one of KKS's most frequent volunteers, including helping raise thousands of dollars at the annual charity dinner. Katie knows that she needs lots more Veronicas.

Step 3: Define the Investment

Like most other nonprofits, KKS has no budget for a new program, so the cost of any new outreach will be the hours of staff time to implement the strategy and measure it. KKS has five people on staff, plus some volunteers who help with outreach. Key to this process will be the fundraising director Jason, and the office manager, Beth, who is the Webmaster, social media manager, and database geek.

Step 4: Define the Benchmarks

Katie asks Beth to pull together last year's fundraising and pet adoption reports. Beth also pulls her Google Analytics reports to see how many people visit the KKS Web site every week, how much time they spend on key pages, and how many pages they typically visit. These numbers will be benchmarks to measure future progress against.

Step 5: Define the Metrics That You Will Use to Judge Progress

The next step is to have a team meeting to get everyone on the same page, define specific metrics to be tracked, and flesh out the ladder of engagement. Given the importance of correctly defining success, Katie decides that she needs a broad range of opinions, so she includes Sally, the marketing and communications director, as well as Jason and Beth. For this meeting, they hang posters on the wall that describe each key performance indicator (KPI) for each rung of the ladder. Katie uses sticky notes to jot down data points that they need to collect for each rung and puts these on the posters. They put more paper on the wall with the following labels "Low-Level Engagement," "Midlevel Engagement," "High-Level Engagement," "Long-Term Engagement and Satisfaction," "Actions," and "Commitment." Then they brainstorm what each stage looks like and how to measure it based on what they know or have observed from their target audience.

They use Veronica's progress up the ladder of engagement as an example. When she moved to town, Veronica's route to work took her past a poster promoting an event to benefit KKS. She also noticed volunteers handing out flyers for the event in front of the grocery store. But although they had reached Veronica's "eyeballs" in a number of ways, the KKS team all agreed that those contacts were merely an opportunity to be seen, not actual engagement.

"So we can all agree what engagement is *not*. But what's the difference between low-, medium-, and high-level engagement?" Beth wanted to know.

Metrics to Measure Low-Level Engagement Jason explained, "Engagement begins only when Veronica takes some sort of action. It might be a simple click that indicates a desire to have further contact—for instance, liking KSS on Facebook or following @KSS on Twitter—but she has to actually *do* something. For example, when Veronica gets an e-mail from KSS that has been forwarded from a friend, if she clicks on it and then visits the Web site for more information about an event, she is clearly beginning to engage. Metrics to measure this low level of engagement would be unique visitors to the event page on the Web site or the number of likes on Facebook."

Metrics to Measure Midlevel Engagement Suppose that Veronica likes KKS's content enough to follow @KKS on Twitter and she regularly retweets their posts. Of late there has been a proliferation of particularly cute cat images on the KKS Web site and adorable new videos on YouTube, so Veronica routinely makes a point of visiting the sites, retweets the links to the videos, and occasionally forwards the images from the Web site to friends. She registers to receive an RSS feed of the blog. Essentially Veronica has now given KSS permission to send her content. She has also expressed potential interest in a longer-term relationship. Through her actions, Veronica is saying, "I like this; send me more." She is midlevel engaged.

Metrics to Measure High-Level Engagement The team at KKS was savvy enough about social media to know that at some point, no matter how good their content is, some percentage of their followers, visitors, or likes will get bored or become passive observers, and their relationship will stagnate. So in order to achieve its goals, KKS needs to measure whether its relationships with the Veronicas of the world are progressing. Beth suggests that they track the following as measures of high-level engagement:

- The percentage of visitors who subscribe to the newsletter
- The percentage of people who visit the site more than three or four times a month
- The percentage who visit more than two pages
- The percentage of people who spend more than one minute on the site

Most important, KKS needs to look at the content and activities that the organization is generating and compare them to the measures to see if there is a connection. When the meeting ended, they had agreed on metrics for the three levels of engagement.

The good news in this scenario is that Veronica hasn't gotten bored. She loves the "Feline Finder App" that she downloaded and is using it to connect her friends with new kittens. She gets positive feedback from her friends on the things she's sent along. She now is ready to move to the highest level of engagement by taking one or more of the most desired actions on behalf of KKS: donating to or volunteering for the shelter, and maybe even adopting a kitten.

Beth pulls up her data about the number of new adoptions, donors, the amount per donation, and the number of visits to the Donate Here page. She has noted the increase over time, not just the raw numbers. Using her spreadsheet, she correlates the increases in traffic to the Donate Here and Adoption pages with the activities that the communications team have been implementing. She also notes the number of people who go to the Donate Here page but then leave the site without making a donation.

Her research shows that when they changed the kitten picture on the Donate Here page from a standard tabby to a long-haired Maine coon cat, the number of people completing the adoption application increased. She makes a note to do some mini pretests on future kittens to star on the page. The discussion that follows this discovery leads to the creation of the Celebrity Cat Contest (more about that in Chapter Seven).

Measuring Satisfaction and Long-Term Engagement Veronica is now firmly settled in the highly engaged category. She recently became the mom of a pair of rescued Maine coon kittens. She is actively participating in Facebook threads, retweeting news updates from the KSS Facebook page, and sending out YouTube videos to all of her friends. And presumably she is convincing her friends to do the same.

Beth wanted to make sure that Veronica was satisfied with her relationship with KKS, so she looked at Veronica's loyalty to the cause. How often does she contribute or volunteer? On average, highly engaged members of the KKS community donate twice a year. Veronica, however, has already donated three times this year and is actively recruiting new donors, so Beth figures that's a pretty good indicator of satisfaction. Beth also tracks Twitter posts and Facebook comments to make sure that no one is expressing any dissatisfaction with KKS. She uses these metrics for long-term engagement:

- Percentage who donate more than once per year
- Percentage increase in average amount per donation
- Percentage increase in number of volunteers

Beth is also worried about donor fatigue, so she keeps a close watch on the ratio between the number of asks to the number of commits and the number of referrals from existing volunteers. She brings the data to a meeting to get answers to the following key questions:

- What are we doing/writing/posting that has convinced all those lurkers and low-level engagement folks to go to the next step?

- What is convincing them to care more about the organization or cause?

- Which posts or tweets or videos contributed to this increase in engagement?

Then they dig into the numbers to decide on goals for the coming year. What are reasonable increases to plan for? They came up with the following key performance indicators for the year ahead:

- A 30 percent increase in low-level engagement, specifically Facebook likes and first-time visits to the Web site

- A 20 percent increase in midlevel engagement, including the number of Twitter followers, the number of YouTube votes, and the ratio of comments to posts on their blog and Facebook page

- A 10 percent increase in high-level engagement, including sign-ups for the newsletter, download of application for adoptions, download of application for volunteering, number of retweets, and the use of hashtags

- A 5 percent increase in important actions: first-time donations, first-time volunteers, and adoptions

- A 5 percent increase in commitment, including multiple donations in one year, automatic renewal of memberships, and formal engagement, for instance, becoming a board or committee volunteer

Step 6: Select the Right Tool to Collect Data

Katie writes a one-page description summarizing the goals for each rung of the ladder and reviews it with staff. At the next meeting, they discuss choosing the best data collection tools, and Katie makes sure that the in-house experts who are using the tools are present. The tools they consider are Google Analytics, Facebook Insights, Twitter metrics, the spreadsheet programs Excel and Convio, and SalesForce or other membership management software. (These are discussed in detail in Chapter Eight.)

Then Katie leads a discussion with the team about how they can collect data efficiently on a regular basis. They realize that the reports will require data from a couple of different places and decide to split up the workload using a Google spreadsheet. To make sure that the staff collect data weekly, Katie declares that they're going to have "metrics every other Monday afternoon," and that Katie will bring ice cream or other treats.

CONCLUSION

Building a ladder of engagement and using measurement is a powerful combination to improve strategy and get dramatic results. Take the time to create a customized ladder based on what you know motivates your audiences. But remember that no matter what your goal or your cause, engagement is never revealed by just one metric; it will always be indicated by a range of actions. The key is to measure on a regular basis and associate shifts in engagement with the activities or content that you are posting.

REFLECTION QUESTIONS

1. What does high-level engagement mean to you? To your boss?
2. How well do you understand where your stakeholders are on the ladder of engagement?
3. What are the specific decisions for which data would be most useful?

chapter
SEVEN

How to Turn Your Stakeholders into Fundraisers

Social Fundraising and How Measurement Can Make It More Effective

Yes, I know Molly only made the minimum donation to your
social fundraising campaign. She's still coming to your birthday party.

When nonprofits marry tried-and-true fundraising techniques with social media, social fundraising is the result. Social fundraising is only a couple of years old and very much an emerging practice, but it has already shown tremendous power and promise in its ability to turn an organization's stakeholders into fundraisers. With 90 percent of nonprofits having a presence on Facebook in 2011 and virtually all nonprofits having some presence in social media, best practices in social fundraising are evolving quickly as nonprofits use measurement to learn what works best.[1]

Social fundraising can be defined as "people asking personal networks to give support." It encompasses more than just the transactional act of making a donation; it includes many ways in which individuals and their friends can support social good efforts. For example, when NTEN launched its annual fundraising effort, it enlisted the help of influential members and asked them to create online social fundraisers and reach out to colleagues. In a social media world, anyone can become a philanthropist for a charity, whether they have been in the organization's database for years or whether they have just connected with the organization for the first time.

The number of nonprofits adding social fundraising tactics to their bag of tricks has been steadily increasing: 46 percent of nonprofits in the NTEN Benchmark Study reported doing fundraising through social networks and social fundraising platforms in 2010, up from 38 percent in 2008.[2] Although the dollar amounts raised by individual organizations may seem modest, with the majority of nonprofits raising ten thousand dollars or less in 2010, the total raised through social giving is increasing. According to the quarterly Online Giving Index published by Network for Good, social giving increased for the first two quarters in 2011 compared to the same periods in 2010.[3]

If measured purely in terms of dollars raised, the future looks bright. Social fundraiser powerhouses and early adopters like charity: water (www.charitywater.org), which focuses on bringing clean, safe water to people in developing countries, have seen dramatic success from their efforts, giving everyone confidence that social fundraising is not just a passing fad but destined to become the cornerstone of fundraising campaigns.[4]

However, social fundraising's value to a nonprofit isn't measured only by funds raised. There can be great value in increasing the size and strength of your network. And there are other benefits of social fundraising, including increasing awareness of your cause, identifying new networks and partners, and growing the lifelong value of your donors.

In this chapter we take a look at social fundraising best practices through the lens of several campaigns and consider how to measure success and improve results.

NEW TOOLS AND TECHNIQUES DRIVE SOCIAL FUNDRAISING

The recent growth of social fundraising practice has been powered by new online tools that allow individuals to easily set up their own pages and solicit support from friends for their personal causes. Also fueling the growth are social giving contests like the Case Foundation's America's Giving Challenge in 2007 and 2009.[5] Contests are designed to encourage people to become champions for their favorite causes by launching personal fundraising appeals, setting goals, and raising hundreds, if not thousands, of dollars. Contests have also helped inspire nonprofits, motivated by cash prizes and lots of technical assistance, to dip their toes into the social fundraising waters.

More recently social fundraising has been popularized by the growth in online social fundraising platforms like Causes, Razoo, Fundly, Crowdrise, and HelpAttack! that make it easier for individuals to raise money for their favorite charity. These platforms help nonprofits empower their most ardent fans to ask their personal networks to donate. These platforms not only make it easy for people to donate online with their credit cards but seamlessly integrate social media into an online campaign.

The largest online giving event in history was Minnesota's Give to the Max Day, which inspired over thirty-six thousand donors to give $14 million to more than thirty-four hundred nonprofits in Minnesota over a twenty-four-hour period.[6] It, and similar "giving days," incorporate social fundraising components and have paved the way for the use of social fundraising techniques by many nonprofits, both large and small.

There are many good resources online about social fundraising techniques such as Network For Good. Some best practices include organizing a group of champions who are closely allied with your community to promote your cause, personalized thank-you notes, storytelling, matching grants, and working with free agents or influencers (see Chapter Nine).

CHARITY: WATER MAKES A SPLASH BY TURNING FRIENDS INTO FUNDRAISERS

September 18 is Paull Young's birthday. But back in 2008, he didn't ask for the newest electronic gadget or a dinner out as presents. This social media consultant wanted to do something meaningful to celebrate his birthday, so he decided to give fundraising a whirl. He joined charity: water, an organization dedicated to providing drinking water to people in developing nations and a pioneer of social fundraising, in its annual September Birthday campaign. He reached out to his family and friends, using social networking tools like Twitter, and his happy birthday raised over eight hundred dollars for charity: water to build wells in Ethiopia.

Fast-forward a couple of years, and social fundraising has been embraced by many more nonprofits. Paull Young is now following his passion for clean water around the world as director of digital engagement for charity: water. The nonprofit continues to be an innovator in fundraising best practices and raises impressive dollar amounts; in addition, 100 percent of the money raised is directed to projects. Measurement has played a huge role in its success.

charity: water founder Scott Harrison launched the September Campaign in 2006 by throwing a birthday party, charging people twenty dollars to attend, and donating all the money to build wells in a refugee camp in Uganda. He then rewarded all of the guests by sending each one photos and GPS coordinates of finished wells. In 2007, ninety-two people gave up their September birthdays to bring water to a hospital in Kenya. Says Young, "In 2008, the year I first participated, even more people joined and raised over $1 million for clean water projects in Ethiopia."[7]

In September 2009, charity: water launched mycharitywater.org, a Web site where anyone can have a birthday celebration in honor of a good cause or run any type of fundraising campaign for clean water at any time of the year. Young reports, "Since then, over 10,000 individual fundraisers have raised more than $11 million—including over $1 million for Central African Republic as part of the 2010 September Campaign to bring clean water to all of the Bayaka people."

The celebration for charity: water's fifth anniversary in 2011 focused on raising money to purchase a drilling rig for a partner in Ethiopia that will provide access to clean and safe drinking water to forty thousand people a year. It met the overall goal of raising $1.2 million online, which came from more than fourteen hundred fundraisers and donors. Before the campaign, Young said, "The campaigns will form a long tail, ranging from a few that can raise tens of thousands, to two-year-olds who can raise two thousand dollars."

Over the years, says Young, staff have tracked conversion rates from page visitors to donors to fundraisers: "We keep a close eye on Google Analytics to ensure that enough people are visiting the campaign page. We also keep a close eye on the video views for the campaign trailer—we think it's a great piece of content so we hope a lot of people will watch it!"

Young describes the September Campaign strategy as mirroring "our overall strategy, which revolves around building a grassroots movement for clean water based on the power of word-of-mouth. First, we aim to inspire with content. We have two videos on the campaign page that have had a great reaction, along with infographics explaining the campaign and images, banners, and other content available for campaigners."

They use a variety of predominantly online tools to spread the message: e-mails, personal outreach to supporters through Facebook and Twitter, and placement of ads in donated media spots such as AOL's Cause Module, Hulu, and Meebo. Says Young, "Once we drive people to the September Campaign page, we inspire them to fundraise. In doing so, they'll set up their own page and begin their own grassroots marketing campaign for the drilling rig. So twelve hundred September Campaigns become twelve hundred word-of-mouth efforts. For example, for my personal birthday fundraiser, I've been communicating regularly with my closest friends and family to connect them with the story of the rig."

Use Data to Make Strategic Improvements

Like the other networked nonprofits profiled in this book, charity: water is a data-informed organization. Young says that it's "one thing to collect data, but it is another thing to transform that information into action and strategic improvements. charity: water is a nimble and fast-moving organization, and our approach to measurement reflects this. We don't spend a lot of time developing formal metrics reports that wind up sitting on a shelf. Instead we keep a close eye on key metrics on a daily and monthly basis and use them to guide decision making."

Young's three-person digital team provides data to the rest of the organization to align all the other teams with the progress of the campaign. "Right now," he says, "we send a daily e-mail to our executive team pointing out the campaigns started and funds raised the day before, as well as our progress toward the goal trended against last year's campaign."

The team does a lot of A/B testing of landing pages and calls to action. Young gives this example: "We used Optimizely to run a test of three different video thumbnails on the page to see which one would drive more engagement from users. We tested an image of our founder, one of the rig, and a shot of a clean water well and then after two weeks chose the image with the best results to remain on the page."

Know the Metrics That Work for You

Young offers this advice about using measurement for social fundraising: "If you are set up to measure something the right way, every test is valuable, even if you don't get the result you hoped for. Define clear objectives that tie directly to your mission and monitor them rigorously." He says that organizations need to know and track the performance metrics that most influence results and offers this example: "For our September Campaign these included traffic to the page, number of campaigns started, and average amount raised by campaigns. In addition, we also know that matching grants and other revenue opportunities contribute to our goal, so we identify those."

Paull has these final words of wisdom about measurement: "There is a plethora of free tools you can use for online measurement, but it is easy to get lost in the details. Identify the key metrics that matter for you, and remember: the greatest analytics engine of all is the human brain."

AUTISM SPEAKS USES SOCIAL FUNDRAISING IN A MULTICHANNEL CAMPAIGN: LIGHT IT UP BLUE

In April 2011, Autism Speaks, the world's largest autism science and advocacy organization, launched its second annual Light It Up Blue campaign, a unique global initiative to celebrate World Autism Awareness Day and garner attention for autism research, awareness, and services.[8] The campaign used social fundraising to encourage hundreds of people with personal stories about autism to reach out to their networks for donations.

Autism Speaks' vice president of social marketing and online fundraising Marc Sirkin, sees the Light It Up Blue campaign as "a critical awareness-raising effort for us and the autism community. Thousands of homes and communities and more than two thousand buildings and landmarks across the world—including the Empire State Building in New York City and the Sydney Opera House in Australia—were illuminated in blue."[9]

This multichannel campaign did more than turn buildings blue. Autism Speaks engaged corporate sponsors in unique partnerships, like Home Depot selling blue light bulbs, to raise hundreds of thousands of dollars and allow families to light their homes blue. In addition, the campaign encouraged thousands of people to create local events.

Sirkin says the social fundraising component brought in both dollars and many new supporters: "Our supporters created more than seven hundred personal blue Web sites, generated more than $36,000 in donations, and reached many new donors."

The blue Web site component enabled the organization's supporters to easily set up a personal fundraising campaign and ask friends, family, and neighbors to make a donation to Autism Speaks. Pauline Murphy, whose son Joey was diagnosed with autism, built a blue Web site to encourage her friends and family to give. Her goal was to raise three hundred dollars, which she surpassed, reaching over twelve hundred dollars thanks to the combination of a compelling story and a personal, heartfelt ask for support to friends and families.

Moving People Up the Ladder of Engagement

Sirkin says the first step was to set measurable objectives that followed a ladder of engagement. The first rung was to ask for pledges of actions that hinged around the simple idea of "lighting it up blue"—where the "it" was selected by the supporter. It brought in over seventy thousand pledges. "Once people get engaged by taking an easy pledge," he said, "we encourage further participation via e-mail lists, social media, and face-to-face relationships. We provided an engagement platform with the Web site, iPhone apps, Flickr photos, and social fundraising tools to allow our community to design and customize how they wanted to 'light it up blue' from anywhere in the world."

"The Light It Up Blue campaign helped Autism Speaks get new supporters," says Sirkin. Autism Speaks begins at the bottom of the ladder of engagement with what Sirkin calls "acquisition": "We used any and all channels to get people to our Web site to sign up for our e-mail pledge, which puts them on our e-mail list. Once we've captured them in the database, we use targeted follow-up e-mail asks. We use engagement on Facebook and the blog as on-ramps. For example, we created a Facebook event for the Light It Up Blue Campaign that had more than 100,000 RSVPs and directed them to the Web site pledge."

E-Mail Segmentation and Customized Asks Prove Their Worth

The key to success was tracking the performance of targeted e-mail messages to different segments of their list, a strategy that Blue State Digital helped create and execute. Figure 7.1 shows the high open rates that resulted from this

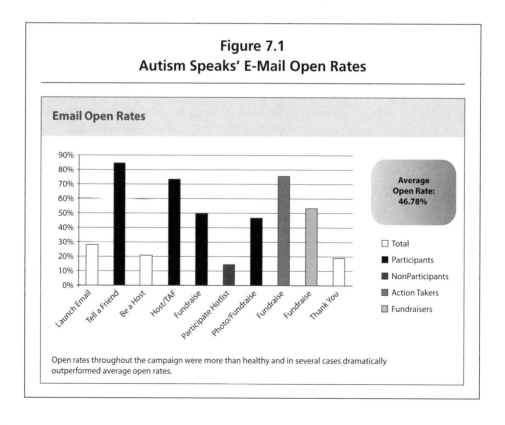

Figure 7.1
Autism Speaks' E-Mail Open Rates

Open rates throughout the campaign were more than healthy and in several cases dramatically outperformed average open rates.

segmentation, in some cases dramatically outperforming average open rates. Says Sirkin:

> Our first ask was to get our supporters to pledge their support to the Light It Up Blue campaign. That got them into our database. We could then customize our follow-up e-mail asks and track the response. We were constantly testing asks based on the level of commitment. For relative newcomers, a soft ask might be to join us on Facebook. But a long-time supporter who has a record of organizing events for us was asked to create a Light It Up Blue event in their community. We had a variety of asks, from setting up a social fundraiser, to tell a friend, etc.

Social fundraising as part of an integrated campaign helps make Autism Speaks more successful. Sirkin identifies "the mix of offline actions, mainstream press, retailer support, e-mail, and social media is what got us results."

SOCIAL FUNDRAISING AS PART OF MULTICHANNEL INTEGRATED CAMPAIGNS

Katya Andresen, chief strategy officer for Network for Good and online fundraising expert, defines *multichannel* as "building our relationships with our communities through more than one means (like direct mail plus online outreach). *Integrated* means we fit those different means together in a coordinated way, with the focus always on our supporters rather than our own internal, sometimes independently operating siloes. These approaches recognize that our donors might respond to direct mail one week and e-mail another. Or they like to have one follow-up on the other."[10]

Being multichannel can raise serious challenges for measurement. Simply adding in a public service announcement (PSA) on top of social fundraising may boost donations, but unless you plan carefully to separate out the results, you will never know if the success of your program was driven by the PSA or the social fundraising. Dealing with this type of difficulty is addressed later in this chapter.

Integrated and multichannel strategies that incorporate social media will deliver results. But are those results always dollars? Yes and no, as the stories that follow will show.

UCSF Challenge for the Children: Dollars Is Not Always the Sole Success Metric

Lena Shaw is manager of social media marketing at the University of California, San Francisco (UCSF). She supports the social media implementation of the university's strategic communications, as well as provides training and support for social media activities across departments on campus. She's a busy woman.

She had been on the job for only a month when she was called into a meeting with the fundraising, marketing, and Web departments to brainstorm how the university could make its first foray into social fundraising. This session led UCSF to join forces with the online fundraising platform Causes to plan and implement a year-end social fundraising initiative, the UCSF Challenge for the Children, to benefit the university's Benioff Children's Hospital. Shaw says they set an initial goal of a thousand donors and $100,000 raised but notes that "increasing community engagement—by tapping into influencers from Silicon Valley and activating new donors—was a more important definition of success."[11]

The campaign recruited individual contributors and team leaders who then drafted groups of supporters through their personal networks. Throughout the eight-week contest, more than fifty teams signed up to compete for various incentive prizes, with the top two teams earning the grand prize of naming rights to a prominent space in the new Benioff Children's Hospital, then under construction in San Francisco.

Susan Gordon, director of nonprofit services for Causes, says, "The UCSF and Causes teams started the campaign by defining what would determine success and the metrics. While dollars raised was important, getting the community involved was just as valuable. To that end, we designed the campaign to measure participation and decided that the grand prize would be awarded to the team that could get the greatest number of donors, regardless of how much they donated. Our final metrics and definition of success focused on how many people donated any amount, how many teams entered the challenge, and how many comments were on the leaderboard."[12]

Coming in first place was Team Zynga, which raised $817,375 through 162,544 individual donations. The social gaming company built a special feature into its wildly popular FarmVille game. Players purchased candy cane seeds for their virtual farms, with 100 percent of the proceeds going to the Challenge for the Children.

Says Gordon, "Once Zynga put the candy cane seeds into FarmVille and designated the proceeds to this challenge, they easily won the contest. As a result, we needed to adjust our measurements and metrics accordingly and always made sure to report numbers 'with Zynga' and 'without Zynga.' It was a wonderful addition to the challenge that generated a lot of money for UCSF. But in order to get a more accurate picture of how this success was actually achieved, it was important for us to measure how many people came in through FarmVille and how many people through peer-to-peer fundraising on Causes."

Shaw points out that this campaign was an unusual opportunity, one that brought in new donors from segments that didn't typically contribute: "Traditionally, most of our donors are at a high level—a thousand dollars or more—so there was often a perception from students or patient families that their smaller donations would not have impact."

Shaw reports that the vast majority of the 160,000 donors who participated in the contest were new. The development office is viewing that as a huge asset—a large pool of potential lifetime donors. She says, "We're cultivating these individuals, keeping them informed of the hospital plans, and continuing to engage with them through the same social media channels that they used to donate."

It's Not All About the Money: Community Engagement Is a Vital Measure of Success

A key aspect of social fundraising is that both community engagement and dollars raised are important measures of success. According to Susan Gordon, there are half a million causes on Causes.com, each with different goals, desired outcomes, and potential impacts on the world: "There are sixteen year olds who start awareness causes to get people to stop using plastic bags and there are also causes run by large international aid organizations. Many of these campaigns have engagement as outcomes, so dollars raised isn't the sole KPI [key performance indicator]."[13]

GiveMN, a collaborative venture to transform philanthropy in Minnesota by increasing giving and moving more of it to online and social channels, also looks at engagement and participation as outcomes, in addition to dollars raised. Dana Nelson, executive director of GiveMN, says that what leads to success is training, so that nonprofits understand how to focus on community engagement as much as the dollars and donors raised.

Geoff Livingston, a marketing strategist and author who designed the strategy for the Washington, D.C., Give to the Max Day event in November 2011, says that the "ultimate success metric for the participating nonprofit goes beyond dollars or donors. Social fundraising metrics for success should be the strength of community and return donors. The DC Give to the Max Day is encouraging nonprofits to build better relationships. Then they won't just be good at social media and fundraising once; rather, they will have higher visits-to-actions conversions and will increase their return donor ratio from an event like this."

Livingston also suggests, "It is about better thank-yous, more relationship building, better reporting, more access to EDs [executive directors] and other NPO [nonprofit organization] leaders. This should all equate to better conversion and return donors. This is what we emphasize as best practices in social fundraising."[14]

MEASURING SOCIAL FUNDRAISING

Measuring social fundraising starts with goals and objectives that are usually easy to articulate. Typically fundraising programs start with a dollar amount that is necessary to meet the budget, build the building, or in some other way help achieve the mission. Raising money may be the immediate objective, but it is actually only a step along the way toward completing the mission. For instance, Habitat for Humanity could build houses a lot faster if it just raised money and hired contractors to build them. But its mission is to eliminate poverty housing and homelessness from the world by inviting volunteers to build houses in partnership with families in need. So without volunteers and partners, its mission could not be accomplished—no matter how much money it raised. The point here is that effective measurement always measures the progress toward the mission, not just the size of the bank account.

Social Fundraising Measurement Has Some Tricky Aspects

Social fundraising brings a number of interesting caveats to the measurement table.

The Big Ask Can Hide Your Progress First and foremost, most social fundraising systems are designed to get large numbers of people to participate, not just raise large amounts of money. In the old days of fundraising, especially for small, local nonprofits, the fallacy was that the only way to raise money was to target a few likely donors and do "the big ask," using personal connections to get someone to write a big check. Other donations would follow once the big boys were on board. This practice was measured simply by whether the charity met its fundraising goals. All too frequently the only metric was: Yes or no? Did the new building get built? Did the XYZ purchase get made?

As we know, you become what you measure, and having just that one yes-or-no metric certainly focused staff and board attention on achieving the goal. But with a yes-or-no metric, you often don't examine the progress you are making along the way or learn about what actual activities are helping you make that progress.

With social fundraising, measurement can take an opposite and much more effective approach. Continuous ongoing metrics provide both the nonprofit and the donor with the information they need to make informed decisions and experiment with tactics until they know what works, what doesn't, who responds, who doesn't, and what is needed to get to the goal.

Social Fundraising Is Typically Not Used Alone Another aspect of social fundraising that changes the measurement landscape is that it is almost always employed in addition to other fundraising activities. Unless the metrics are carefully planned in advance, isolating the impact of the social fundraising component is very difficult.

Not Too Small to Measure Finally, social fundraising campaigns may suffer from a "too small to fail" complex. Major campaigns that include PSAs, media tours, direct mail, and events all have very visible costs, so return on investment (ROI) becomes an important metric. Yet today's technology makes it so easy and inexpensive to implement a social fundraising campaign that making the effort to quantify the return may be considered not worth the effort. And therein lies a great fallacy. Measurement is always worth the effort if it helps you make better decisions in the future.

Six Steps to a Well-Measured Social Fundraising Campaign

With those qualifications in mind, we offer the following steps to measuring your social fundraising campaigns.

Step 1: Know Why You Exist Every measurement program begins with establishing SMART objectives, and to set these, you need to understand your organization's mission and reason for existence. This may seem obvious, and one might wonder whether someone who doesn't know the answer should even be part of the discussion. But you might be surprised at how your employees' knowledge of your mission varies. It is important to the process to get everyone to articulate and agree on the organization's goals.

To help define objectives, whether for the organization as a whole or a particular project, one exercise is to gather a diverse group of leaders and managers and have them complete a questionnaire that includes the following:

1. How do you define success?

2. How do you define failure?

3. If someone says, "We're getting our butt kicked!" what does that mean?

4. If someone says, "Congratulations! You're really kicking butt!" what does that mean?

Then get specific and ask the same questions about the social fundraising programs.

If the answer to all those questions starts with a dollar sign, then you have your metrics. But chances are it's a lot more complicated than that. One person will probably mention relationships, another will say it's about meeting the budget, and someone else will talk about expanding the donor base. You may end up with three or ten goals. The point is that you need to prioritize the goals and get everyone on the same page, or else your metrics, and perhaps your program, will surely disappoint some fraction of the team.

Ideally you'd be meeting in real life to go through this exercise. We recommend handing out a million dollars in play money to everyone in the room and then have them spend it on whatever goals they think are most important. They can spend it all on one goal or distribute it among the goals. Then the pot that gets the most money becomes the first thing you measure. Depending on your budget, you can add other goals to measure.

Step 2: Prioritize Your Stakeholders One thing that sets most nonprofits apart from their for-profit counterparts is the number of diverse and frequently conflicting stakeholders who hold the keys to their success: new members, active members, dormant members, old members, nonrenewing members, former members, not-yet members, board members, donors, volunteers, staff, partners, and everybody's networks of friends and families, plus all the other individuals in your market who aren't even in your network yet.

You need to understand how a good relationship with each group can benefit your organization and how a bad relationship can hurt it. Good relationships with long-standing members of your organization may bring in significant membership dues, but their value may be much greater than donations if that's where your pool of leadership talent resides. Similarly, new members have value far beyond their dues, since they may help spread the word, be the most active volunteers, or become attendees at new events.

So make a list of all your constituencies, and next to each one list the benefits that a great relationship with that group would bring to your organization. Resources are never unlimited, so while you have your leadership team in the room with all that play money, get them to prioritize your stakeholders as well. Give them another million dollars to spend, and see where they spend it.

Step 3: Establish a Benchmark If your development manager tells you that your social fundraising program brought in $10,000, you have no idea if that's good or bad. It could be that the most recent event you held raised $150,000, so the contribution from social fundraising is paltry. Or if your typical direct mail campaign brings in only $5,000, $10,000 looks pretty good. Typical benchmarks for nonprofits are prior years' performance, but comparisons with peer groups are also recommended. Measurement is a comparative tool, and in the nonprofit sector, you are always competing for share of wallet as well as share of volunteer time and passion. So whether you are measuring fundraising, new memberships, or community engagement, you either need to benchmark against your own work over time or find another nonprofit to share data with to understand how good your numbers really are.

Step 4: Audit Your Data Supply The key to any measurement program is the availability of data. A problem today is that "warehouses" controlled by different parts of an organization typically keep the data. It is not uncommon to find a single nonprofit with a dozen different measurement systems, all operating independently. Public affairs departments will have a traditional media monitoring system in place, those in development will own the fundraising data, the membership staff control the customer relationship management (CRM) system, and the Web folks are happy with their Google Analytics. Meanwhile, the social media team gives up trying to get data out of any of them and goes out and hires its own measurement firm. One key to effective measurement is to get all these systems and the people who control the data to talk to one another.

Your mission is to find out who is measuring what in your organization. You may need to get a little technical. Find out what data is being tracked, over what period, how it's stored, and how it can it be exported. Is anyone doing any statistical analysis of the data? You need to make a list that includes all surveys that are conducted, any Web analytics collected, any media monitoring programs, and any conversion data being stored. Don't be surprised if you end up with a very long list.

Step 5: Choose Your Metrics Social fundraising can drive behavior in many forms beyond just donations, including increasing the size of your network, the sharing of information, subscriptions to your newsletter or RSS feed, Web traffic, e-mail responses, attendance at events and trade shows, and votes, to name a few. All are relatively easy to measure once you have a tracking system in place.

Typical metrics might be:

- Percentage increase in number of donors
- Percentage increase in size of donations
- Percentage increase in frequency of donations
- Percentage increase in first-time donors
- Percentage reduction in time between donations

If you are comparing social fundraising to other tactics, you might want to add some cost ratios to your metrics such as these:

- *Cost per donor acquired.* Count the number of new donors each month. Divide that number into the total amount (including salaries) that you spend trying to get those donors.
- *Cost per volunteer acquired.* Track the number of new volunteers you've signed up each month. Divide that number into the total amount (including salaries) that you spent in recruitment efforts.

Don't forget to investigate the lifetime value of your donors. Every new contact, donor, or member will be a resource for your organization for some length of time into the future. Many of them you will never hear from again, but some will become steady donors or supporters for years, and some will eventually even leave you money in their wills. The lifetime value of a donor will vary greatly from organization to organization, but the point here is that you can use your data to understand what it is for your own nonprofit. If you can determine how to increase this value even slightly, over a large number of donors it can make a significant difference.

Step 6: Design Your Program to Measure the Contribution of Specific Tactics Social fundraising is typically part of an integrated campaign, so measuring it is like trying to track the flight of one arrow among many. It is possible, but it requires commitment and planning. Standard fundraising practice is to define a goal and associated metrics for an entire campaign and launch all aspects of the campaign at once. However, if you are going to measure the contribution of social fundraising, you need to be willing to roll out the campaign in phases and measure progress along the way.

A good measurement program looks at as many different influences as the budget allows. At the very least, take into account what your stakeholders are seeing in the media, what they're exposed to online, and what they're hearing from you.

KATIE'S KAT SHELTER MEASURES A CAPITAL CAMPAIGN

Social fundraising is such a new field that there are as yet few case studies of its measurement. But Katie's Kat Shelter (KKS), the hypothetical charity we introduced in Chapter Six, will serve as an example to demonstrate the measurement of social fundraising in an integrated campaign.

Suppose that the faltering economy results in record numbers of cats being dropped off at KKS and that the local population is not adopting them fast enough to keep pace. The board has realized that it needs to expand its facilities and authorizes a capital campaign to identify and purchase a new shelter. However, Jason, the fundraising director, fears that the local supporter base of cat lovers and businesses might be tapped out. So Beth, KKS's social media guru, suggests starting a social fundraising program as a way to expand their network and get new cat lovers involved in the organization. The team quickly jumps on the idea of doing a campaign around World Cat Day on August 8 that will connect cat lovers from all over.

The campaign will roll out in several phases:

- A social media launch publicized with a series of tweets, a new Facebook page, and a barrage of cute cat videos.

- A traditional PR push

- A virtual Celebrity Cat Show in which local movers and shakers who are cat fanciers post pictures of their cats on Facebook to compete for cutest cat

- A PSA that airs on the three local TV stations

Before launching anything, Katie, the executive director, pulls together a meeting of the development, information technology, and digital groups to find out what data already exists. They brainstorm and ultimately define the following metrics as possible indicators of success that can be tracked weekly:

- Percentage increase in number of donations from online versus offline

- Percentage increase in number of individual donors from online versus offline

- Percentage increase in new revenue from online versus offline sources

- Percentage increase in RSS subscribes

- Percentage increase in Facebook likes

- Percentage increase in number of Facebook comments

- Percentage increase in shares

- Percentage increase in video views

- Percentage increase in Twitter followers

- Percentage increase in retweets

- Percentage increase in number of mentions in all earned media

Keeping track of so many metrics would raise hackles on the tamest tabby, so before everyone got overwhelmed, the group reexamined their priorities and narrowed down their metrics to three that they would compile into a weekly dashboard:

- Percentage increase in higher levels of engagement as measured by number of retweets, Facebook shares and comments, video views, RSS subscribers, and users of their social fundraising tool

- Percentage increase in number of donors
- Percentage increase in the size of the network as measured by total subscribers, members, followers, likes, and social fundraising connections

Beth volunteered to set up a spreadsheet to track the various campaign activities on a daily basis:

- A list of any press releases
- The number and subject of tweets
- The number and subject of Facebook posts and comments

By tracking specific activities against the three metrics, they could easily identify which activities helped move the dashboard needles the most and, more important, which ones weren't helping at all.

Once the measurement strategy had been agreed on, they were set to roll out the program. First, they signed up with a social fundraising platform and posted the information on their own Web site. They carefully noted the results they received from the platform's metrics and from their own Web site, and after a few days, they spread the word on Twitter and Facebook, tracking results daily at first and then weekly.

After three weeks of exclusive social media activity, sufficient data had been gathered to show its impact. Then it was time to roll out more traditional promotions. First, the PSA was launched and ran repeatedly on local media. Again, the team noted any changes in results after each airing. Then the traditional media push announced the Celebrity Cat Show. Again, key metrics were tracked daily and weekly to see the cumulative impact of the traditional media push. Finally, when the Celebrity Cat Show started, they again noted any increase in donations, donors, and engagement driven by it.

The campaign ended with financial success: donations were more than enough to purchase a new shelter. Moreover, Katie and her team had documented that while the PSA and traditional media push all moved the needle incrementally, the clear winner was the Celebrity Cat Show, as local celebrities and wannabe celebrities had escalated their battles to both bring in new donors and win the contest on behalf of their cat. The KKS board was delighted and is considering a greatly expanded budget for next year's Celebrity Cat Show.

CONCLUSION

Many nonprofits, especially smaller ones, have begun social fundraising and the measurement of their success using small experiments on social fundraising platforms. Whatever the size of your effort, remember to begin with SMART objectives, track results, and determine what works and what doesn't. If the direct dollar results from a campaign are small, it is easy to assume that it isn't worth the effort. But success isn't measured in just dollars raised: social fundraising can expand your network and create a pipeline of new donors into your database. Although there are a number of tactical best practices, social fundraising is more effective if it is integrated with other communication channels and includes a well-thought-out measurement plan.

REFLECTION QUESTIONS

1. Does your executive director or board consider dollars raised the sole measure of success for social fundraising? If so, how can you use the stories and tips presented here to educate them about the importance of measuring community engagement?

2. Do you have an upcoming campaign for which it makes sense to integrate and measure a social fundraising pilot?

3. If so, what can you test to learn about community engagement from your social fundraising campaign?

4. What is the SMART objective of your social fundraising effort? Remember to quantify both engagement and dollars.

5. What is your organization's suggested path to get people from awareness, to engagement, to donations, to repeat donations? Do you have strategy for each? Do you have a way to measure success for each?

Measurement Tools

How to Choose and Use the
Right Tool for the Job

Just how many dashboards do you need to track one Twitter feed?

easurement tools and systems have advanced tremendously in the past decade or so. Gathering data, whether from media outlets or customers, becomes faster and cheaper every year, and new tools and techniques are developed all the time. There are currently more than 250 tools that a networked nonprofit can choose from to measure its results. This chapter covers the major categories of tools you will need, but the only way to stay on top of new developments is to continually educate yourself. (For a list of educational resources for measurement tools, see the last section of this chapter.)

The reality is that to measure social media effectiveness, nonprofits need to go beyond just using social and Web analytics. Your organization must have three types of tools in order to do measurement correctly:

- *Survey tools:* to measure what your stakeholders are thinking, feeling, believing, or perceiving
- *Content analysis tools:* to determine what people are writing and saying about you
- *Web and social analytics tools:* to determine whether, as a result of your efforts, anyone is taking any action or becoming more engaged

This chapter discusses these three categories of tools and how to use them to collect specific types of data to measure progress toward your goals. Chances are that your nonprofit will need to use two out of the three categories of tools, but which ones will depend entirely on your goals and what you want to measure.

Many nonprofits tend to lean on Web analytics tools, mostly due to the popularity of free tools like Google Analytics. In November 2011, Trudel MacPherson and Sen Associates released the findings from "How Strong is Your Social Net?" their national survey of the use of social media by over one thousand arts nonprofits.[1] Says Mary Trudel, "About three-quarters of participants said they were using Web and social analytics tools. There was a big gap compared with use of other tools, including online surveys (28 percent) and content analysis. These lower-scoring tools also offer opportunities for nonprofits to learn what stakeholders do and say so organizations can more effectively calibrate their strategies."[2]

The most important thing to remember about measurement tools is that they will do only what you tell them to do. Collecting data is easy, but collecting the right data to answer your questions requires careful planning and appropriate tools. If you think about it, every online click leaves a data trail that can be captured. Measurement tools, especially Web and social analytics tools, can collect lots of data. The challenge is to figure out what data really matters to you. And if you try to decide which specific tools you will need before you figure out what you want to measure, then you'll wash away in a tsunami of data.

THE INDISPENSABLE SPREADSHEET

There is one other asset you will definitely need: a person to be your spreadsheet ninja. When nonprofit measurement mavens were surveyed for this book, the secret they most often shared is that no matter what data and tools are available, they all need someone in their organization to become a spreadsheet expert.

Spreadsheets are the Swiss army knife of measurement tools, whether it is a Google spreadsheet shared online or a Microsoft Excel spreadsheet stored on your desktop. Shonali Burke said, "Spreadsheets are especially valuable for nonprofits with limited resources. As long as you are tracking data points consistently, you can use simple correlation formulas to see how your efforts are impacting your outcomes."[3] Burke notes that most measurement tools have the ability to easily export data, and analyzing the data in a spreadsheet is easy and inexpensive.

Holly Ross, executive director of NTEN, also loves spreadsheets: "I pull in metrics from all over the Web to get instant snapshots and create graphs that show changes. While it takes a little bit of time, the tool is free."[4] Ross says being focused is very important because the more you track, the more time you spend on this.

Many nonprofits think that fancy analytics or monitoring software will provide them with actionable information with just a click or two. This is seldom the case. Analytics and monitoring tools are great at scooping data—lots of data—from the social Web, but to make sense of the data and glean valuable insights requires additional work. That work means a little effort but does not require genius-level talent or root-canal-like pain. It's often actually fun and even exciting. (We discuss data analysis in depth in Chapter Nine.)

THE RIGHT TOOL FOR THE JOB

It used to be that the biggest barrier to measurement was cost. Today, with the proliferation of tool choices, the biggest barrier is figuring out just which ones you need to collect the data that will lead your nonprofit to success. Even the most sophisticated measurement tool is worthless if it can't measure progress toward your goals. If your goal is awareness, for instance, no amount of simple media content analysis will tell you if you are achieving it. You must use some technique that will measure the degree to which your publics are truly aware of your brand, your brand benefits, or your messages. Table 8.1 provides some examples of program objectives, typical metrics for measuring those objectives, tools to gather the data, and sample vendors to supply those tools. These are just a few examples from the many options available; what you actually use will depend on the details of your program.

Table 8.1
Selecting Measurement Tools to Measure Your Goals

Objective	Key Performance Indicators	Tools
Increase inquiries, Web traffic, recruitment	Percentage increase in traffic Number of click-throughs or downloads	Web analytics: Google Analytics, Omniture, Webtrends
Increase awareness or preference	Percentage of audience preferring your brand to the competition's	Survey: Online (SurveyMonkey) or by mail
Engage marketplace	Conversation index greater than .8 Rankings Percentage increase in engagement	Web analytics or content analysis: TypePad, Technorati, Omniture, Google Analytics
Communicate messages	Percentage of articles containing key messages Total opportunities to see key messages Cost per opportunity to see key messages	Media content analysis
	Percentage aware of or believing in key message	Survey

TOOLS TO DETERMINE WHAT YOUR MARKETPLACE IS THINKING: A VERY BRIEF GUIDE TO SURVEYS

If your objective is to increase awareness of your mission or issue or your goal is to educate an audience, you need a tool that measures opinion. Polling and opinion research is by far the oldest and most widely used form of measurement. Pre- and postsurveys and A/B testing are commonly used to determine if a particular program changed opinions or awareness. An initial study establishes a baseline, and a follow-up study determines if opinion has shifted.

Depending on your goals, you will need different types of surveys.

If Your Goal Is to Increase Awareness

Awareness is the extent to which an audience is conscious of something. The change of awareness brought about by a certain program can be determined only by surveying members of the audience at which that program is directed.

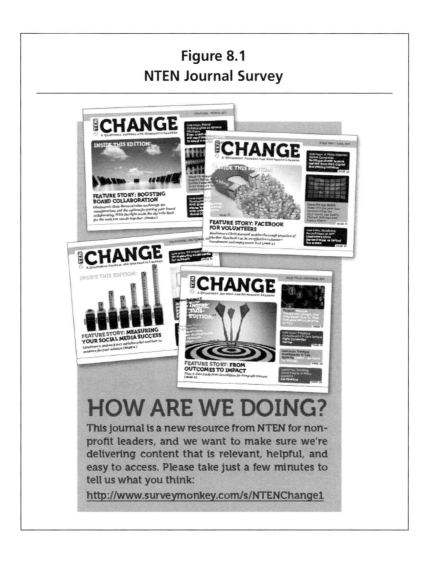

Figure 8.1
NTEN Journal Survey

If you are introducing a program to promote something that has never been seen or discussed before, it is reasonable to assume that prior to your program, awareness of that something is zero. If it already has some presence in the marketplace, then you will need to establish a baseline measurement against which to measure any future changes in awareness.

Best practices for measuring awareness are covered in the Advertising Research Foundation document "Guidelines for Market Research." (See the Resources section at the back of the book for this and other references.)

If Your Goal Is to Increase Preference

Preference implies that an individual is making a choice. Therefore, all preference measurements must include alternatives—typically organizations with which you compete for share of attention or share of wallet. To measure a program's impact on audience preference, you expose the audience to the specific tactic or activity (for instance, a photograph, article, white paper, or speech) and determine whether it leaves the audience more or less likely to support your organization. This exposure can be done in focus groups, panels, or by surveying a randomly selected sample of the population. The last method is the most expensive but will generate the greatest certainty about your audience.

If Your Goal Is to Improve Relationships

No one would argue against the notion that using a thermometer is a better measure of the health of your child than simply feeling her forehead. Similarly, you need a precise measurement tool to assess the health of your relationships with your stakeholders. The Grunig Relationship Survey is that tool, and it is discussed in detail in Chapter Ten. It was developed from research on the nature of relationships and is designed specifically to measure the strength of relationships and their components.

What Sort of Survey Should You Use?

There are literally dozens of different types of surveys.[7] Before you even consider a vendor, you need to be clear about the types of data you need and therefore the type of survey you need to conduct:

- *Polls:* Typically short surveys of no more than three to five short questions that provide a sense of what people are thinking. Questions are exclusively closed-ended, and therefore the analysis can be done quickly. Polls are typically repeatable, using the same questions each time, so you can easily determine if people's opinions are changing.

- *Snapshot survey:* A survey that consists of individuals or objects that are observed or measured once.

- *Longitudinal survey:* A survey that consists of different individuals or objects that are observed or measured over time. Examples are annual membership and volunteer surveys in which the individual members may change but the questions still test the same opinions.

- *Omnibus survey:* An all-purpose national consumer poll usually conducted on a regular schedule (once a week or every other week) by major market research firms. It is also called a *piggyback* or *shared-cost* survey. In the non-profit sector, these are typically conducted by consulting firms and national associations such as NTEN.[8] They are generally less expensive than polls or longitudinal surveys.

Polls and snapshot surveys are the most common nonprofit applications of surveys, particularly to collect information about content preferences, awareness, and activity.

CONDUCTING SURVEYS

Traditionally most surveys and polling have been conducted by telephone. However, the "Do Not Call" rules have made it difficult to get people on the phone. Increasingly, households are canceling their landlines and using cell phones only, and there is no readily available phone book in which to find their numbers. Although you can obtain lists of cell phone numbers, such lists tend to be expensive and the number of completed calls is low. Phone surveys can be faster, but their real downside is that they can cost many times more than comparable online or mail surveys. (See Table 8.2.)

While talk of the demise of the post office may be popular these days, the oldest and, some would argue, the most reliable type of survey is by mail. The problem is that although mail surveys are relatively low cost, they tend to skew results toward older people who are more likely to have the time and inclination to fill something out in hard copy. But if you are dealing with a population that does not have ready access to a computer, a mail survey may be your only option.

Thus, the most common survey technique today is online. Online surveys tend to produce results faster and, depending on the quality of your list, may yield a higher response rate. They are cheap and relatively easy to field. However, they are valid only if all of your publics have equal access to a computer and an e-mail account. While online audiences are to a certain extent self-selecting, the data has been shown to be reliable and, in many cases, far more robust than phone sampling. Later in this chapter we discuss controlling the costs of surveys. For a complete list of survey research options, refer to Dr. Don Stacks' *Primer of Public Relations Research* (see Resources for Tools, Tutorials, and Assistance at the end of the book).

Table 8.2
Comparison of Survey Tools

Tool	Strengths	Limitations
Online survey	Easy to program	Most are English only
	Fast	Convenience sample (only for those who have e-mail addresses)
Paper survey	Inexpensive	Self-selecting audience
	Better sampling (reaches everyone)	Slow
Phone survey	Fast	More time to code and analyze
		More expensive
		Low response rate

A serious drawback for surveys can be the time they take to conduct. Typically results from a mail survey take four to eight weeks. If you are in a situation that is changing rapidly, you may not have the luxury of time. We recommend conducting shorter pulse check surveys that can be administered electronically or by phone very rapidly on a regular basis, typically every quarter.

SEVEN STEPS TO CONDUCT A SURVEY

There are seven basic steps to conducting a survey:

1. Define the objectives for the research.

2. Define the universe you are going to survey.

3. Define the answers you want.

4. Create a survey instrument.

5. Test the instrument.

6. Field the survey.

7. Analyze the results.

Step 1: Define the Objectives for Your Research

By now you should know that the first step in any measurement program is to define what you are trying to measure and why. Consider Katie's Kat Shelter, the hypothetical nonprofit introduced in Chapter Six, as an example. If its goal is to test awareness, both prompted and unprompted awareness questions are needed—for example:

Q1: Are you familiar with any local organizations that provide kittens for adoption? If yes, please name those organizations.

Q2: On a scale of 1 to 5, with 1 being not at all familiar and 5 being very familiar, how familiar are you with the following organizations?

❐ KKS

❐ North Country Animal Services

❐ Dave's Doggie Day Care

Step 2: Define the Universe You Are Going to Survey

Figuring out exactly whom you are going to survey is more challenging than you might realize. You need to be very specific about your audience. Here is an example of the sort of snafu you can find yourself in if you are not careful. One Connecticut-based nonprofit wanted to conduct an awareness study of the issue around which a campaign was being organized.[9] To save money, the first round of research used what is known as a *snowball sample*—a type of sample in which individuals who are interviewed are asked to suggest other individuals. The list was derived from the nonprofit's own list of contacts and interested persons. The results, not surprisingly, showed that the issue of interest enjoyed a fairly high level of awareness.

The idea was that the study would be a longitudinal survey in which Connecticut residents were studied over time to see if their awareness and attitudes changed. The problem was that when the survey was fielded a year later, the response level was so low that it was necessary to purchase an e-mail list of Connecticut residents age eighteen and over.

Because this survey went to a very different list than did the first snowball sample, the results were radically different. The second year's results showed a sharp decline in awareness of the problem, so the first year's results could not be compared to the second.

Another problem was that in the second year, responses from the purchased list were heavily skewed toward wealthier counties, where people had greater access to computers and presumably more time to fill out surveys. The solution was to oversample in other counties and limit the number of responses from the wealthier ones.

To avoid these sorts of problems, be as specific as you possibly can be about exactly who and where you are asking questions.

Step 3: Define the Answers You Want

Writing a good survey means designing individual questions that answer the questions you need answers for. The hardest part of any survey is to be clear about the answers you want. A good exercise is to imagine that the results are in and you are

QUALITATIVE VERSUS QUANTITATIVE RESEARCH

Focus Groups Provide Insight

Focus groups are guided discussions among a relatively small group of individuals. They allow you to probe in-depth to discover the real issues that concern people. If the major messages aren't getting through, what is? It is important to keep in mind that qualitative research (focus groups, one-on-one in-depth interviews, convenience polling) is usually open-ended, free response, and unstructured in format. It generally relies on nonrandom samples, and its results are rarely generalizable to larger audiences.

Surveys Provide Facts; Polls Provide Data

Although it may contain some open-ended questions, quantitative research (for instance, a poll by telephone, mail, mall, Internet, fax, or e-mail) is far more likely to involve the use of closed-ended, forced-choice questions that are highly structured in format. It generally relies on random samples and usually is projectable to larger audiences.

writing a press release about them. What does it say? What are the headlines you'd like to see from the survey's results? Let's say that you'd like the headline to be, "Social Media Increased Donations by 40 Percent over Last Year." To get the data, you would need to understand all the factors involved in the increase in donations, so you would ask the respondents what media they had seen, what events they had attended, and what other organizations they gave money to.

Step 4: Create a Survey Instrument

Once you have the answers defined, you can create a draft set of questions, a deceptively tricky and difficult job even for experienced researchers. We strongly recommend finding a research group at your nearest university or hiring out the survey development part of your project.

One reason to use established survey instruments like the Grunig Relationship Survey is that they have already gone through rigorous testing. Many survey tools, like SurveyMonkey and Qualtrics, for example, have some standard and tested survey questions available.[10]

Step 5: Test Your Questions

Whatever the source of your questions, rigorously test the survey instrument with people outside your department or organization to ensure that you will get useful responses. You must test, retest, and retest again to make sure that the data you will receive is the data you need—especially if you have not hired a professional to develop the questionnaire.

Step 6: Field the Survey

Once the instrument has been tested and shown to produce reliable, repeatable results, you need to field the survey. If you are using e-mail to distribute the survey, we strongly recommend against using your own e-mail service. It is difficult to get unbiased results when respondents know who is sending the survey out. You should make sure that your e-mail service allows mass mailing and that the survey doesn't get bounced on the receiving end.

Most survey tools (including SurveyMonkey, Qualtrics, and Constant Contact) allow you to embed a link to the survey in a tweet, blog, or Web site, which allows anyone to access it. However, if you use this method, you need to make sure that you have good qualifying and screening questions in the survey to guarantee that you are reaching the appropriate respondents.

Finally, be patient. Depending on the survey methodology you chose, it will take between two and six weeks to get results. Do not jump to conclusions after a few days. At the end of the first week, check to see how many responses you have. If necessary, resend or repost the survey to boost the response levels.

Step 7: Analyze the Results

The most valuable part of any survey is not the overall results but the breakout of data by age, gender, geography, education level, and other categories. It's one thing to conclude that 60 percent of people are aware of an issue, but what can you do with that information? If you know that of those people who are aware of the issues, 70 percent are women under the age of thirty, you can put together a strategy to address the 30 percent who are not aware. Use Excel, WinCross, SPSS, or some other analysis tool if you have it. Again, a local university is a great resource.

A TOOL TO MEASURE WHAT PEOPLE ARE SAYING ABOUT YOU: MEDIA CONTENT ANALYSIS

In an ideal world, you would poll your entire audience to see what they read and how they react to everything you do. A more realistic alternative is to read and quantify what people are saying about you in the media, on social networks, as well as in blogs, microblogs, and communities. This technique, *media content analysis*, is one of the most valuable and commonly used tools in measurement. If your objective is to increase exposure and communication of key messages, measuring media content is essential.

In the past, people believed output measurement was simply counting numbers of all the mentions or column inches that appeared in the media. But with the proliferation of social media channels, measuring what they are saying about you encompasses far more than calculating sheer volume. This means looking at the content of each item to determine whether it contains your key messages, how the article leaves the reader feeling, and what messages it communicates. In other words, you need to measure the *quality* of your output as well as the *quantity*.

To understand this, consider the following example. What do you think demonstrates a more successful program: a fat notebook containing five hundred news items or a skinny folder containing seventy-five items? The answer, of course, is "neither." Without examining the content, you have no way of knowing.

The former might represent a surge in negative references about the organization. The latter might represent a program in which the client communicated its key messages in a whopping 75 percent of the items and reached all of its target audiences.

FEEDING AMERICA TRACKS CONVERSATIONS

Feeding America's strategic plan has a broad goal to mobilize the public in these outcome areas: donations, public policy advocates, brand awareness, and stakeholder engagement. As Dan Michel, digital marketing manager, says, "We spend time identifying and building relationships with superadvocates online and engage them—similar to the way you engage major donors or champion advocacy constituents. We track what people are saying about us. We look at the quantity of conversation on social media channels using Radian 6, a tracking/monitoring tool. We look at share of conversation. We'll do pre/post share of conversation about hunger for a campaign. But understanding the quality of the conversation is just as important: Who is talking about the hunger issue, and are the key messages we want being communicated? We also do a content analysis." (See Figure 8.2.)

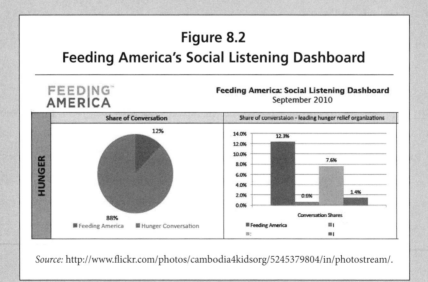

Figure 8.2
Feeding America's Social Listening Dashboard

Source: http://www.flickr.com/photos/cambodia4kidsorg/5245379804/in/photostream/.

Manual or Automated Content Analysis?

Media content analysis can be done with human readers or automated with computers (Table 8.3 provides a comparison). Although computer analysis can be effective at some very gross measures, such as share of conversation compared to other organizations, it is highly unreliable for more subtle aspects, such as detecting key messages. Computers are also lousy at differentiating between irony and sarcasm, and they are not likely to pick up regional variations. If I say that I had a "wicked time at the benefit last night," the computer doesn't know I'm from northern New England and that "wicked" translates to "very good." Or, if I say, "Yeah, saw the movie, read the book," the computer can't figure out

Table 8.3
Comparison of Manual and Automated Media Content Analysis

Tool	Strengths	Limitations
Automated content analysis	Can analyze large volumes of articles quickly to determine share of discussion, share of visibility, and share of positioning	Accuracy can be less than 50 percent because the system doesn't differentiate real content from spam.
		Doesn't pull out influencers and spokespeople well
	Very fast	Doesn't determine tone accurately
	Very efficient	Can't determine subtle and complex messages
		Many non-English networks are not available
Manual content analysis	Excellent for pulling out complex messaging, tonality, and subtle differences	Usually slow
		May need to use samples to fit a budget.
		Can be slower and more complex to set up.
		Labor intensive.
		Readers can be biased or inconsistent

if I'm recommending the book or panning the movie. Our recommendation is to use computers to do the heavy lifting and humans to detect the subtleties.

How to Select a Media Monitoring Tool

To do media content analysis, you will need to collect the media or the conversations in which your organization is being discussed. The simplest way to do this is to set up a Google Alert for all the terms that are relevant. If the volume becomes overwhelming, you may want to select a media monitoring tool or vendor to search for and retrieve the mentions you are interested in tracking. Selecting a tool can be a deceptively complex and difficult effort. There are a great many options to consider, and there are many companies that want your business. (For help in this often-daunting task, see Appendix D, "A Checklist for Monitoring Services.")

Elements Coded for in a Media Content Analysis

The following is a list of the most common elements that should be coded for in a content analysis.

Types of Media   Today there are literally dozens of places in which your brand or organization can be discussed, including these:

Blogs	Forums
Micro blogs (Twitter)	Geo-based networks
Photo-sharing sites like Flickr	Podcasts
Video-sharing sites like YouTube	Forum and message boards
Social networks, for instance, Facebook and LinkedIn	Wikis
Communities	Print media
Broadcast	Online news media

For each of these, the author, reporter, or creator of the conversation has a different level of influence—typically called *authority*. Authority used to be determined by the circulation of a publication, so a reporter with *The New York Times*, with a circulation of over 1 million readers, had more authority than a reporter with the Berlin, New Hampshire, *Daily Sun*, with a circulation of under ten thousand. However, with the arrival of social media, many of the most influential sites may have only a few readers, but if their posts are picked up by

The New York Times, they carry a lot of weight. So in social media, there are a number of ways to define authority. Twitalyzer, Technorati, and other sites and services assign grades to sites based on some variation of the following:

- The number of followers a user has
- The number of unique references and citations of the user in Twitter
- The frequency at which the user is uniquely retweeted
- The frequency at which the user is uniquely retweeting other people
- The relative frequency at which the user posts updates

    Authority can also be defined by the number of links to a blog site:

- *Low authority:* 3 to 9 blog links in the past six months
- *Middle authority:* 10 to 99 blog links in the past six months
- *High authority:* 100 to 499 blog links in the past six months

Visibility: Prominence and Dominance A great deal of evidence shows that the more visible your brand is in an item, post, or article, the more likely it is that viewers will remember the brand and message. *Prominence* is defined as the location of the first mention of the organization within an item. Although it doesn't really apply to Twitter, the placement of your brand within a blog post or on a Facebook page may have an impact on how memorable it will be. So typically you would record whether the brand was first found in:

- *The headline*: The organization is first mentioned in the headline.
- *The top 20 percent:* The organization is first mentioned in the top 20 percent of the item body
- *The bottom 80 percent*: The organization is first mentioned in the bottom 80 percent of the item body

In addition, memorability is increased if your brand is mentioned throughout an item rather than just in passing. We recommend classifying each mention according to these categories:

- *Exclusive:* Only the organization or brand studied is included in the article.
- *Dominant:* The organization is the main focus of the item but not the only one mentioned.

- *Average:* The mention of the organization is one of many integral parts of the story or is equal to other parts.
- *Minimal:* No one would miss it if the mention of the organization were gone.

Tone The tone of an article or mention is the attitude or opinion toward something or someone. Tone is broken down into four categories:

- *Positive:* You are more likely to work with, support, or refer someone to the organization. Positive coverage is desirable.
- *Neutral:* The item doesn't give you enough information to form an opinion of positive or negative.
- *Balanced or Mixed:* The item gives information that is equally positive and negative.
- *Negative:* You are less likely to work with or support the organization. Negative coverage is undesirable.

Messages Communicated Whether online or in print, the conversation about your brand can convey a variety of messages; some are desirable, and some are not. You will want to track key messages established by the organization as well as the opposite of those messages. Typically the rating would be:

+3: Amplified key message

+2: Full key message

+1: Partial key message

  0: No message

–2: Wrong or opposite message

Sources Mentioned or Quoted Influencing the influencers is key for almost all successful programs. You will want to know if academics, funders, or experts are picking up your key messages. Who is quoted in your coverage, and what do they say?

Conversation Type The nature of the conversations in social media as well as traditional media can reveal a great deal about what people are saying and thinking about you. Research has identified twenty-seven types of conversations that take place:[11]

1. Acknowledging receipt of information
2. Advertising something
3. Answering a question
4. Asking a question
5. Augmenting a previous post
6. Calling for action
7. Disclosing personal information
8. Distributing media
9. Expressing agreement
10. Expressing criticism
11. Expressing support
12. Expressing surprise
13. Giving a heads-up
14. Responding to criticism
15. Giving a shout-out
16. Making a joke
17. Making a suggestion
18. Making an observation
19. Offering a greeting
20. Offering an opinion
21. Putting out a "wanted for free" ad
22. Rallying support
23. Recruiting people
24. Showing dismay
25. Soliciting comments
26. Soliciting help
27. Starting a poll

KATIE PAINE ON DOING SOME TRICKY ANALYSIS FOR THE USO

When we did a media awareness study for the USO, its target audience was very specific: people currently serving in the armed forces or their families. We had a tight budget, which meant we had to narrow down the media list to a manageable size. So for the content analysis, we decided to focus on areas of the country with the highest concentration of people serving in the military. It took a Freedom of Information Act (FOIA) request to get that information, but once we had it, it was easy to put together a targeted media outlet list.

I'd been looking forward to writing up that year's report because we also do USO's traditional and social media tracking, and I knew that in terms of basic impressions, it had had a threefold increase in overall exposure. All of that increase was either positive or neutral, and a majority mentioned the nonprofit prominently. So I was convinced we were going to find a major bump in awareness.

Imagine my surprise when awareness *declined*. From a statistical perspective, it wasn't significant—less than 2 percent—but enough to make every alarm go off. How could USO enjoy more exposure and more favorable exposure than ever before and still see awareness go down?

We checked and rechecked the data and isolated every factor we could think of. And that's how we finally figured it out: our awareness study survey used a sample of the entire U.S. population, but our client is geared entirely toward active members of the U.S. military and their families. As it happens, only about 40 percent of our study respondents had some connection to the military. So we redid our analysis, looking at only those respondents who acknowledged a tie to the military. We compared the survey data with the news coverage that appeared in the FOIA-created list and found a high degree of correlation. In other words, the more the target audience saw the key messages, the more likely they were to support the mission.

Aha! Awareness went up, relationship scores went up, and willingness to volunteer or donate went up. Our client had actually done a terrific job reaching its target audience, but we had assumed that exposure would mean awareness for the entire national audience, and we were very much mistaken. Awareness had indeed gone up—but only among people who had a reason to support the organization.

TOOLS TO DETERMINE WHAT YOUR MARKETPLACE IS DOING: WEB AND SOCIAL ANALYTICS AND BEHAVIORAL METRICS

The ultimate test of the effectiveness of your efforts is whether the behavior of the target audience has changed as a result. This is also the most difficult to measure because of all the factors that can influence the results of your programs. The most straightforward way to isolate behavior change attributable solely to your efforts is to study programs with results that can be attributed only to the work of your team—for example, a PR program designed to increase traffic to a museum.

With the proliferation of Web and social analytics and business analytics, it has become much easier to determine the impact of various efforts. Any organization that uses e-commerce has a tremendous wealth of information on how, when, and where customers purchase. Your online museum gift shop, for instance, is not just another income stream. It can also be a valuable source of information on who your visitors are and what they are interested in. Customer service data can also indicate satisfaction (or lack of it) with various programs.

HOW THE LONDON SYMPHONY ORCHESTRA TUNES UP TICKET SALES USING SOCIAL MEDIA DATA

The London Symphony Orchestra uses social media channels not only to engage with audiences, but to generate ticket sales. Jo Johnson, digital marketing manager, says they use a combination of tools to track the ticket sales goal: "We use Google Analytics hooked into our online shopping cart with a tracking code so we know if they clicked through from Twitter, Facebook, e-mail, or a Web site. We look at the conversion rates, but this is not the whole story. We also know that ticket buyers use the phone and/or purchase at the box office having seen the information on Facebook or Twitter. So we use snapshot surveys at the point of purchase to ask how they heard about the concert."[12]

Your Web site is a tremendous source of data that can be used to measure the impact of various programs. Most sites already use some form of traffic analysis such as Google Analytics, Webtrends, or Omniture. These systems can tell you very specifically how many people go to what pages on your site. So if you provide a specific URL for a specific press release, you can track editors' and consumers' behavior by following the traffic to that URL.

Organizations frequently want to be able to isolate the impact of one effort from others. One way to do this is to maintain advertising and other promotional efforts at a constant level for a given time, typically twenty-six weeks. Collect data to determine the baseline level of awareness, Web traffic, and donations. Then introduce your new campaign and continue collecting data to measure changes in awareness, Web traffic, and donations. If you are in an environment in which advertising or other communications programs are changing, and thus presumably producing changes in awareness in addition to the changes produced by your new tactic, then to sort out the various influences you will need to use factor analysis or other sophisticated statistical techniques.

FEEDING AMERICA TRACKS CONVERSIONS

Feeding America measures conversions for every campaign, whether it is a conversion for an advocacy action or a donation. For example, for Hunger Action Month in September, Feeding America created a tab on its Facebook page where people could share a different action every day. The theme was "30 Ways for 30 Days." (See Figure 8.3.) Dan Michel, digital marketing manager, says, "We measured that through each action, and each was trackable. At the end of the month, we had data on what calls to action resonated best across our different channels."

Feeding America tracks conversions for donors using Google Analytics in order to follow the path of the donor—from a like or comment on Facebook to an online donation form: "It is still a little clunky and requires work but that information is very valuable," explains Dan. "We are low on the donation conversions, but we are seeing social

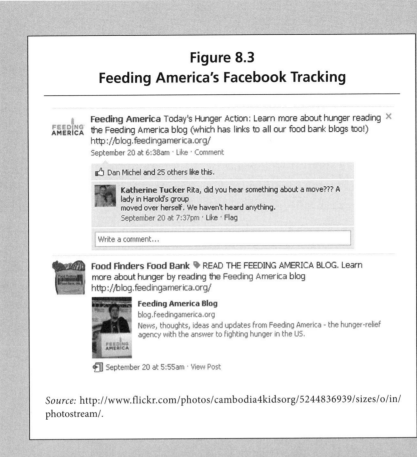

Figure 8.3
Feeding America's Facebook Tracking

Feeding America Today's Hunger Action: Learn more about hunger reading the Feeding America blog (which has links to all our food bank blogs too!) http://blog.feedingamerica.org/
September 20 at 6:38am · Like · Comment

👍 Dan Michel and 25 others like this.

Katherine Tucker Rita, did you hear something about a move??? A lady in Harold's group moved over herself. We haven't heard anything.
September 20 at 7:37pm · Like · Flag

Write a comment...

Food Finders Food Bank 🚩 READ THE FEEDING AMERICA BLOG. Learn more about hunger by reading the Feeding America blog http://blog.feedingamerica.org/

Feeding America Blog
blog.feedingamerica.org
News, thoughts, ideas and updates from Feeding America - the hunger-relief agency with the answer to fighting hunger in the US.

September 20 at 5:55am · View Post

Source: http://www.flickr.com/photos/cambodia4kidsorg/5244836939/sizes/o/in/photostream/.

media become very important in helping with public policy efforts, like our advocacy efforts to support the Child Nutrition Bill. We saw a lot of interest and click-throughs from Twitter, particularly." To see where traffic came from, Feeding America used Google Analytics for advocacy pages and bitly for click-throughs on Twitter.

GOING MOBILE AND MEASURING IT

The latest challenge to measurement has been the proliferation of mobile marketing. Many nonprofits now have mobile apps to facilitate donations or find a location. Fundraising via SMS and other outreach using mobile phones and tablets is now almost expected for nonprofits.

In today's world, if your stakeholders can't find you in places they are accustomed to looking, they will go elsewhere. So if they can't get your Web site on their phone, that's a problem. They want basic information and tools for action. Look at your own Web site on a mobile phone. Are the basic information and calls to action right there? Probably they are not, which means you need a mobile version of your site that is stripped down. The same goes for e-mail; make sure your e-mails look good on mobile phones (and, yes, millennials still use e-mail for some purposes).

Allyson Kapin, a blogger who writes about the use of mobile tools for non-profits, says, "While there are a variety of mobile strategies and tools in the toolbox that nonprofits can integrate right now, they come at different price points and degrees of success and risk. These include apps, text-to-give campaigns, and text-to-engage. People will be purchasing more smart phones and mobile devices in 2012 than personal computers. So the most important mobile strategy nonprofits should focus on first is making sure their Web site and e-mails are optimized and mobile friendly."[13]

To help guide decisions about getting Web site content mobile ready, she says:

> You can now use Google Analytics to track how many people are visiting your Web site on mobile devices, track mobile users' engagement paths, and look for trends such as:
>
> - Where are they coming from?
> - Where are the main drop-off points?
> - How much time are they spending on your Web site?
> - What are the bounce rates?
> - What are their sign-up rates?
> - What percentage is going to key pages such as campaign landing pages, donation pages?

Measuring Mobile

Measurement of all of these device-specific efforts is essentially the same as with any other digital source. You need to build in metrics up front, and then examine your Web analytics to see the number of refers and actions that come from specific sources. Of course, be clear about your goals.

The best way to test a mobile platform is to conduct an A/B test against campaigns or programs that do not use mobile. Evaluate whether donations or expressions of advocacy increase with the addition of mobile and, more important, if the increase is worth the expense of creating a mobile app. Many nonprofits have jumped on the mobile app bandwagon without any benchmark in place to determine if the investment is worth it.

Goodwill Develops a Mobile Site

Goodwill Industries International provides job training and employment services, job placement opportunities, and postemployment support through its network of 179 community-based agencies worldwide. There are over twenty-six hundred Goodwill stores around the world that sell gently used and new items, providing an important revenue stream for its programs.

When Goodwill was planning its mobile site, it knew from Web analytics that the most popular feature would be the store locator; more than 7 million visited the Goodwill Web site in 2011, and more than 6 million of those visited the locator. Arlene McCrehan, senior director of online media, says, "We knew that Web site visitors tended to use that feature as they're walking out the door to drop off a donation. We felt we could offer better service to our patrons if we set up a mobile site for the store locator."[14]

Goodwill considers this first year an experiment. It's tracking use patterns of the mobile site against donation volume data by location. Says McCrehan, "We want to fulfill our mission. We saw the potential for mobile, and we knew we wanted to get in quickly. We knew it wasn't going to cost too much. We needed to learn the technology and, more important, how to measure to improve and make decisions about what to do next."

Another experiment with mobile is also mission driven. Says McCrehan, "With the recession, there is higher demand at Goodwill's stores. That's why we started the Donate Movement. As part of that strategy, we've incorporated a mobile component: a Donation Impact Calculator for people who want to organize drives. It calculates the impact of their donation, from keeping items out of landfills to benefiting their community by supporting Goodwill."

Goodwill has learned from measuring its mobile strategy. "We've seen the use of our mobile site grow dramatically, from dribs and drabs to twelve hundred unique visitors per day. We learned that we have to be in this space and be very strategic about the content we deliver," says McCrehan. The team at Goodwill

ROOTS OF CHANGE

Roots of Change is a networked nonprofit that works with leaders and institutions in California with an interest in establishing a sustainable food system. This network includes food producers, businesses, nonprofits, communities, government agencies, and foundations that share a commitment to changing food markets and policies.

Its leaders launched the Food Movement Rising campaign with a group of organizational partners to encourage people to sign a petition on food policy in the state using the online petition site Change.org. They discovered that Change.org was not just a platform, but was home to a community of activists standing ready to spread their campaign. They used the landing page as a platform for A/B testing with Google analytics, analyzing what worked best to get conversion—images, less or more text, the placement of a "sign petition" button, and so forth. They learned that images are really key for conversion.

has learned that measuring mobile is not different from measuring anything else. McCrehan advises, "Start with asking what mobile strategy fits best with your objective and how you can best deliver your program or message."

WHAT DOES MEASUREMENT REALLY COST?

For those nonprofits on a tiny budget, the rule of thumb is to allocate 5 to 10 percent of their overall project budget for measurement: half for upfront research, the other half for evaluation. The primary driver of expense is the amount of data you collect. The more people you interview, postings you study, or articles you analyze, the higher the cost. There are many estimates of cost for both surveys and media analysis, but they change with each advance of technology. Your best estimating strategy is to prepare a detailed request for proposal and submit it to a variety of vendors to get a true apples-to-apples comparison.

Controlling the Cost of Surveys

The following factors influence the cost of surveying an audience:

- *Number of questionnaires administered.* You can probably get most of the information you need from talking to 250 people. If you are skeptical, note that it's possible to get a representative sample of the entire United States with only 500 people. So don't get talked into surveying thousands if you don't really need to.

- *Length of questionnaire.* It's always a good idea to keep questionnaires as short as possible, which will both hold down the cost and bring up your level of response. A quantitative survey should take no more than ten minutes to administer.

- *Cost of collecting names.* In some research (if you are studying an event, for example), you collect names and phone numbers during the event and then interview by phone later. That way, you know what respondents remember about you, not just what their initial impression was.

- *Difficulty in getting people to respond.* You may need to offer incentives to get people to respond or repeatedly ask them to respond. Marketers, for instance, are notoriously difficult to survey; even journalists and doctors are easier. You also need to make sure that every member has an equal opportunity to participate: the more random your selection, the better. Self-selecting groups— for instance, people who come to your Web site—are much less desirable, because those interested in your topic are more likely to participate, thus skewing your results. What you may really be interested in are the opinions of people who are *not* going to your Web site.

- *Customized versus syndicated research.* On any given day, thousands of research projects are going on designed to ask the general public their opinions on a given topic. These omnibus studies are carried out by a variety of market research firms, and you can add questions to these studies at around three thousand dollars per question.

Controlling the Cost of Media Content Analysis

Commercial clipping organizations charge between one and three dollars a clip to gather articles, and analysis firms can charge upwards of ten dollars per article to analyze the content. You can expect these costs to come down as technology makes this work faster and easier. Automated data collection systems generally charge on an annual basis, and a typical contract starts at ten thousand dollars a year. For more sophisticated programs that are more customizable, plan on spending five to ten times as much, depending on the size of your organization.

Another cost influence is the number of media outlets you are analyzing. Eighty percent of your most meaningful and effective coverage will come from 20 percent of your outlets. Therefore, the easiest way to cut down on cost is to cut down on media sources and limit your search to the 20 percent that really matter.

Broadcast coverage is another expensive addition to a content analysis program. Typical broadcast monitoring companies charge six thousand dollars and up per year to collect broadcast spots and provide an estimate of audience reached. You need to decide whether you need quality broadcast coverage or can get by with what shows up on the broadcast channel's Web site.

The next question you need to ask is: Do we need to collect everything, or just stories that have the greatest likelihood of influencing our target audience? Coverage in *The Wall Street Journal* may please the boss, but it probably isn't going to influence any teenagers to show up at your after-school program.

In addition, many conversations, even in top-tier blogs or media, will not be relevant to your study. These include such articles as weddings and acronym confusion (KKS, for example is also an abbreviation for King Kool Savas, a German rapper). You will need to filter such mentions out of your data.

IF YOU HAVE NO BUDGET AT ALL, BECOME SOMEONE'S HOMEWORK

Katie Paine's organization, KDPaine & Partners, was previously located in Durham, New Hampshire. It was blessed by the proximity of the University of New Hampshire, which has an excellent market research lab. Most M.B.A. programs and undergraduate colleges offer some sort of survey research class. With a bit of luck and persuasion, you can get help there in conducting research.

And if you're still faced with more articles than you know what to do with, limit your selection to articles that mention you in the headline or lead paragraph. That's all the average reader pays attention to anyway. These articles are the ones that will have the biggest impact in the long run.

IF YOU DON'T HAVE AN ANALYTICS GURU ON STAFF: THE ANALYSIS EXCHANGE

Many small and midsized nonprofits operate on limited budgets with finite resources and often do not have the technical expertise on staff to set up analytics programs to track everything they need. That's why many nonprofits like the American Leadership Forum are turning to the Analysis Exchange. This free service matches seasoned analytics professionals with nonprofits to help them set up their system, configure software, and set up reporting systems at no cost.

American Leadership Forum—Silicon Valley (ALF) is a network of regional leaders committed to serving the common good in Silicon Valley. Through its fellows program, ALF brings together demonstrated leaders to explore collaborative leadership that can strengthen their capacity to address public issues. The organization has a eight-member staff. Debbie Ford-Scriba, vice president of network relations, is responsible for overseeing online presence and communications strategy, which is 15 percent of her job. Says Ford-Scriba:

> There is only so much time in the day, and smaller organizations like ours don't typically have the luxury of hiring someone to do social media full time or analytics. We got help from the Analysis Exchange, which provides volunteers who will help your nonprofit make better use of analytics. Our volunteer helped us figure out an analytics framework as well as what analytics tools we needed.
>
> Our organization is very disciplined in using measurement and data, but we just didn't have the social and Web analytics technical expertise. We had goals and SMART social media objectives—and our volunteer helped us map those to specific social media metrics and set up the analytics tools for us. Also, she helped us improve our use of spreadsheets.[15]

Here is an example of a program set up with help from the Analysis Exchange:

Objective: Increase engagement among current supporters on a certain issue.

Social Media Goal: Extend conversation rate within target market segments to exceed internal benchmarks by 20 percent during 30 days before and after an event.

Conversation Rate Metrics

- *Facebook:* Average number of audience comments per post
- *Twitter:* Number of @replies per tweet
- *YouTube:* Number of video responses to videos

EDUCATE YOURSELF ABOUT MEASUREMENT TOOLS

New measurement tools are being developed rapidly. The only way to stay on top of this change is to continually educate yourself. A good place to start is at one of the best research Web sites, that of the Society for New Communications Research (www.sncr.org). The Institute for Public Relations (www.instituteforpr.org) also has a library of free papers on measurement.[16] (See also www.themeasurementstandard.com and kdpaine.blogs.com.) Beth Kanter maintains a listing of social media tools that nonprofits are using that also includes links to tutorials and other resources and other users (http://measurenetworkednonprofit.org). In addition, NTEN has an ongoing series of Webinars and other educational opportunities for learning about measurement tools for nonprofits. Idealware (http:/www.idealware.org) specializes in doing reviews of software used by nonprofits and they regularly review measurement and social media tools.

CONCLUSION

The key to a successful measurement program is not the tools but the clarity of the goals. Remember that picking a tool is the second to last step in the seven steps of measurement, so don't make any decisions about tools until you've gone through the first five steps (see Chapter Four). Just because a tool exists and sounds as if it might be the perfect answer does not mean that it will answer your questions. Before collecting data, make sure the tool measures the objectives of your program.

REFLECTION QUESTIONS

1. What are your goals, what are you measuring, and what data do you need?

2. Based on this information, what types of tools do you need to collect the data?

3. What are your budget and time line for doing the data collection and analysis? How can you make them efficient and streamlined?

4. Are you or someone else in your organization a spreadsheet ninja? What types of templates can you set up based on the answers to the first question?

5. Have you considered crowdsourcing or secondary research to develop your benchmarks?

Measurement and the Aha! Moment

Using Your Data to Tell Stories, Make Decisions, and Change the World

Our cat adoption numbers tanked this quarter. But the important thing is, our YouTube views are **waaay** up.

Congratulations! You have spent weeks or months collecting data, and now it is time to understand what it has to say. It's time to chart, graph, analyze, and comprehend the story that your data is telling you. It's time to present this story to other people. In short, it's time to use your data to improve your programs. That's how measurement helps you change the world.

This chapter is about all those things, but especially about what makes measurement really thrilling: the process of examining your data and gleaning conclusions. This is where the magic happens and when the mysteries are revealed. It's when the results of your months of hard work make themselves known in the most direct and useful way.

As we said at the beginning of this book, over-the-top-successful nonprofits know measurement is more than simply collecting data—they collect the right data and then use the information. They achieve dramatic success because they:

- Start with a plan to collect data that they know will answer questions and help make decisions.

- Use dashboards to organize and report on the data and summary statistics that are most important to their goals.

- Have regular processes for reviewing the data and reflecting on both successes and failures. This leads to continuous improvement and better decision making.

- Make improvements to their programs and processes based on decisions informed by their data. Then they go out and collect data on the improvements.

- Use reports to generate discussion with internal stakeholders (like board, senior management, and staff) and external stakeholders.

- Know how to tell stories with their data and their results.

YOUR AHA! MOMENTS, AND HOW TO GET MORE OF THEM

Your data consists of just numbers on a spreadsheet until you organize and analyze them and understand what they have to say. Many people find this puzzle-solving, cause-and-effect nature of data analysis to be the most rewarding part of measurement. Just ask any data geek.

We've all had those profound experiences called "Aha! moments" by psychologists (and Oprah), when facts come together in a moment of clarity to open up some significant insight. We aren't going to promise you an epiphany with every spreadsheet, but dig around in your data long enough and you will have Aha! moments of all shapes and sizes. Here are some examples:

- Mothers Against Drunk Driving had an Aha! moment in 2009 when its data revealed that donations increased if they focused media attention on victims and the victims' services that MADD provides.

- An Aha! moment arrived for the USO when social media results demonstrated that its Twitter hashtag and Facebook programs gave a boost to its normal fundraising efforts.

- The Federal Reserve Bank of Cleveland's recent Aha! moment was when its Web traffic data showed that its most popular vehicle for communicating with the public was its YouTube series of Drawing Board videos, which explain complex economic concepts using "Really bad drawings, real simple explanations."[1]

Getting from the raw data to an Aha! moment or even to just a logical and useful conclusion is not always easy. Analyzing data is both an art and a science, and it helps to bring experience and a sharp mind to the job. A little creativity doesn't hurt either. If you enjoy playing Scrabble, Sudoku, and Tetris, then you will probably find rummaging about in your numbers highly enjoyable and productive. But even if Rubik's Cube isn't to your liking, there are tried-and-true techniques to encourage your data to reveal its secrets. Here we offer a few of them.

KATIE PAINE ON HER FIRST MEETING WITH A SPIDER CHART

One of my biggest Aha! moments was when I was introduced to the spider chart. I had just joined the board of a local nonprofit medical center and was attending my first board meeting. Among the fifty or so pages in the meeting packet was a colorful and utterly incomprehensible chart (see Figure 9.1). I was informed that it included all the information I would need for the meeting. I stared at it, clueless, for about five minutes, until finally the chief marketing officer bailed me out.

He explained that the lines represent performance against goals, and the quadrants represent the divisions within the organization (the hospital, Visiting Nurse Association/hospice, sports center, and physicians' network). Each score represents how they were doing relative to their goals. It was the equivalent of a twenty-page PowerPoint presentation on one page!

That's when I understood the mentality of this board and why they rolled their eyes at typical PR reports: it wasn't that they wanted less information; they just wanted it in a way that they were used to seeing.

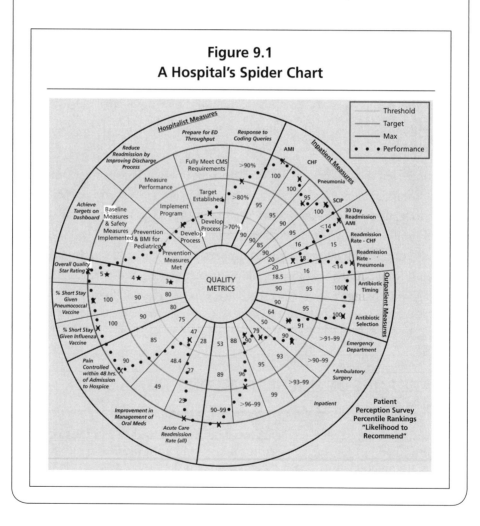

Figure 9.1
A Hospital's Spider Chart

Look for Failure First

Yes, it is very, very nice to have proof that your brilliant idea actually got brilliant results. Well done and congratulations! But you'll find that you get the most bang from your measurement buck if you look for failure first: find out what didn't work, and get rid of it to make room for something more effective. Then move resources from what is not working to what is.

This book started with the story of MomsRising as a shining example of a data-informed organization, and there is much to learn from how it operates. Says Ashley Boyd, campaign director, "One thing we *don't* do when we analyze the data is to use it to pat ourselves on the back. In fact, we look for failures first. We have even given ourselves permission to do that by calling 'Joyful Funerals' on tactics that don't work! We'll even joke and ask: 'Is it time to send flowers?'"[2] The humor removes the stigma, but it always leads the team to reflect on why something might not have worked and suggest ways to improve it.

Like MomsRising, you need to look at your benchmarks and ask yourself: "What didn't work?" If everything worked to a certain extent, ask, "What were the worst-performing programs? Where do we need to pay attention? What can be improved?"

Ask "So What?" of Every Result

Every time you think your data is telling you something, summon up every ounce of skepticism you've ever had. For every slide, chart, table, or graph that shows that one thing seems to be related to another, ask, "So what?" Make sure you can answer that question in a way that relates the numbers back to the mission of your organization or at least of your department:

"So what if our stakeholders had fewer opportunities to hear about us? Does it affect our online donations or our volunteer recruitment?"

"So what if we had more Facebook likes? What changed in our ability to fill the needs of our community?"

"So what if we didn't get our messages out? Did that give greater visibility to opposition groups? Does it mean that we have a harder time attracting and keeping talent?"

Ask "So What?" Three Times

Sometimes you are confronted with data that stubbornly refuses to speak to you. A particularly effective technique to tease out results that are related to your organizational goals is to ask, "So what?" three times, each time digging deeper into how the data relates to your mission. For instance, suppose you notice a distinct shift in the nature of your conversations. Interesting, but *so what?*

So you dig deeper and discover that conversations are changing because more people are expressing support for your organization. Great, but *so what?*

So you compare donations to the frequency of positive messages about your organization and find a positive correlation between frequency and donations. *So what?*

So you've found it! There's your connection between a change in the nature of conversations about your organization and its bottom line.

Make Sure Your Data Is Fresh from the Oven

Data is like homemade bread. When the bread is still in the oven, smelling great but not quite ready, the anticipation is huge. You can't wait for it to be done. When you take it out of the oven, it's perfect. You can use it for anything. You serve it with dinner, then have it for breakfast, and make sandwiches with it for lunch. After a while, it gets old and stale, and you stick it in the freezer. A few months later, you take it out, and all you can do is make bread pudding with it.

When data is fresh, you can mine it for all kinds of data and insights, but the older it gets, the less useful it is. Eventually it makes for a good benchmark but isn't really that useful anymore. That's why MomsRising's Metrics Mondays are so worthwhile: the data is fresh and at hand when MomsRising has to make decisions about the next campaign.

Use Correlations to Get from Data to Insights

One of the simplest forms of statistical analysis is correlation. What a correlation does is tell you whether there is any connection between two sets of data. We want to emphasize the difference between *correlation* and *causation*. With the exception of certain text-to-donate campaigns, few nonprofits can say definitively that activity A (for example, Twitter activity) definitively *caused* people to respond by doing B (for example, donating). What you can tell is that

TELLING CAMPFIRE STORIES WITH THE DATA: MOMSRISING'S WEEKLY DATA STUDY GROUP

Every Monday morning for the past five years, the twelve-person staff at MomsRising has had a thirty-minute meeting to review their weekly dashboard report. Says Ashley Boyd, "Our Metrics Monday meeting is about telling campfire stories with the data. We review our dashboard, which is really just a shared spreadsheet. We examine every piece of data to see if it supports our goals of growing the movement and winning legislative policy changes. These are two key results areas that we use for every single campaign. This is our true north and our feedback to know whether we're on track."

MomsRising's dashboard presents different views of its work, from the big picture down to the smallest metrics. The team reviews metrics for e-mail, social media, and Web site conversions for action alerts across different campaigns. Boyd says they look for stories and context, not just at the numbers: "We've been tracking results over several years, so we know immediately if something is performing below or above average. We review highlights and themes from qualitative feedback like e-mail and comments. Then we use them to flush out something that is not making sense in the quantitative feedback."

MomsRising considers Metrics Mondays a valuable exercise for the staff, since everyone has the same information and is getting the same learning. Says Boyd, "At first we had just one person as our stats person. But by including everyone, we're spreading the knowledge so everyone can benefit from the insights . . . We love our dashboards because they help us make better decisions; it's not a sideline activity so it doesn't feel like an extra element of work. We have two staff members who gather the stats: one who looks at the Web site and e-mail and another for social media. It takes a couple of hours of their time per week."

The weekly dashboard includes Twitter follower growth and retweets, but they also look for larger patterns and insights that could improve their tactics. Says Boyd, "Doing a formal content analysis of our qualitative feedback helps generate insights that lead us to better campaign decisions. And that ultimately gets us better results."

the frequency of donations is positively correlated with the presence of this particular Tweet or hashtag. When you bring two or more sets of data together (for example, Facebook likes, positive mentions, and online donations), you use a correlation function (available in Excel) or some related form of statistical analysis to prove that there is a connection.

Make Sure Your Data Passes the Sniff Test

Once you've analyzed your data, ask yourself, "Does the data make sense?" Don't blindly depend on some software or calculations to make your conclusions. Sit back and take a good look at your data, analysis, and conclusions. Anything fishy there? If it doesn't look right to you, it certainly won't look right to your board. If the data is accurate, make sure you have an explanation. If you find a flaw in the data, postpone the meeting until you can make sure that all the data is accurate.

Tear Down Those Cubicles and Share Your Data

The insights that you glean from analyzing your data tell the best stories in the world. So to borrow a phrase from Ronald Reagan, "Tear down those cubicles!" Take your accounting, information technology, and development folks out for cocktails. Get to know them and their data. You're all on the same team, and it's hard to argue with the notion that you all want to improve.

Silos are the biggest barriers to effective measurement-driven change. In most organizations, the accounting department (or at least the data in the accounting department) doesn't talk to development, and neither talks to public affairs. It doesn't have to be this way. One solution to this problem is to bring all the data together in a single dashboard.

Use Dashboards to Share Data and Summarize Progress

Call it a dashboard, a cockpit, or whatever other buzzword you chose. At some point, you have to pull summaries of all your important data into one place and figure out if what you are doing is making a difference to your organization.

Dashboards were introduced sometime in the last part of the last century, with the idea that, similar to the dashboard in your car or the cockpit in a plane, you'd have a system that would sit on your desktop and flash warning lights to indicate what areas you need to pay attention to. This concept led to a lot of fancy software that delivered all kinds of information, but also a lot of confusion and very little insight or recommendations.

Finding an appropriate tool isn't the problem. Many nonprofits, particularly small ones, can get by with using a shared spreadsheet. The real difficulty is getting people to share their data and agree on just what metrics measure success. There is more discussion of dashboards later in this chapter.

Lather, Rinse, Repeat: The Whole Point Is to Do It Again, Only Better

One of the most significant aspects of measurement is its iterative nature. It's not measurement unless you learn something from your data and then apply that knowledge to your next effort. It is a learning process of trying, learning something, and trying again, only better this time. The real reward, the real excitement of measurement, comes when you see, right before your eyes, that an adjustment you've made has improved your results.

Knock Their Socks Off: How to Present Your Data Like a Pro

So it's time to present your results to your boss, the board, the weekly brown bag lunch meeting, or maybe even a session at a regional conference. You've got less than a minute to give the powers that be a reason to keep listening to what you are saying, so the first thing to remember is that they are much more interested in what your data says than the actual data. They want to hear the exciting story of what your data has revealed. And therein lies the secret to a successful presentation: give your listeners their own Aha! moment. Make sure your results are as exciting to them as they are to you.

Data without insight is just trivia, and most of the time it's up to you to provide the insight. Everyone can look at the chart you put up on the screen, and quite a few of them will understand what it says. But few people will actually get what it really means for your program unless you tell them.

Nothing makes a meeting go south faster than someone pointing to a PowerPoint slide and saying, "There's a big spike in June." People want the story behind the conclusion illustrated by the chart, as in, "There was a big spike in online donations in June due to the effort we put into growing our follower base." These story statements are called *conclusionary headlines*, and every chart and PowerPoint slide you show should have one.

Tell Stories with Your Data

Rod Stewart was right: every picture tells a story. When it comes to presenting results, every chart, dashboard, table, and report should tell a story. Whether you are sharing your data on a public dashboard on your organization's Web site, presenting the results to your board, or sharing the weekly report with other staff members, you need to make sure that your reports tell a story—and not just a boring, dead-end story but one that leads to an action.

A story is something that happens over a period of time. So if you want to tell a story of progress or decline, show how your data trend over time. Present your data for at least thirteen weeks, but if possible, show thirteen months so you accommodate any seasonal changes. And often you can tell an even better story if you compare your data or your campaigns to those of your peers.

Don't Waste Their Time: Get to the Point, and Make It a Good One

The dollar value of the time of your board members and leadership team or external stakeholders is probably a pretty large number. This means that the first page of your report is some of the most expensive real estate in the world. If you get them to pay attention to your report or your dashboard for more than a minute, you should consider it a victory. So do not waste their time with numbers or graphics that do not tell your story. Just as *USA Today* figured out years ago and Twitter has now reinforced, what you used to need three pages to express can now be done in 140 characters if you're good.

KATIE PAINE ON WHY MEASUREMENT IS SEXY

I think if you want to understand why measurement is sexy, just look at why so many people find data geeks Abby and McGee (from the TV show *NCIS*), MSNBC's Rachel Maddow, and *Freakonomics* (the book by Steven D. Levitt and Stephen J. Dubner) sexy. They all present data in entertaining and interesting ways. It's all about using data to provide surprising—and surprisingly useful—results. It's not just the Aha! moment—it's the "Aha! My mind is blown by this data!" moment.

Pie Charts Do Not Tell Stories

If a chart, graph, or table doesn't tell a story, it probably doesn't belong in your report. And pie charts do not tell stories. Certainly pie charts can be simple and effective ways to present data, but chances are they don't tell much of a story, especially if there are so many slices you can't tell what is what or if there is only one big slice.

Words, Charts, and Tables: Use All Your Channels to Reach All Your Audience

Researchers have known for years that children learn in different ways. Some need words to learn, others need pictures, and others just need to do something. Here's a secret: we don't change much as we grow up. There will be people to whom you report who will only look at your words, and others who will only look at the charts, and still others who look only at numbers in a table. So use all three in your reports.

HOW THE SMITHSONIAN SHARES DEPARTMENTAL DASHBOARDS AND REPORTS

C. Daniel Chase, a Web developer with the Smithsonian Institution Archives (SIA), was charged with designing and implementing a dashboard to share Web and social media analytics across departments.[3] Chase's team looked over how they were defining success and selected the metrics that were most critical in revealing whether they were pushing the needle.

The SIA uses social media to support two core areas of their mission:

- Offering a range of reference, research, and records services and creating products and services that promote understanding of the Smithsonian and its history

- Tracking what content and services are used in order to measure their success in achieving their mission

Chase says that their key performance indicators (KPIs) boiled down to two: requests (how many queries for information about SIA's collections were received from Smithsonian employees, outside researchers, and the general public) and ratings of the usefulness of their content. "These serve as indicators of how well we are serving our audiences," he notes. "The first is by demonstrating our goal of making SIA resources accessible and used, and the second is a broader indicator of how useful people find our new content, information, advice, and outreach."

He admits that too much data can be overwhelming if you try to review and use it all. He has found that dashboards are best when they summarize information to answer the following questions:

- Is there a problem I need to react to, or is everything running smoothly?
- Is what we are doing working?
- What isn't working?
- Are we spending our time and money on the right things?

"The ultimate success of a dashboard," he explains, "is whether you actually look at it and make decisions from the data. Making sure that happens is an important part of the design process, especially if you want departments to share a dashboard. At SIA, we have monthly reports and meetings to review the numbers, as well as the specific content that is doing well—or not."

Chase also said that it's necessary to incorporate multiple views of the data into the design—for example, "We upstream our data to management of the Smithsonian Institution as a whole (the Archives is just one of many units at the Smithsonian). Our IT department has developed a dashboard to be used by each unit, which has summary abilities to provide that information to Smithsonian Institution leadership. We don't want to maintain both separately, so the plan is to develop an export of our data in a standardized format. We get to automate our part, and still contribute to the wider organization's summary information."

Dashboards shared across departments require certain characteristics:

- Dashboards should have a centralized, high-level view that clearly shows KPIs for senior management.
- Each department should have a subview or tab that shows more detail on the KPIs. Departments have to agree to the same format and structure. One way to do this is get department leaders to agree on the structure and then present it to the other people in the department as, "This is what your boss wants" or get the senior leader to present it.
- An automated dashboard is a good idea, perhaps as a database.
- The most important thing is the consistency and centralization of the data collection format. Make sure to get everyone to agree on the display of the top and department levels.

THE POWER OF SHARING DASHBOARDS

A big component of working in a networked way is working transparently, with ongoing sharing of insights, resources, and activities between organizations and between organizations and their stakeholders. But dashboards often work against this valuable transparency, because they are almost always kept private for internal use by staff and boards. Sometimes they're not even shared among departments.

What if these reports were shared more broadly? What if the default setting was for nonprofit organizations to share dashboard reports or results metrics with their network? Sharing with peer organizations helps organizations learn from others' experience. And sharing organizational dashboards with everyone helps to achieve external accountability. This is more commonly a practice of governmental departments. Nevertheless, more and more nonprofits are sharing their performance data openly on the Web with their peers, donors, and communities and are engaging in conversations in the open with stakeholders.

Sharing Dashboards with Peer Organizations

Sean Redmond, a Web developer at the Solomon R. Guggenheim Museum in New York City, has created an online list of several hundred museums that compares Twitter and Facebook benchmarks and includes a top fifty performance list. Based on weekly data, Redmond blogs about social media best practices and standards for museums.

Redmond originally collected the data in a Google spreadsheet, using a time-consuming manual process. To avoid data error and ease the collection chore, he created an automated version with data collected automatically via application programming interfaces (APIs). The open dashboard is now a powerful vehicle for peer organizations to learn in public. For example, if one institution has a sudden jump in fans or followers, it can be a good opportunity to start a conversation with peer institutions about what techniques it is using.

Says Devon Smith, arts blogger and self-described data nerd:

> I think of collaborative dashboard sharing with peers in much the same way as institutional data collection and analysis. You're looking for outliers, bright spots, or dark spots that help point you in the direction of where you should be spending your time digging deeper into the data. Data collection has to come before data analysis, and this list is a great example of collection.

A simple dashboard like this has the potential to connect the social media teams at these institutions with each other, and gives them a foundation to build on . . . Inevitably there will be new and better APIs that collect more of the information we want. And then of course we'll want new and different data. You have to start somewhere, and this automated collection of "data that is easy to collect" is a huge leap forward over a Google spreadsheet.[4]

Anthony Brown, social media manager at the San Francisco Zoo, was interested in improving his institution's use of Twitter but wanted a reference point for his industry: "So, I set up an online dashboard that tracks the Twitter stats from peer aquariums and zoos. Because we're all on Twitter, we can easily have a dialog about Twitter best practices before our annual conference."[5]

Humberto Kam, who oversees social media strategy for the Monterey Bay Aquarium, says, "It is really useful to have an open dashboard where your organization measures itself against other organizations with similar size, resources, and demographics."[6]

Sharing Dashboards and Reports with External Stakeholders

In 2007, the Indianapolis Art Museum launched its learning in public efforts by posting its institutional dashboard to a Web site for everyone to use. Today, five years later, no other organization has done as good a job.

While sharing performance dashboards with the public may not yet be standard practice for nonprofits, more and more are doing so by using infographics to share with audiences. Lucy Bernholz, a well-known blogger and author of the annual Philanthropy and Social Investing Blueprint, an industry forecast for philanthropy and social investing, says that nonprofits' use of infographics to share data is on the rise: "The age of big data that we're living in has set loose the age of infographics. Infographics include cool interactive maps, Venn diagrams of apparently unrelated events, and trend lines everywhere. Infographics are the ultimate 'pictures that say 1000 words.' Like so many buzzy things, infographics are running on their own adoption cycle, from the rare and cool to over-hyped and over-used."

Take, for example, the infographic in Figure 9.2 about reaching 1 million fans on Facebook that the Humane Society shared with its external stakeholders (which we chronicled in the opening chapter of this book).

Figure 9.2
The Humane Society's Infographic to Report Results

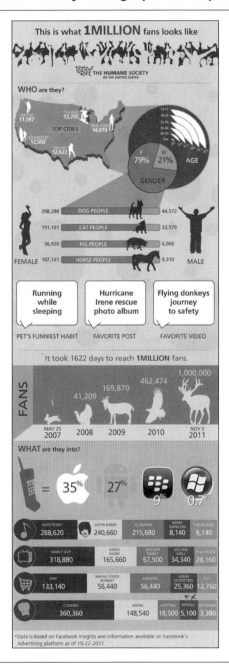

HOW BETH FOUND INSIGHT FROM THE DEVIL'S TOWER IN HER FACEBOOK INSIGHTS DATA

The goal of my Facebook page is to listen to nonprofit practitioners and their ideas, concerns, and needs on using social media effectively. My result metrics are the number of good ideas I get in return, and the time I save by getting ideas for blog posts, curriculum development, and presentations.

I know that in order to generate good ideas from my network, I need to feed and tune it. By "feeding," I'm talking about posting engaging and useful content that resonates. So that's why I track my content against two metrics in the new Facebook Insights: reach and virality. That's all well and good, but the data—in and of itself—is pretty useless unless I use my sense-making skills. Here is how I do it.

I check my Insights monthly against my editorial calendar. My first step is to look at the visuals on the dashboard (see Figure 9.3). The upper line represents weekly reach. The lower line represents people talking about

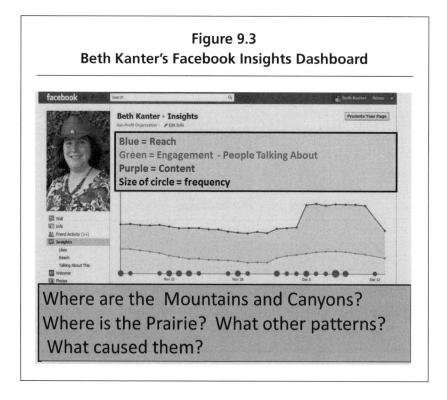

Figure 9.3
Beth Kanter's Facebook Insights Dashboard

my posts. And those circles along the bottom represent the frequency of my posts; a bigger circle means more frequent postings, and no circle means no content posted.

I like to use metaphors, so I ask: Where are the mountains? Where are the valleys? Where is prairie?

While staring at the visual, I immediately noticed a small canyon and a big Devil's Tower—a spike that stays high for a few days. When I compared the data with my posts, I discovered that the canyon was just after Thanksgiving, when I didn't post and my readers were less likely to visit.

Next, it was time to visit the mountaintops. I've noticed different types of mountains and hills in my Facebook analytics and Google Analytics over the years. One of them is the Devil's Tower: I get excited whenever I see one!

One of the posts that I shared at the beginning of the "Devil's Tower" was a practical piece of content that was visual, geeky, and fun. It was just the kind of material that I know my audience loves, but usually traffic just spikes and then comes down. This time it stayed high for a few days. So what? What does this tell me?

My next step was to look at the comments to see if there were any patterns or further clues. I discovered that two social media gurus with large networks had shared my post. I also noticed that several people in my network shared it and called the post a "Fun Friday Geeky Share."

All this is fun to do and interesting, but I took my coauthor Katie's advice and once again asked myself, "So what?" I thought hard about my content strategy and goals. Remember that I was looking to encourage more engagement and interaction. So as I planned out my editorial for the following month, I decided that I would post geeky, visual, fun stuff on Fridays. Over the next couple of months, the "Fun Friday Geeky Shares" continued to produce mountains, sometimes a few hills, and even another Devil's Tower.

If your takeaway from this post is, "Hmm. I should post geeky, visual, fun stuff on Fridays on Facebook," then you've missed my point. It is more important to practice and sharpen your sense-making skills through a process of analyzing your data.

THE KAT'S MEOW: KATIE PRESENTS
HER RESULTS TO THE BOARD OF TRUSTEES

To illustrate how a dashboard comes to life, we return to the adventures of Katie's Kat Shelter, the hypothetical nonprofit introduced in Chapter Six.

It's time for the quarterly meeting of Katie's Kat Shelter's board of trustees. To make sure the data she needs is up to date, executive director Katie has pulled together the development, accounting, marketing, PR, and social media staff two weeks before the meeting. Once the data is verified and complete, it gets turned over to Beth, who uses an Excel spreadsheet to combine and examine everything. Using the Pivot table function in Excel, she analyzes the data to see what has changed, what stands out, and which numbers look odd or off. Then the department teams get together again for a thorough discussion of the events of the past few months. They go through the data and develop preliminary conclusions that will form the headlines on the PowerPoint presentation for the board.

Beth prepares the presentation and presents it to the team. It consists of a table, a summary spider chart, and four individual charts. Once it has passed departmental muster, it gets turned over to the board a week in advance of the meeting. Katie knows there are a few very engaged board members who are sure to question a few things. She wants to make sure that they have time to dig into the data.

At the board meeting, she spends 20 percent of her allotted time reviewing the data and 80 percent informing the board of her plans for the upcoming quarter. All of her plans include improvements to programs and processes suggested by the data. The board congratulates her on an excellent job and cheerfully signs off on her proposals.

CONCLUSION

Data is one of the most powerful tools a nonprofit has in its arsenal. With good data and the insights that come from it, a networked nonprofit can improve its programs and its ability to achieve its mission. It can learn from mistakes and find shortcuts to success. Ultimately measurement will show where resources are working effectively and where they are failing. But if the data is stuck in a drawer and never presented, those opportunities will remain locked away. It is only by presenting, sharing, and learning from the data that success is achieved.

REFLECTION QUESTIONS

1. When you look at your data, do you see failures as well as success?

2. How can your data help you make decisions? How can it help you generate ideas to improve your next campaign?

3. Does your organization have a structured and regular process for reviewing data and generating insights? How can you institute one? Who needs to be involved?

4. Is your organization missing learning and insight opportunities because data is confined to silos in different departments? How can you change this?

PART THREE

Advanced Measurement Concepts and Practices for Networked Nonprofits

Measuring What Really Matters

The Importance and Measurement of Relationships

And you, Amanda: on a scale of 1 to 5, where 5 is "I do," 3 is "Meh" and 1 is "Heck, no"...

Networked nonprofits are passionate about their missions. They know that the world's problems are too difficult and its needs are too great for them to take on alone, so they can't risk discouraging those who want to help or alienating those who have helped in the past. This is why networked nonprofits work hard to build lasting relationships with their supporters and all their stakeholders.

To build strong relationships, nonprofits need to value their interactions with people, and they need to show their appreciation honestly, sincerely, and publicly. Networked nonprofits use social media to initiate and nurture relationships with their audiences, thereby building networks of friends, clients, donors, volunteers, and stakeholders of all types, including other aligned organizations. This chapter shows you how to understand and evaluate those relationships and, in the process, improve the ability of your organization to connect with and motivate your stakeholders.

Relationships are especially important for nonprofits in today's connected environment, where people can easily find each other and work together to change the world. For a person to support an organization, financially or otherwise, he or she must have some sort of a relationship with that organization. The person must trust that the organization has the ability to do what it says it is going to do and that it will be financially responsible with their money. Just ask United Way, Greg Mortenson, or any of the religious organizations that have recently come under scrutiny for financial misbehavior. A key to the long-term success of an organization is the ability to inspire commitment in its supporters and provide them some level of satisfaction. As the examples in this chapter and the rest of this book demonstrate, the most successful nonprofits build relationships with their supporters that move them from passive bystanders, to active supporters, to evangelists for their causes.

THE BENEFITS OF FRIENDS: GOOD RELATIONSHIPS PROVE THEIR VALUE

Good relationships with stakeholders provide many benefits for organizations besides increasing donations and volunteers, as the two examples that follow show. For SeaWorld, good relationships paid off in risk mitigation, and for the

American Red Cross, they proved their worth by rescuing it from an embarrassing situation.

SeaWorld's Relationships Blunt the Impact of a Crisis

In early 2010, a trainer was drowned by a killer whale at SeaWorld, an apparent accident. Despite the usual handwringing by PR pundits about the horrible situation, it was hardly the PR disaster they forecast. The reason? SeaWorld's strong and beneficial social media relationships.

Ever since SeaWorld took the social media plunge with Kami Huyse's help several years ago, and thereby realized the value of having direct conversations with roller-coaster bloggers, SeaWorld has been an object lesson in the measurable benefits of social media for marketing.[1] Over the past few years, SeaWorld has developed relationships with a sizable community of fans on Facebook, their blogs, and Twitter.

After the tragic accident, SeaWorld received a wave of negative publicity, and its brand was under attack by People for the Ethical Treatment of Animals (PETA) supporters. There were posts and comments that disagreed with SeaWorld's decision not to put the offending whale down or to release it. But the negative comments were counterbalanced by a flood of sympathy for the victim's family and support for SeaWorld's actions. Thanks to SeaWorld's large social network, it had an army of followers agreeing with its decisions and defending it. SeaWorld fans dismissed PETA's arguments as being uninformed. In fact, when SeaWorld pulled down the Twitter handle @shamu, explaining that under the tragic circumstances, it just wasn't appropriate to continue Tweets from someone pretending to be a killer whale, there were lots of fans who still wanted to hear from "Shamu."

By responding quickly and openly, having a social media community to rely on, sharing decisions with all publics, and making senior management available throughout (including answering all tweets and blog and Facebook comments), SeaWorld was the quintessential twenty-first-century company in a crisis. The value of its efforts to build relationships with fans could be quantified in terms of the amount of staff time required to deal with the crisis (which would have been significantly higher if the fans hadn't taken on a lot of the work themselves). Ultimately, however, the value of SeaWorld's social media relationship-building efforts was proven by the protection of the SeaWorld brand and the mitigation of risk.

The Red Cross's Strong Relationships Turn a Twitter Faux Pas into a Fundraiser

In February 2011, Beth Kanter received a direct message on Twitter from Wendy Harman, social media manager of the Red Cross. The message said, "The dreaded tweet! Our network took care of it."[2]

What Wendy was referring to was an epic Twitter mistake or embarrassing mistweet. These image-bruising blunders occur when the person who manages an organization's Twitter account sends an inappropriate tweet to that account, usually one that was intended for a personal account. The most tabloid-friendly of these tend to befall politicians and the business world: think of Congressman Anthony Weiner, sending a revealing photo of himself, and London's National Theatre, discussed in this chapter.[3] But for the Red Cross, the mistweet transformed from a PR disaster into a fundraising opportunity. This happened because the Red Cross took swift action, was wise enough to admit its mistake, and, above all, had strong relationships with supporters.

The Red Cross's Twitter faux pas occurred when an employee sent out a tweet about drinking beer to the organizational account: "Ryan found two more 4 bottle packs of Dogfish Head's Midas Touch beer . . . when we drink we do it right #gettngslizzerd."

The compromising Tweet was out in the wild for only about an hour, but it did not go unnoticed by Twitter followers, beer bloggers, and, of course, Wendy Harman at the Red Cross, who was awakened in the middle of the night by a call from a staff person in Chicago.

Thinking quickly, they deleted the rogue tweet and addressed the situation with a clever yet clearheaded follow-up: "Rest assured that the Red Cross is sober and we've confiscated the keys." The next morning, the Red Cross admitted on its blog that it accidentally tweeted something that was intended for a personal account.[4] The mistweeting employee apologized to her personal account, and the organization did so as well in a blog post.

Meanwhile, Dogfish Head Craft Brewery, which has its own host of devoted followers, helped to finesse the situation by acknowledging the incident and asking fans to donate to the Red Cross on Twitter. The witty pitch cautioned potential donors not to drink beer before or after they gave blood.

THE NATIONAL THEATRE GETS HECKLED AND DISCOVERS RELATIONSHIP PROBLEMS THE HARD WAY

Not until a rogue tweet sparked an honest and revealing exchange did London's National Theatre realize how very valuable it would have been to be keeping a closer eye on what its audience felt. It started during summer 2010 in a public hearing about London's South Bank arts precinct. Mayoral advisor Steve Norris declared, "The National Theatre should have a Compulsory Demolition Order." In a fit of pique, someone at the National Theatre responded with a stunningly inappropriate mistweet, calling Norris a four-letter word. This lapse of judgment prompted a Twitter storm and mainstream media coverage.

The theater's Twitter followers began to respond immediately—but not in the way you might assume. They were horrified, yes, but they also found the tweet, in the words of one follower, "refreshingly human." And another wrote, "Best. Tweet. Ever." It seems that the theater's audience was enjoying a bit of honest personality in its communications.

The next morning the National Theatre deleted the rogue tweet and sent out a message blaming the mistake on an anonymous hacker. But it was soon clear that the audience didn't buy into the phony damage control. Said one follower, "To be honest, I thought their tweeting of the c-word was less offensive than their selected tweeting of good reviews." It was becoming apparent that the theater had bigger problems than one mistweet.

A few tweets, of course, don't tell the whole story, and that's why the theater should stage regular relationship surveys to measure the feelings of its audience. The lesson here is not to wait until the greasepaint hits the fan before you assess the state of your relationships.

The generous and forgiving response from the networks of both the Red Cross and Dogfish Head turned the mistake into an opportunity that raised almost ten thousand dollars for the Red Cross. In fact, it attracted so much traffic to the site that the server crashed. The hashtag #gettingslizzerd, a reference to drinking beer, trended on Twitter.

MEASURING RELATIONSHIPS: THE GRUNIG RESEARCH AND RELATIONSHIP SURVEY

Much of this book so far has concerned the importance of identifying the goals of your social media programs. No matter what your goals, their achievement ultimately depends on the health of your relationships with your stakeholders.

The good news is that relationships have been studied, analyzed, and quantified. University of Maryland professors James and Larissa Grunig developed the science of relationship measurement in the 1990s, and numerous academics and measurement professionals have tested and used their techniques since then.[5]

Businesses and nonprofit organizations have been measuring their relationships for years. No matter how squishy it sounds, you can measure the extent to which people trust their local social service agency or whether they feel a commitment to a particular charity. Using survey research and content analysis (see Chapter Thirteen for more on these tools), you can quantify the health of relationships between people and organizations. You do not need to become an expert on measuring relationships to use and benefit from the techniques we discuss here. (To learn more about relationship research, see Appendix A.)

Just consider these data points. Kang, Garciaruano, and Lin found that the health of an organization's relationships was directly connected to the spread of rumors about the organization—a major concern in a world full of "Twitstorms," #FAIL, and viral parodies.[6] The study found that people who had low relationship satisfaction with an organization showed a stronger intention of passing along negative rumors than did those with high relationship satisfaction. In addition, people with good relationships with an organization were more likely to verify negative rumors before passing them along.

An organization's involvement in social media has also been shown to have a direct impact on the trust people have in the organization. Sisco and McCorkindale found that the credibility of an organization in the minds of potential donors was strongly correlated with the transparency of the organization and its communication effort. Specifically, organizations that tweeted more and had more likes, more followers, and more overall tweets were seen to be more transparent and credible by virtue of activity alone. The organizations that updated less frequently appeared to be less transparent. Thus, organizations appear to benefit from both quality and quantity of communications.[7]

FOR THE ASPCA, HEALTHY RELATIONSHIPS MEAN HEALTHY SUPPORT

When the ASPCA wanted to measure its success a number of years ago, it took a very comprehensive approach, using survey research to measure relationships, development data to understand what drove donations, Web analytics data to gauge traffic and interest, and a detailed content analysis of all media mentions in specific areas of the country. Specifically, they wanted to know how the health of their relationships and opportunities to see the brand affected fundraising.

Part of this question was straightforward to answer. Web data showed that the greater the exposure to the brand, the more Web traffic resulted. And there was a direct correlation between greater Web traffic and donations.

However, the data also showed that some types of news drove more revenue than others. One campaign was specifically designed to spread the word about what to do if you suspected your pet had been poisoned by contaminated pet food. This campaign evoked a communal response in the sense that, "You are helping me save my pet. You care about *me*; therefore I will care about *you*." This campaign was highly successful.

A very different campaign centered on the investigation into football player Michael Vick's dog fighting exploits. In this instance, the ASPCA, which was involved in the investigation, was unable to talk about details of the case. So the campaign, hampered by its limited ability to communicate, did not evoke the pet food campaign's level of communal response and thus did not generate anywhere near as many online donations.

More interesting, however, was that when the relationship survey data was overlaid on the exposure data, there was a direct correlation between high levels of trust and satisfaction with the organization and respondents' likelihood to volunteer, donate, or purchase ASPCA branded products.[8] For the ASPCA, the health of relationships is closely connected to support for its mission.

HOW TO MEASURE THE COMPONENTS OF RELATIONSHIPS

The work of the Grunigs and others has shown that relationships between people and companies or brands have distinct measurable characteristics, including:

- *Exchange relationship.* A relationship in which one party gives benefits to the other only because the other has provided benefits in the past or is expected to do so in the future. Exchange relationships (which were called transactional relationships in *The Networked Nonprofit*) are the basis of much of human commercial activity.[9] In an exchange relationship, there are no expectations on either side beyond the transaction.

- *Communal relationship.* A relationship in which parties provide benefits to each other because they are concerned for the welfare of the other, even when they get nothing in return. For most public relations activities, developing communal relationships with key constituencies is much more important to achieve than developing exchange relationships. When the relationship is communal, you will be more readily forgiven for mistakes, you will get past a crisis faster, and people will be more likely to take action on your part and recommend you to their friends.

- *Control mutuality.* The degree to which parties agree on who has the rightful power to influence one another. Although some imbalance is natural, stable relationships require that organizations and publics each have some control over the other.

- *Trust.* One party's level of confidence in and willingness to open oneself to the other party. There are three dimensions to trust:
  - Integrity: The belief that an organization is fair and just.
  - Dependability: The belief that an organization will do what it says it will do.
  - Competence: The belief that an organization has the ability to do what it says it will do.

- *Satisfaction.* The extent to which each party feels favorably toward the other because positive expectations about the relationship are reinforced. A satisfying relationship is one in which the benefits outweigh the costs.

- *Commitment.* The extent to which each party believes and feels that the relationship is worth spending energy to maintain and promote.

You can measure these relationship components by surveying your stakeholders. For each component, the Grunig research has validated a series of statements that evaluate it. These statements are known as the Grunig Relationship Survey and are provided in Appendix A. This set of questions has been thoroughly tested and shown to be a highly effective measure of how customers or members perceive their relationships with an organization. You present these questions to your stakeholders in a questionnaire and ask them to agree or disagree with each one on a scale of 1 to 5. You can do this by phone or in person (a very expensive choice) or by mail or e-mail.

The way to discover changes in your relationships is to do before-and-after surveys. Administer the survey prior to starting a specific campaign and then after the campaign is compete. The difference in the results will tell you how the campaign has affected the various components of your relationships. Then use this knowledge when designing your next campaign: How do you want it to affect your relationships?

Can Social Media Be Used to Measure Relationships?

Interest has been growing in the use of social media metrics to judge the health of your relationships.[10] Social networks, according to many, can be used like giant focus groups to provide insight into what the world thinks of you and your services. There are now numerous vendors of systems that analyze sentiment in social media messages, and they tout their products as substitutes for reputational surveys. It is intriguing to consider the possibility of mining social media to measure relationships, but the current state of the art of sentiment analysis does not make it an accurate proxy for relationship surveys.

Relationships Revealed by Engagement To a great extent, you can judge the health or progress of your relationship with an audience based on the state of engagement of that audience with your organization. Recall that Chapter Six discussed the topic of engagement, and the typical nonprofit member was seen to move through steps of engagement, from becoming aware of the organization to taking desired action on behalf of it. The actions that indicate engagement also indicate the presence of certain of the Grunig relationship components. So it is possible to gauge, in a rough fashion, the state of your relationships with an audience by understanding their engagement with your organization. In some cases, this may save you the effort of doing a survey.

To illustrate this, consider the hypothetical example of Veronica, the fan of Katie's Kat Shelter (KKS) introduced in Chapter Six. When Veronica purchases a greeting card with a cat on it, she accepts the card in exchange for a payment to the person behind the counter. This is an example of an exchange relationship.

But when Veronica takes an action that expresses her interest in KKS, such as following @KKS on Twitter, joining KKS's LinkedIn group, or forwarding a YouTube video, the relationship becomes a communal one. By taking an action that more closely associates her with KKS, Veronica is essentially saying, "Because KKS and I have similar interests, I'm interested in its future."

A very big and desirable step for nonprofit engagement is when interested persons become donors. In relationship terms, when Veronica donates to the cause or encourages a friend to donate, she demonstrates her trust in the organization. By taking this action, Veronica is expressing her belief in the organization's integrity, dependability, and competence.

When Veronica increases her involvement even more, say by making a recurring or auto-renewing pledge or offering to serve on the board, she is expressing her commitment. Commitment, as defined by Grunig and Grunig, is the extent to which each party believes the relationship is worth spending energy to maintain and promote.

Ultimately you need to look at the long-term aspects of Veronica's involvement with KKS to determine her level of satisfaction. Does she show up at board meetings? Does she lobby on behalf of the organization? Does she adopt another kitten? All of these actions are illustrative of her ongoing satisfaction with the relationship.

What Caused Veronica to Take Action? An important part of measurement is determining the context of your results and the drivers of the changes they indicate. In other words, you need to understand what was going on and provide an explanation of what made your results go up or down.

A major point of analyzing Veronica's engagement metrics is to determine what types of content have inspired her to move to a particular stage. Cute cat videos, for instance, are no doubt a strong driver of engagement at certain levels and for certain audiences. But are they really the most effective content for encouraging your long-term membership to increase their donations? This is the kind of question you want your data to answer.

KATIE PAINE HAS AN AHA! MOMENT THANKS TO ASPCA RELATIONSHIP STUDIES

My company had been tracking the ASPCA's traditional and social media for several years, and we'd just completed our first survey to determine whether its media exposure was having any impact on its Web traffic or online donations. At first glance, the results showed nothing all that surprising. However, we had inserted four relationship questions taken directly from the Grunig Relationship Survey because we wondered if respondents' relationships with the ASPCA might be related to exposure or to their behavior.

Surprise! It turned out that there was a high level of connection between respondents who had better relationship scores and their likelihood to purchase ASPCA-branded products. We also identified a connection between those relationship scores and exposure to local media (as opposed to national). In other words, in areas where the local media covered ASPCA the most, people's relationships with the organization were the healthiest.

HOW TO MEASURE RELATIONSHIPS IN EIGHT STEPS

The following approach to measuring relationships will help you determine if your strategies to improve your relationships are actually effective (see Chapter Eight for a detailed discussion of how to do surveys):

Step 1: If you don't already have a regular online survey tool, sign up for one. Qualtrics and SurveyMonkey all have free versions. Convio, Constant Contact, and other mailing list programs have survey programs built in.

Step 2: Determine whether your survey tool has analytical capabilities or if anyone in your organization has SPSS, SAS, Wincross, or any other software that can analyze and cross-tabulate data. If not, approach your local university and enlist its help. Perhaps your program would be a good case study for them.

Step 3: Define the universe that you will send the survey to. Are you surveying just your membership or the entire community? If you are surveying the entire community, you will need to acquire a list of community members. If you are surveying only your members, you will need to start the survey with qualifying questions about how they know you and if they know and understand that they are members.

Step 4: Go over the list of statements in the Grunig Relationship Survey in Appendix A. Select the ten that are most appropriate and applicable to your organization.

Step 5: Program the statements into your survey research tool. Check with your e-mail supplier to make sure that it won't reject the survey or related e-mails.

Step 6: Test the survey on people outside your organization. Here is where your local university can be a big help. Review the test results and revise your questions as necessary to ensure that you are getting the data you want and that you are able to segment those data sufficiently.

Step 7: Distribute the survey. Make sure you have a good cover letter that introduces the survey, explains its purpose, and ensures anonymity. Then distribute it in a way that ensures valid data.

Step 8: Wait at least two weeks for data to come in. If you do not get sufficient response, you may want to repeat the distribution.

Step 9: Analyze the data by date, gender, location, length of membership, and as many other different data points as possible. Look for anomalies—numbers that are abnormally low or abnormally high. Rank responses by worst to best. Draw conclusions and present results.

CONCLUSION

Many of today's nonprofits are obsessed with "building brand" or "enhancing reputation." What they don't understand is that you can't force brand and reputation down anyone's throat. Reputation is the end product of all your relationships. And without healthy relationships, all the branding in the world won't stop a nonprofit's reservoir of volunteers, supporters, and donors from drying up. Unless you are regularly taking their temperature, you may not know how healthy your relationships are until it is too late.

REFLECTION QUESTIONS

1. How might measuring relationships with your stakeholders improve the effectiveness of your communications strategy?

2. Have you planned any research projects for which the collection of relationship data would provide useful insight?

Understanding, Visualizing, and Improving Networks

No wonder we're lost... this is a map of my LinkedIn network!

The nature of a networked nonprofit, as opposed to a traditional nonprofit, is that it shifts its focus from working as a single organization to working as part of the larger social networks that exist beyond its institutional firewalls. Working this way enables these nonprofits to create a network of passionate supporters for an idea or to solve a problem quickly and at little cost. In fact, given the massive scale of the problems most nonprofits are working on, working in this kind of networked way is the only way to make meaningful progress. As Annie Leonard describes in the next section, it isn't just about the technology and tools; it's about working to harness the power of social networks, online and offline.

Networked nonprofits engage with networks of people and organizations to help meet their goals. To understand how these networks work, they can use measurement techniques in the form of mapping and visualization called *social networking analysis* (SNA). SNA can help networked nonprofits identify and cultivate influencers.

It requires effort for an organization to develop an effective network, including the work of introducing people, cultivating connections, and building relationships. In *The Networked Nonprofit*, this activity is described as *network weaving* and is critically important for the use of social media in fundraising, crowdsourcing, or volunteering. If you are responsible for this on-the-ground work and want a more in-depth guide, we suggest that you read *Network Weaver Handbook* by June Holley. If you are curious about the details of networked practice, look at "A Funder's Guide to Networks: Growing Social Impact in a Networked World" for additional and recent resources.[1]

In this chapter we look at methods for using SNA to improve the functioning of networks. We also discuss how to measure the impact of a network, although that is an emerging practice. To better understand exactly what you do when you measure a network, let's look at a very successful network, "The Story of Stuff."

THE STORY OF STUFF: WHY THE NETWORK IS THE HERO

When Annie Leonard and her friends at Free Range Studios set out to share what she'd learned about the way the United States makes, uses, and throws away consumer goods, one of their metrics for success was to get fifty thousand views for their "twenty-minute cartoon about trash."[2] Today, with over 15 million views since its release in 2007, *The Story of Stuff* is one of the most watched environmental-themed online movies of all time. It's been translated into dozens of languages and has inspired curricula for high schools, a ballet in Boston, a puppet show in Palestine, and floats in parades. People have even spray-painted the URL on bus stops.

The Story of Stuff is a fascinating and powerful critique of contemporary American culture. But what makes it truly amazing is the way it was developed and produced. Traditionally documentary films have been carefully crafted by a filmmaker in relative isolation and in complete control of the finished product. For distribution, a filmmaker would try to interest independent theaters in booking the film and then hope that an audience would show up.

But Leonard turned this model inside out. She created "The Story of Stuff" Web site and used social media to leverage and extend the film's impact by developing a network of people who discuss the issues and are passionate about building a more sustainable world. Today the online network includes over 250,000 activists, and the project partners with hundreds of environmental and social justice organizations around the world to create and distribute the film, curricula, and other content.

Leonard credits her success to letting the network help create the film. Not only did the network promote it, but many people provided feedback and content for the film. For *The Story of Stuff*, the network is the hero.

The story behind *The Story of Stuff* is about the networked leadership approach that created it and spread its message. The difference between a networked approach and the traditional organization-centric approach is the difference between an infrastructure of connections for widespread engagement and a tightly coordinated, top-down communications strategy. Leonard experienced this difference firsthand, and in making *The Story of Stuff*, she orchestrated a change between the two.

Leonard's innovation is that she harnessed the power of working in networks to mobilize people. But it didn't come quickly or easily. She spent nearly two decades investigating and organizing on environmental health and justice issues. She has seen with her own eyes the horrendous impacts of overconsumption around the world. She has visited hundreds of factories where products sold in the United States are made, as well as the dumps those products are trashed in when the next version is produced.

After lecturing people for years about this important issue, Leonard became exasperated that the ugly underside of American consumerism was being ignored. She had worked as a communications staffer in a large environmental action organization and was annoyed that people did not seem to be paying enough attention. She was frustrated that people around the world were not taking action.

In time, she realized that working within a single organization was not enough to inspire people to change their behavior, so she took a network-centric approach to address the problem. She spent years building relationships with groups all over the world and building a network of organizations to address the issues in the film. She also got lots of feedback about the film while it was being created.

By the time the film officially launched in 2007, it was already on the Web sites of hundreds of groups around the world. Hundreds of advocates and allies helped create it and had a stake in its success. She says it was a "network-held" resource: "When you have a group of people who are facile with social media and online tools all working together in a network culture, it can be unstoppable."[3]

HOW THE STORY OF STUFF PROJECT KNOWS IT HAS THE RIGHT STUFF

Says Annie Leonard, founder of The Story of Stuff project, "We love feedback, which comes in a variety of forms, from data about our online community to actual letters, e-mails, and questions at public forums. We are firm believers that systems can't self-correct without feedback and we depend heavily on it to get better."

The Story of Stuff is constantly testing different message topics and tone, and uses bitly to understand what the network responds to. Here is an example of how they judge the response to a message:

• Fewer than two hundred clicks usually indicates that the subject matter, source, or tone lacks relevance.

- Clicks numbering in the range of five hundred to seven hundred indicate that people were interested but not necessarily moved.

- Over seventeen hundred clicks indicates that it really resonates with their network, so they build out the theme further.

Says Leonard, "We look at who's referring people to us so we can get a more complete picture of our network and how information flows within it. This helps us deliver better content and media, especially to the people who are clearly nodes. We're not superactive in posting tweets, but Twitter is very useful in keeping tabs on what's happening around us."

Annie's next film, *The Story of Broke*, is now in progress. After 28,011 views of the initial teaser, 15,665 were from embedded YouTube players. Here is the breakdown of those views by Web site, which helps to reveal which audiences are most interested in the content and which channels are most effective for its distribution:

- 13,677 from storyofstuff.org, the teaser page

- 806 from treehugger.com

- 132 from Facebook mobile

- 68 from Google Plus

- 60 from redgreenandblue.org

- 1,888 from Facebook

- 1,658 from mobile devices

- 1,432 from YouTube subscribers

SOCIAL NETWORK BASICS

At its simplest, a social network is a structure that identifies relationships between people and organizations called *nodes*. The connections, communications, reciprocity, similarities, and relationships between nodes are called *ties*. The nodes are important, but without the ties, the network doesn't exist.

A network's *core* is the closely connected inner circle of people who do most of the work on any project or effort. Depending on the network, the core might comprise the organization's staff, volunteers, and key supporters.

Hubs are groups of strongly connected nodes within a network, meaning the people or organizations with close relationships. *Influencers* are nodes with many connections and strong connections throughout the network. They enjoy sharing information and connecting people to one another and resources.

Clusters are groups of people who are connected to one another but have fewer connections to the rest of the network. Clusters are often isolated from the rest of the network and require intentional efforts if you wish to connect them.

The *edge* or *periphery* of a network is the location of people or organizations who are not well connected to the network. Traditional top-down, command-and-control organizations don't pay much attention to the periphery because it doesn't appear to have as much value as the influencers. But from a networked point of view, the edge is vital to growth because these people or organizations are likely to be part of other networks. By incorporating them into your network, you can bring in new perspectives and energy.

SOCIAL NETWORK ANALYSIS: VISUALIZE YOUR NETWORK TO IMPROVE IT

SNA is a technique for helping understand, map, and measure the networks of social relationships that connect people and organizations to one another. Network visualization, through either maps or SNA, can reveal current and potential network resources and provide important insights. Nonprofits that want to build or improve their networks can use the art and science of these techniques.

The value of SNA is its ability to investigate questions that other research techniques cannot. SNA makes visible the otherwise invisible relationships, connections, and information that flow between nodes in a network. *Social network maps* provide a guided journey through the social landscape of your networks. Using them, you can visualize and explore the patterns that connect your organization's fans, followers, and friends. You can even analyze the connections and ties between people who use your organization's hashtags on Twitter.

Social network analysis and theory is a relatively recent set of concepts and techniques, largely developed by social scientists, academics, and mathematicians during the twentieth century. A field of intense study at graduate schools in universities, it has changed the way we combat terrorism, study ecologies, fight disease, and evaluate organizations.[4]

Social network visualizations provoke discussion and action about the people and organizations in a network. Visualizations reveal how they might better connect and work together toward achieving specific outcomes.

Seeing a picture—or map or diagram—of your network can be a powerful way to ignite ideas and conversation about your strategy. For example, suppose you want to learn who are the people most interested in your message and how you should cultivate them. Seeing a map of Twitter users who have participated in a Twitter chat can help you quickly identify new people and introduce them to your organization's work.

Social network analysis is not limited to looking at networks of people or individuals but can include networks of organizations as well. Networked non-profits can use this approach to analyze aligned partner organizations and to study the dynamics within a specific sector or discipline. An example is how the National Wildlife Federation used network mapping to identify aligned partners for advocacy around a bill, as discussed later in this chapter.

Q&A WITH MEG GARLINGHOUSE ON VISUALIZING YOUR LINKEDIN NETWORK WITH INMAP

Meg Garlinghouse is head of employment branding and community at LinkedIn.[5]

Q: What is an InMap?

A: An InMap is an interactive visual representation of your LinkedIn networks. We use information about how people in your network are connected to you and each other to create your personalized map. Groups like colleagues, people you went to school with, and friends are separated into color-coded clusters. With your InMap, you can visually understand how to better leverage your professional network to help pass along job opportunities, seek professional advice, or gather insights.

MEASURING THE VALUE OF NETWORKS

To measure the value of networks, you need to take the same basic steps as for any other measurement program: identify success, translate it into value, then collect and use data to chart your progress toward success.

Investing in networks requires patience and a willingness to embrace unexpected outcomes in addition to the original goals. A key challenge in measuring networks is showing near-term returns. Roberto Cremonini, network expert and former vice president at the Barr Foundation, expresses this challenge well: "You never know when the value of a network will become clear. This can be difficult for those that seek a linear return on investment. Yet as networks grow, they build upon many small acts of relationship building, problem solving, and knowledge sharing. The key is patience: Networks may lie dormant for a while, but will activate quickly when necessary."[6]

For Networks, Size Doesn't Matter; Quality Does

The quality of a network is much more important than its size. Put another way, the reach of your network is only one aspect; how it is clustered is far more important.

One SNA metric is called the *average path length*, which refers to the average number of degrees of separation between any two people in a network. The smaller the average path length between people is, the less effort is required to reach between them. If a nonprofit's emphasis is on expanding its network by adding random friends or followers, this will most likely result in longer path lengths, so the simple addition of new members will not necessarily increase the quality of a network.

People's relationships with one another are the building blocks of the social world. Social networks and sets of relationships combine to create patterns of connections among people, organizations, and things. The insights from SNA come from looking at what is between people, not simply counting them.

Social Network Analysis Can Be Used to Inform and Evaluate Strategy

A social network analysis or map done at the beginning of a project can be used as a baseline to gather a detailed understanding of a network to help inform strategy and tactics. It can also be used to take a snapshot of the same network after the project. Now compare before and after: Is the network more connected and denser as a result of the project?

Social network analysis requires examining connections between people in the network and looking at the network holistically. How are different groups of people connected? How might they influence other people and their connections? Using an SNA approach can help your organization more easily identify influencers and better pinpoint the best conversations to follow and people to cultivate for relationships.

This type of measurement is different from that discussed in Chapter Ten for measuring relationships. Participation statistics such as retweets or number of comments on a post can provide important insights about the engagement of a network or community with an organization, but they do not provide detailed information about the connections between people. Network analysis can help explain important social phenomena such as a group formation, overall community health, group cohesion, social roles, and individual influence. Combining participation and engagement metrics, relationship measures, and network metrics can provide a panoramic view of your network.

SOCIAL NETWORK MAPPING TOOLS: HOW TO VISUALIZE YOUR NETWORKS

Social network mapping tools run the gamut from simple to complex, free to expensive, and low tech to high tech. High-end social network analysis software can generate dazzling pictures that yield myriad interesting data and insights about who is connected to whom.

Don't be dismayed if your organization can't afford the expensive tools; you can still map your network in simple, low-cost ways. One is to map an organization's ecosystem by hand by simply drawing networks on paper or with sticky notes. The other is using a free online tool to map a social network on a social media channel like Facebook or Twitter. This is what TechSoup Global does.

TechSoup Global Maps and Studies Its Network

Susan Tenby is the director of online community development for TechSoup Global, a company founded in 1987 on the belief that technology is a powerful enabler of social change. She has worked there for over a decade and is fluent in using social media tools like Twitter and Facebook to help expand and knit TechSoup's vibrant network of individuals and organizations around the globe. Tenby organizes and hosts many online and offline events such as Twitter chats, and she is constantly engaging with her network to identify individuals and organizations whose work is valuable to share.

Tenby used a free Excel plug-in called NodeXL to build an SNA map of people who used the word *TechSoup* on Twitter (Figure 11.1). When she and her team sat down with the map, it prompted new ways of thinking and new tactics to build and weave their network. They looked at the hubs and thought about whom they should invite to participate in Twitter chats. The map made them think of new resources to add to their how-to materials.

What was most exciting was their discovery of networks of people who were interested in TechSoup but whom the team did not yet know existed. They discovered individuals who were on the edge of TechSoup's network but were hubs in other networks.

Tenby and her team developed ideas about how to improve their online events and community-building strategy simply by looking at the visualization and asking questions like these:

Figure 11.1
Social Network Analysis Map of Tech Soup

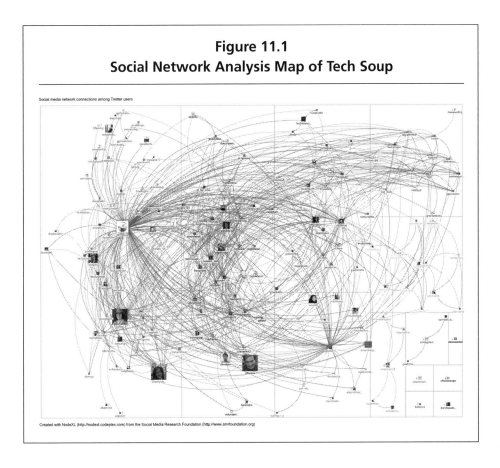

Social media network connections among Twitter users

Created with NodeXL (http://nodexl.codeplex.com) from the Social Media Research Foundation (http://www.smrfoundation.org)

- Is the network dense or sparse?
- Are there many connections among many groups, or are there silos?
- Who are the hubs or individuals who are most connected to other users?
- What groups are on the edge? What are the bridge connections to the core?

Says Tenby, "We can use this before social network analysis and compare to an after map that we build after we test new techniques. Did our strategies and tactics help us make the network denser and more connected?"[7]

It came as no surprise to Tenby that the TechSoup organizational account was a hub with many connections. But it wasn't the only hub. Key members of her team, including Tenby herself, were also hubs and were connected to other clusters of people. Their SNA map was clearly illustrating a key principle of

The Networked Nonprofit: for social media to scale, nonprofits need to use a combination of the organization's and individuals' networks.

As Tenby and her team explored the hubs and their networks, they noticed some interesting patterns. Many of the hubs had people who were connected to other networks. The map identified several smaller clusters that are part of the edge and may be connected to other networks.

Using the map as a guide, the TechSoup Global team might cultivate influencers, perhaps inviting them to be part of a Twitter chat or asking them to share it with their networks. Also, they might research and reach out to those people on the edge and see what networks they are part of and whether they are hubs for those networks. This might provide some ideas for future themes or guests for Twitter chats to grow the network.

BETH KANTER ON MAPPING HER LINKEDIN NETWORK

When LinkedIn released InMap, a free SNA mapping tool that lets you see your LinkedIn network and better understand it, I immediately put my own network to the test. My network looked like a virus, and as I later learned, this is a good thing because it means that I'm connected to many well-connected people.

What I found most compelling about my network map is that it allowed me to peer into my network, notice connections, and remind me of people I had not thought about in years. More important, it made me ask the "So what?" questions: What do I want to accomplish?" and "How can this network help me?"

As I stared at the visualization, I asked myself:

• What patterns exist?

• What surprises are revealed?

• What might I do differently with my network?

I learned a lot by browsing through the visualization of my network. What surprised me was how densely connected people are who work in nonprofit technology. When I examined the map in detail, it revealed a minihistory of the field. Viewing my whole network in this visual format helped me to remember people who I haven't recently been in touch with and how valuable their knowledge is.

National Wildlife Federation Uses Sticky Notes and Markers to Map Its Network

Danielle Brigida is the social media manager at the National Wildlife Federation (NWF) and an accomplished network weaver. She tweeted a photo showing how they were mapping one of their networks with a popular low-tech tool: sticky notes (Figure 11.2). Daniel Chu, vice president of affiliate and regional strategies and resident network weaving enthusiast, was facilitating a network mapping activity with NWF's education advocacy staff. They wanted to visualize their network for a specific purpose: getting a national bill (the Moving Children Outdoors Act) on President Obama's desk for signature by October 2012.

Figure 11.2
Using Sticky Notes to Map National Wildlife Foundation's Social Network

Staff members were at the core of the map. Chu asked each staff person to add a sticky note with the name of a "go-to person" for this issue for his or her group and location. This became the next ring of sticky notes. They discussed any common contacts, if any two staff who shared the same contact were aware of it, and if they had a coordinated relationship strategy for that contact. ("Closing the triangle" is a network weaving technique that means introducing people in your network to one another.) They also discussed relationship building:

- What is the strategic value of investing in the relationship with that person?
- Are you the right staff person to have an intensive relationship with that person?
- Is there another staff person who makes more sense to bring into the relationship?

The next step was to look for patterns, so they reorganized the map into clusters—for example, all clusters associated with formal education or advocacy. This prompted a strategy discussion about how the staff teams might reorganize so that each cluster would have a lead weaver.

Finally, they discussed identifying important potential influentials to expand each cluster or create a whole new cluster with a set of influentials that would be strategically important to build out.

Chu made this observation about the value: "Such analysis allows the team to be more intentional about weaving a national network for a specific campaign or advocacy outcome."

CONCLUSION

Networked nonprofits engage and build relationships with networks of people and organizations to reach their objectives. They take the time to visualize and understand how their networks work, and with those insights they can help make these networks more vibrant. A vibrant network—one that responds to and engages around an organization's issues and programs—leads to more powerful social change. Visualizing your network can help catalyze people in your network to action. And when they do, wonderful things can happen.

REFLECTION QUESTIONS

1. What is the goal of your network? If your organization has a presence on Facebook, Twitter, or other networks, try mapping your network to see what it looks like. Who are the influencers and hubs? How can you use your map to improve your network?

2. What types of tactics or ideas can you use to weave and knit your network? After you use these tactics, what does your network look like? How has it changed?

3. Are staff members or board members on LinkedIn? Take a look at your collective profiles on LinkedIn. Are there influencers or important nodes in these networks you need to cultivate and build relationships with to get work done?

Influence Measurement

How to Determine Your Influence and That of Your Organization, Free Agents, and Nonprofit Champions

I clearly said our nonprofit needs to measure "social media influence."
Not "social media people *under* the influence."

B ack in the days before Facebook and Twitter, before crowd-sourcing and the cloud, communications directors and PR managers at nonprofits depended on spiral-bound directories to identify media outlets and reporters who were best at reaching the specific demographics they were interested in. These directories were based on readership surveys that purported to identify who read what publications. The assumption was that if you could get your story in those publications, it would "influence" your stake-holders. It was a pathetically inexact science.

In reality, if you'd worked in an industry long enough, you knew exactly who the influencers were. If you were operating a local nonprofit, you knew the three reporters in the area who were likely to cover you and the four local philanthro-pists and business owners who believed in your cause. If you were running a national organization, you pretty much knew who your influencers were because you ran into them at conferences, or they called you to talk about your issues. Those spiral-bound notebooks were most useful to people newly established in the field who hadn't yet accumulated the gray hairs and the relationships to know where the bodies were buried and who was buttering which side of whose bread.

Then along came Facebook, Twitter, and the democratization of social media and the world seemed to redefine "influence" over night. Influencers were popping up everywhere: moms in their bathrobes, teenagers with cell phones, and folk musi-cians from Canada were causing major headaches for brands around the world. In the nonprofit world, these influencers are sometimes called *free agent fundraisers*, a term Beth Kanter coined in 2008.[1] Free agent fundraisers combine their social media savvy with their passion for social causes to organize, mobilize, raise funds, and communicate with constituents outside the walls of nonprofits. In the old days, nonprofit organizations could dismiss free agents as not worthy of their time and attention, and without the connectedness of social media, they might have been able to afford to ignore them. But today they are viewed as valuable partners.

INFLUENCE REDEFINED (NOT)

Influence means the power or ability to affect someone's actions. Philip Sheldrake, in his book *The Business of Influence*, sums it up nicely when he writes, "You have been influenced when you think in a way that you wouldn't otherwise have thought, or do something you wouldn't otherwise have done." Brian Solis, in his book *Engage*, provides a more eloquent definition: "Influence is the capacity to have an effect on the character, development, or behavior of someone or something, or the effect itself. Effect is key in understanding influence and its role in societies online and in the real world. In social media, it's the ability to cause measurable actions and outcomes."[2]

Influence is frequently confused with popularity. Just because someone has lots of followers on Twitter does not mean that he or she has influence over any audience, let alone the one you are trying to reach. Justin Bieber has lots of followers, but he's probably not going to influence anyone to change his or her social media measurement system.

Influence is also confused with *influential*, a term derived from Elmo Roper's Influentials model of 1945, that identifies those consumers in a society whom others are more likely to turn to for advice on which products and services to buy.[3] (Today, PR people use the term *influencer*, and the terms are largely synonymous.) These influentials were found to be individuals who are more likely to go to meetings, pass on recommendations, and express opinions. Earlier in this century, Roper updated the theory to include online word-of-mouth and showed that profiles of influentials almost exactly matched the characteristics of bloggers.[4] The result was that more and more consumer marketers started paying attention to social media. With the publication of Malcolm Gladwell's *Tipping Point*, influentials became all the rage.[5] Every organization was suddenly on the hunt for its influentials.

A debate ensued about whether you can "tip" a market by getting a few key influentials to talk about your organization. Traditional marketing and advertising types believe that if you can reach the most influential people in society (for instance, Lady Gaga, Ashton Kutcher, Chris Brogan, or whoever else is the next in line) and get him or her to endorse your cause, you will make all your revenue targets. However, recent research has upended this old-school wisdom, revealing that many celebrities do not effectively raise money for nonprofits. In fact, lesser-known people can raise more money, particularly those who:

- Have a personal connection to the cause
- Are willing to engage a preexisting network that is passionate about the cause
- Have an authentic relationship with the cause[6]

On the other side of the argument is Duncan Watts, who has been research-ing influence at Yahoo! and whose latest research concluded that "word-of-mouth information spreads via many small cascades, mostly triggered by ordinary indi-viduals."[7] This has become the rationale for many nonprofits to create Facebook pages and Twitter accounts in hopes of generating such a cascade. But Watts is confusing the way networks operate with how people's actions are affected by the opinions of others.

What Watts and others have done is to use retweeting, linking, and other social media actions as proxies for influence, leading to a popular belief that because lots of people hit the "like" button on Facebook, masses of people will donate or show up at an event. In reality, the degree to which people show up, donate, or do any-thing else you ask them to depends on who is asking them, what else is going on in their lives at the time, and the strength of their affiliation with your cause.

Influence is far better understood by psychology and sociology than by Web analytics. In those fields, it is commonly understood that influence happens either one-on-one—your mother influences your choice of clothing (God forbid she *tells* you what to wear)—or socially—your peers influence what event you wear that clothing to. In the end, it still comes down to individuals.

In reality, there is no substitute for an individual's knowledge and experience with the market from which you are trying to raise money or the cause that you are trying to help. Influence implies a personal, persuasive relationship between the individual and the audience being influenced. No investor relations or analyst rela-tions professional would dream of relying on mass e-mails to explain a new strategy to a financial or industry analyst. Today's influentials for nonprofits are no different. They authentically care about the cause and can influence a network of other people to care about it too. In the nonprofit world, a given organization's influentials are frequently people who are not necessarily already known to that organization.

This chapter discusses two distinct aspects of the measurement of influence: how to discover who is influential to your stakeholders and in your marketplace, and how to measure and improve your own influence.

HOW FREE AGENTS HELP NETWORKED NONPROFITS CHANGE THE WORLD

Free agents are nonprofits' uber-influentials. They use their expertise in social media to help nonprofits solve social problems, achieve fundraising goals, and educate about a cause. Thanks to social media, they can be found just about anywhere. They can be famous or unknown, with deep pockets or no pockets at all. Their common denominator is passion. Free agents are people who want to give their money, time, or personal endorsements to a cause or organization that can help solve wicked problems facing our world today. (Wicked problems are those that are not solvable by traditional methods and are difficult or impossible to solve at all because of incomplete, contradictory, and changing requirements. The effort to solve one aspect of a wicked problem may reveal or create other problems.) Free agents come in all shapes and sizes, from eight-year-old Grace who raised a thousand dollars for the National Wildlife Federation to help wildlife harmed by the Gulf oil spill, to Amanda Rose, a passionate millennial who helped charity: water inspire people to self-organize fundraising events in over 150 cities worldwide, raising more than half a million dollars in twenty-four hours.

Here are a couple of their stories.

Shining a Light on Homelessness: Mark Horvath and InvisiblePeople.TV

Mark Horvath (@hardlynormal) knows from personal experience what it is like to be homeless and live on the streets or in a shelter. He was frustrated that the stories of homeless people were being ignored, and so in 2008 he launched his video blog Invisible People.tv to tell the stories of homelessness and the agencies trying to help. "I'm pushy—screaming loud to end poverty. I'm supporting the organizations working on the front line and I'm doing the best I can to fight homelessness," he said.[8]

Horvath is an expert at using social media to connect his work with a broader network of people and organizations sharing his goal. On the face of it, his Web site doesn't seem to be set up to collect money. It's simply video story after video story of the homeless. However, the material is so powerful that after watching a few videos, many people find themselves scrambling to find the page where they can donate.

Over the past few years, Horvath's' network of homeless advocates, organizations, and homeless people keeps getting bigger, continuing to be a catalyst for change. Since 2009, he has received funding from large companies, foundations, and government to take an annual coast-to-coast road trip and collect stories about the homeless.

In response to Horvath's efforts, thousands of people and organizations have rallied to house the homeless. Others have created housing programs; a farmer, for example, donated land that is now being used to help feed low-income families. In 2011, YouTube allowed InvisiblePeople.tv to curate its home page for a day. That one day resulted in 1.6 million people encountering homelessness—some of whom might never have rolled down their window at a stoplight for a homeless person asking for help.

In 2010, Horvath won a special Pepsi Refresh contest that awarded him fifty thousand dollars to build a program and Web site, WeAreVisible, that helps those who are homeless gain social media skills to connect with others and help improve their situations.

Shawn Ahmed Talks to World Leaders About Disaster Relief and Saving Children

A lecture by world-renowned economist Jeffrey Sachs in September 2006 propelled Shawn Ahmed to put his graduate studies on hold, liquidate his savings, and buy a plane ticket to Bangladesh. Since then, the twenty-nine-year-old's videos have given a voice to rural Bangladeshis. The Toronto video blogger has managed to attract a huge following on YouTube, where his work has been described as changing the way people think about global poverty.

More than eighty thousand people subscribe to Ahmed's videos—that's more subscribers than Save the Children and UNICEF have attracted. He founded the Uncultured Project, which he describes as his journey to make the world a better place by inspiring people "to believe that we can be the generation that ends extreme poverty." He has also partnered with large charities in the United States, including the American Red Cross and Save the Children, for which he has leveraged his networking and video skills to fundraise.

In 2011, the World Economic Forum invited Ahmed to its annual meeting in Davos, Switzerland, after one of his videos was selected, from one hundred entries, as the winner of the Davos Debates. There he had an opportunity to address world leaders and share successful examples of networked nonprofits working with free agents.

MEASURING WHO INFLUENCES STAKEHOLDERS: THE BLUE KEY CAMPAIGN

Assisting refugees around the world is the work of more than six thousand staffers of the Geneva-based United Nations High Commissioner for Refugees (UNHCR).

USA for UNHCR (www.unrefugees.org) raises funds and awareness in the United States to provide funding and support for UNHCR. The goal is to provide protection, food, shelter, and care that refugees need to open the doors to a new life.

The plight of refugees is so far removed from our comfortable lives in the United States that we don't automatically think of donating to organizations that work to support them. That's why USA for UNHCR created the Blue Key Campaign in early 2011 to increase awareness of this issue. Donors of five dollars to the campaign receive a Blue Key pin or pendant that symbolizes the one thing many people in the United States have and that refugees don't: a key to their own home. This effort was designed to dovetail with the observance of World Refugee Day on June 20, 2011.

USA for UNHCR wanted social media to be a major part of this campaign and so hired social media consultant and long-time measurement maven Shonali Burke to create and implement a plan. Marc Breslaw, then executive director of USA for UNHCR, knew that with existing staff resources stretched thin, bringing on an experienced consultant would help manage expectations for the campaign's results, as well as provide learning opportunities regarding best practices and the efficient investment of staff and consultant time going forward.

An online community of influencers was to be a centerpiece of the campaign. That is where the idea of the Blue Key Champion came in. Blue Key Champions would be active and passionate U.S.-based bloggers who would help spread the word and get more keys ordered. The efforts of these influentials would ultimately help refugees make a better life.

The Blue Key Campaign Builds Measurement in from the Start

As with any other program that incorporates proper measurement, the Blue Key Campaign started with clearly defined goals. Identifying key performance indicators (KPIs) for this project was relatively easy: they would be the number of champions and how many blue keys were purchased. But determining the exact targets to set was uncharted territory. Says Burke:

> When the Blue Key site was launched in December 2010, its social/digital aspects were relatively new, so there was not a lot of data to base our KPIs on.

We decided that phase 1 of the campaign would have two objectives: to secure at least three Blue Key Champions and to get 6,000 keys ordered between May 9 and World Refugee Day on June 20. These goals were important to USA for UNHCR because first, with a limited budget for traditional outreach, we were relying on willing bloggers to help us get the word out, and second, the success of the entire Blue Key Campaign revolved around people purchasing keys.[9]

Finding Influencers to Recruit as Champions

With Burke's help, USA for UNHCR designed and implemented an influencer program using the Blue Key Campaign Blog.[10] Burke's team used a tool called Traackr to identify influencers using keywords (see Figure 12.1).[11] She says, "We also looked at other tools, so it was a combination, but Traackr was the most helpful (and relevant). We also used good old-fashioned elbow grease: Internet and blog searches, Technorati, and Alexa. And finally, my personal knowledge, since I'm plugged into both the nonprofit and social media/PR worlds. But there were a lot of my friends, particularly in the latter,

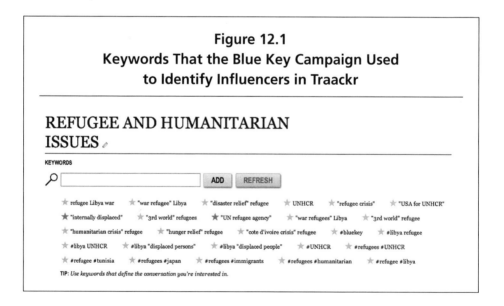

Figure 12.1
Keywords That the Blue Key Campaign Used to Identify Influencers in Traackr

that I didn't reach out to, because it wouldn't have been a good fit for their blogs."

The campaign quickly and easily exceeded its objective, recruiting forty bloggers to write about the cause and spread the word. Burke enthused about the success:

> The Champions are working great. The Blue Key is a great conversation starter, as many of our Champions have noted when they wear them. The more we can get people talking about it, the better our chances of reaching not just the "key" goal, but of truly building a community of support for refugees.
>
> Since the Champions are engaged and active, they hold much more weight in their communities. Of course, they have to get really involved with the campaign, and that takes time. In addition, everyone has different levels of participation, which again is completely normal.[12]

Following best practices for influencer outreach, Burke provided source materials for the bloggers so they had background to work with. The campaign also created a private Facebook group to connect the bloggers with each other and communicate with them about campaign victories, another best practice.

The Blue Key Campaign identified creative ways for champions to use social media channels. The success of each of these activities was measured by the number of Blue Key pendants that were purchased and the amount of traffic referred to the campaign Web site.

One of these activities was a one-day Tweetathon held a week before World Refugee Day. On that day, several champions tweeted in shifts about the refugee crisis from 9:00 A.M. to 9:00 P.M. In addition, Roya Hosseini, wife of Khaled Hosseini (the author of *The Kite Runner*) and manager of the Khaled Hosseini Foundation's Twitter account, signed on as a special guest between 1:00 and 2:00 P.M.

The Campaign Tracks Its Results

In addition to tracking Blue Key purchases on a weekly basis, the campaign tracked hashtags to gather data on how many tweets used its #bluekey hashtag. They also used Google Analytics to look at their Web site traffic sources (Figure 12.2).

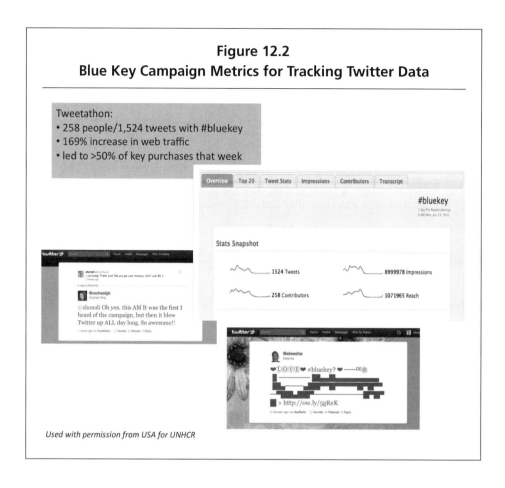

Figure 12.2
Blue Key Campaign Metrics for Tracking Twitter Data

Tweetathon:
• 258 people/1,524 tweets with #bluekey
• 169% increase in web traffic
• led to >50% of key purchases that week

#bluekey

Stats Snapshot

1524 Tweets   8999978 Impressions

258 Contributors   1071965 Reach

Used with permission from USA for UNHCR

Burke enthused about the results: "The Tweetathon was very successful. All told, there was a 169 percent increase in Web site traffic that day, compared to the previous high point a few weeks prior. We get real-time confirmation every time someone orders a key, so we knew the Tweetathon was generating donations. Finally, by tracking traffic to campaign URLs in Google Analytics, we determined that Twitter was the main driver of traffic after the Tweetathon."

While the Tweetathon was unfolding, the team did real-time tracking by paying attention to what was getting retweeted and to the tweets that got the most responses. "Periodically, we would post [this information] to the Blue Key Champions' Facebook group," explained Burke, "so that those who were about to sign on for their shift could adjust their tweets to suit the interests of the audience."

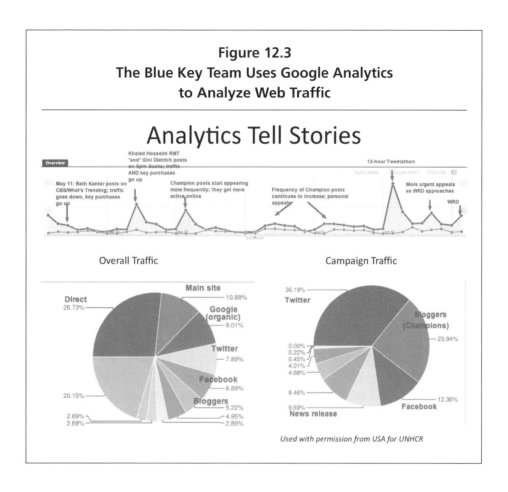

Figure 12.3
The Blue Key Team Uses Google Analytics
to Analyze Web Traffic

Used with permission from USA for UNHCR

Data in Context: Determining the "Why?" and the "So What?"

Figure 12.3 shows how the team used Google Analytics to analyze Web traffic and trends for phase 1 of the campaign, May 9 to June 20. The dash-dot line shows the traffic during that time period, and the line below it with squares shows traffic for the previous six weeks.

To help identify cause and effect, Burke used the annotation feature on Google Analytics to make notes on the chart that relate the activities that occurred during that time to the spikes in traffic: "I reviewed the campaign activities (Champion posts, a radio media tour that Khaled Hosseini had done for USA for UNHCR, the Tweetathon, etc.) and ongoing reports of key purchases. Then I annotated the chart accordingly."

Learning from Experience to Set New Goals

USA for UNHCR understands that measurement and learning are iterative processes to help figure out what is effective and what is not. So doing after-action review is embedded in the organization's way of working. Says Burke, "Information is one thing, but if you're not going to draw conclusions from it and apply them, then it's not very useful. We wanted as many insights as possible, both for internal dissemination and to share with the Champions about the results of their work."

During the phase 1 debriefing process, they looked for both successes and failures of the campaign activities. The results reports were not viewed as a report card, but rather as a tool to help the team set objectives for the next phase and to help keep blogger volunteers motivated.

One phase 1 goal that was not met was to sell six thousand keys. For phase 2, the team set an objective—six thousand keys sold through December 31, 2011 (a goal they exceeded)—based on past performance data rather than the educated guess they had used for phase 1. Burke notes that they had "the benefit of a benchmark based on our past performance, and I'm happy to say we met that phase 2 key sales objective."

When the team saw how effective the Tweetathon had been, they decided to include one every month for phase 2 of the campaign. They also set a new objective to bring in more champions, and more quickly than they had during the first phase. "We learned from our data that the champions' posts really helped spread awareness of the campaign," says Burke, "and they brought the Blue Key site higher in Google searches. So we are continuing to bring more of them on board."

Burke points out that it is one thing to identify champions, but then there is a lot more work to do afterward:

> Take an initiative like the #bluekey tweetathons, for example. It needs buy-in from engaged community members to really work. If the Blue Key Champions were not engaged, they would never have come up with the idea in the first place, nor would they have made the time to participate. When you look at the results, the first tweetathon in June resulted in 66 key purchases. Our second tweetathon resulted in 159 purchases, almost triple the June number! This was because the Champions went all out to make it work. So their value

is far more than simply blogging about the program or retweeting; they are true evangelists for the organization's mission, helping to convert other people into supporters and, ultimately, donors.

MEASUREMENT OF INFLUENCE

There are three things you can measure when it comes to influence:

1. Who is influential to your organization
2. The effectiveness of free agents and nonprofit champions
3. How influential you are

How to Identify Your Organization's Influencers in Three Simple Steps

Finding those people online who influence your stakeholders or mission—or, as for the Blue Key Campaign, who would make excellent champions for your campaign—takes some legwork. While identifying someone with a lot of followers who writes about your space may seem easy, it actually requires a bit of forethought and skill. We offer three steps for finding your own organization's influencers, but you can also use them to locate the influencers on any topic you are interested in. Identify champions for your cause by measuring influence; then measure the success of your champions by whether their participation helped move the needle on your defined goals.

Step 1: Learn What Data You Already Have Available The first step in locating your influencers is to check the data you already have. If you've ever done a survey or are about to do one, see if you can find out or ask your stakeholders where they go for information. What reliable sources do they turn to?

If you are already monitoring your media coverage or your social conversations, examine the previous three months of coverage and identify anyone who has mentioned you more than three times. Someone who is writing about you more than once a month probably has influence on your stakeholders.

Step 2: Use Search Terms to Work Backward to Discover Who Writes About You If you don't have any survey data and aren't doing any monitoring at all, brainstorm within your organization on ways that people might describe or search for you. Check your Google Analytics data to find the words that people use to find your site. You can also use tools like Google Keyword finder or WordTracker to check your list.

Once you've identified the search terms and key words that are commonly used to describe or find you, set up a Google Alert to look for posts that include them. Track the authors of the posts that show up. If you have a budget for this effort, you might want to a find a service that allows you to search for influencers by topic, like Appinions, Traackr, or eCairn.

Katie's Kat Shelter (KKS, the hypothetical nonprofit we introduced in Chapter Six) would consider as possible influencers former adopters, veterinarians, pet stores, and board members and their friends and families. KKS will very likely find that just looking for mentions of "cats" and "kittens" will overwhelm them with posts from a large number of people who aren't local and don't care about this shelter. So they might want to start with a list of people on Twitter and Facebook who are from the local area and monitor their posts for mentions of cats, kittens, purring, fur, or similar indications that they like cats. If there are only two thousand people in KKS's area who can use their services, a cat-liking international celebrity who never interacts with his or her 15 million followers is not important to KKS. What is important are the people who influence those two thousand people.

Step 3: Make a List, and Check It Twice: Once for Action and Again for Trust Remember that the definition of influence specifies that someone who has been influenced takes action or at least changes his or her mind. That means that ultimately you need to check to see if the influencers you have identified do in fact change anyone's mind, intent, or action. Check your Web analytics to see how many referrals come from the blogs of the key influentials you've identified and use techniques similar to those set out in the Blue Key case study.

To winnow down your list to the most important, rate your influencers according to the following four criteria:

1. *Frequency:* How often are they writing about you?

2. *Relevance:* Are they writing about topics that are relevant and interesting to your mission or stakeholders? Are they producing content that is interesting?

3. *Resonance:* Do stakeholders find the content interesting enough to forward, share, like, or retweet?

4. *Trust:* Do people actually trust the information that these influencers are putting out there?

Measuring the Effectiveness of Free Agents and Nonprofit Champions in Achieving Your Goals

Measuring the impact of free agents and nonprofit champions is simply a matter of following the basic rules of measurement that we established in Chapter Four. It all starts with your mission or goal. What do you want free agents to do for you? Raise money? Get people to an event? Raise awareness of your message? Educate the public about a cause?

The point is to measure the impact on your organization. How you define that impact is up to you. Remember these rules:

- Ask, "So what?" to make sure you understand the end result. "So what if we double the number of likes. How does that affect the likelihood of success?" "So what if traffic to the site increased by 10 percent? Did they just go to the landing page and leave, or did they hit the 'donate here' button?

- Get agreement on the goals. Make sure that everyone shares a common definition of success.

- Establish a benchmark and track over time. In order to know if your free agents are successful, you need to measure their progress. Ideally, you'd do a benchmark audit of where your organization is today, add in the free agents, and measure again after several weeks or months. If you already have free agents working for you, measure progress toward your goals week to week to see if an increase in free agents is helping you move towards ultimate success.

Measuring How Influential You or Your Organization Is in Social Media

Determining how influential you or your organization is in social media is thought by many to be simple ego gratification. But there are some legitimate reasons to measure your own influence level:

- You want to demonstrate to potential funders or sponsors that your voice is spreading.

- Your mission is to change minds about a topic, and you need to measure whether your voice is making headway on that topic.

- Your mission is to counter a louder voice on the opposite side of an issue.

- You want to demonstrate to aligned partners that working together is more efficient and can have more impact.

There is no shortage of online tools that claim to help you figure out your "influence score." Most base the results entirely on your levels of activity on Twitter or Facebook and offer little guidance on what the score means or why it makes a difference. The important thing to remember is that it isn't about the activity; it's about the impact.

A perfect system to measure online influence would test perceptions along with activity. Perception metrics might include:

- Percentage of quotes in the media as compared with someone else

- Percentage shift or increase in positioning in media coverage as a leader as opposed to one of the pack

- Percentage increase in invites to guest blog or post

- Percentage increase in speaking invitations or solicitations of papers

- Percentage increase in stakeholder perceptions of you as a thought leader

Activity metrics might include:

- Percentage increase in an influence or impact score over time

- Percentage increase in an influence or impact score relative to the opposition

How you calculate an influence or impact score is a matter of which tool you use. There are about a dozen of them out there, including Tweetlevel, Twitalzyer, Kred, and Klout. Which tool you use doesn't matter as much as consistency: pick one, and stick with it. Track your score over time to see if it is improving or declining. You should also identify a peer group of influencers against whom to benchmark your results.

If your score is going up, then clearly you are doing something right. Check changes in your score against the content you are producing to see what topics and content improve your numbers. If your score is going down, you need to examine both your network and your content. The key to influence is to be interesting and authentic.

According to a recent study of influence conducted by Brian Solis and Vocus, 90 percent of people attribute influence to the quality or focus of a network, and 85 percent say the quality of content is the top attribute of influence.[13] When they asked why people followed others, the story became clear: 37 percent followed because they post interesting content, 62 percent followed because of relevant content, and 43 percent focused on a personal connection.

THE LEADERSHIP LEARNING COMMUNITY

The Leadership Learning Community is a national nonprofit dedicated to transforming the way leadership development work is conceived, conducted, and evaluated, primarily within the nonprofit sector. It combines expertise in cutting-edge ideas and promising practices in leadership development with access to a network of hundreds of experienced funders, consultants, and leadership development programs. The objective is to drive the innovation and collaboration needed to make leadership more effective.

In 2012, the Leadership Learning Community will release an important report on the intersection between leadership and networks. The goal is to use the report to encourage nonprofit leadership programs to use networked strategies to increase their impact. Integrating the use of social media with the release of the online report, they hope to encourage downloads of the report, inspire online conversations about network leadership, have enthusiasts self-organize events to discuss the topic offline, and encourage programs to put the ideas into practice.

Natalia Castañeda, marketing and communications director, says, "As part of our strategy, we've identified influencers and thought leaders on the topic of networked leadership, and we will work with them to spread the report's findings on Twitter and other channels. More importantly, our ultimate result is spreading the practice of networked leadership. We measure the effectiveness of the program by looking at the number of reports downloaded and a survey to track whether or not programs are adopting these practices."[14] They will also track how their own influence has increased by doing a before-and-after content analysis of online coverage and using a tool like Klout to see if their influence score has gone up and why.

CONCLUSION

Measuring influence in any program needs to be approached in different steps. It's not just about who has the most followers; it's about who has the greatest potential to influence stakeholders to take action on behalf of your organization. Who is influential, and to what extent is their influence dependent on your goals? Do you want the audience to donate or to write a letter to Congress? There will be different influencers for each case. But identifying influential people to cultivate and work with you is the first step. To realize success, robustly support those relationships, measure activity and perception over time, and make adjustments.

REFLECTION QUESTIONS

1. What program or campaign is your organization planning that could greatly benefit from cultivating and supporting influencers and free agents to work with?

2. What keywords are most associated with your cause or organization?

3. Once you've identified influencers, what will you ask them to do for your organization?

4. How will you measure the success of your influencer program?

5. Given your organization's goals, how important is it to track its influence? What will you track for perception and activity?

How to Be Naked and Measure It

Transparency Is a Networked Nonprofit's Best Friend

In the interests of transparency, I should disclose that
transparency gives me the willies.

Transparency is a relatively new and developing practice for nonprofits, and the field of measurement of nonprofit transparency is embryonic. There are as yet few case studies of transparency measurement. But tools and opportunities are in place to make this an important field for future development.

This chapter provides an overview of transparency and discusses some techniques for how networked nonprofits can measure its benefits. First, let's look at why and how transparency helps networked nonprofits work more effectively.

GREATNONPROFITS, A RADICAL EXPERIMENT IN TRUE TRANSPARENCY

Perla Ni was more than a little nervous the first time she presented the concept for her brainchild, GreatNonprofits. It was back in 2007, and she was hoping to partner with a group of nonprofits, the Greater Pittsburgh Nonprofit Partnership, to help pilot and launch her initiative.

Designed as a sort of Yelp for nonprofits, GreatNonprofits was an idea ahead of its time—a radical experiment in true transparency. It would provide an online site for nonprofits to set up a public profile linked to their financial reports and other organizational documents. People would visit the site to learn about organizations they were interested in. Those who had direct experience with particular nonprofits could write reviews and rate them on their effectiveness. These public reviews would encourage other visitors to find, review, and share information about great—and perhaps not-yet-great—nonprofits.

Ni was nervous because she knew the nonprofit sector had been slow to adopt almost any level of transparency. Even as recently as 2009, a study on voluntary disclosure practices conducted by GuideStar, an online repository of information on hundreds of thousands of nonprofits, revealed that only 43 percent of the nonprofits surveyed posted their annual reports on their Web sites. Thirteen percent posted their audited financial statements, and a minuscule 3 percent posted their respective Internal Revenue Service letters of determination, the official document that confirms tax-exempt status.[1]

Ni's presentation went better than she had expected, and she was pleasantly surprised by the results. After she explained how the site works and the benefits of transparency, the executive director of a well-respected nonprofit stood up and enthusiastically endorsed the project. And then all the nonprofits in the room agreed to participate in the testing. This first pilot paved the way to GreatNonprofits' continued success today.

"I was curious," recalls Ni. She approached the executive director after the session and asked why her organization wanted to embrace transparency. Didn't she have concerns? The executive director responded that she had been a seller on eBay for years, and she'd found the open ratings and feedback system valuable. Ni recalls the executive saying, "On eBay, sharing feedback from other buyers in a transparent way, both good and bad feedback, has a direct impact on getting better results—in this case, more customers and sales. Why wouldn't we want to get results for our nonprofits?"

Since its founding and first pilot in Pittsburgh, GreatNonprofits has quickly grown into the leading provider of reviews and ratings of nonprofit organizations throughout the United States. This valuable resource helps donors, volunteers, journalists, and concerned citizens learn about nonprofit services available in their communities and beyond.

WHAT EXACTLY IS TRANSPARENCY?

For a nonprofit to be transparent means that it is open, accountable, and honest with its stakeholders and the public. Transparency exists to a lesser or greater extent in all organizations. Greater transparency is a good thing, not just because it is morally correct but because it can provide measurable benefits. *Disclosure*, a component of transparency, means releasing the information you have to and want to. *Transparency*, on the other hand, can often mean releasing information that you don't want to and don't have to.

When organizations work in a transparent way, they consider their staff, board, and people in their networks as resources for helping them to achieve their goals. This is not about being transparent for transparency's sake; working transparently is an opportunity to improve the results of organizations' programs. Transparent and open organizations are clear about what they do, and they know what they are trying to accomplish. They are enriched by outside feedback.

And, yes, the notion of transparency is a bit daunting. Vincent Stehle, executive director of Grantmakers in Film and Electronic Media, expressed the uncomfortable aspect of transparency by putting it this way: "We want to be transparent except when it matters."[2] And noted academic Brad Rawlins, dean of the College of Communictions at Arkansas State University, writes, "Transparency will expose your organization's weaknesses, and areas that need improvement. Hiding these does not make them go away. Positive feedback that everything is okay, when it isn't, only reinforces the debilitating behavior. Sure, transparency might make an organization feel uncomfortable, but it will also motivate it to improve."[3]

Organizations that are not comfortable with transparency should note that it does not mean "no privacy or confidentiality." Transparency can exist at all different levels. Jacob Harold, program officer of the Philanthropy Program at Hewlett Foundation, gives this advice: "Foundation transparency should move from 'opt-in' (default is not to share) to 'opt-out' (redacting small pieces with good reason)."[4]

To develop greater transparency, organizations need to ask how they can do a better job of sharing information beyond their boardroom, file cabinets, and department boundaries. And they should solicit and listen to their networks, then use what they learn.

LEARNING IN PUBLIC

Learning in public is part of the practice of being transparent. It is the process of receiving public feedback from stakeholders and engaging in a conversation about it. Learning in public is a way of thinking and being that is critical for nonprofits that want to embrace a broader network of individuals and organizations.

Nonprofit organizations engage in learning in public when they take any of these steps:

- Allow input and feedback in the development of programs, plans, or strategies.

- Use social media as an early warning system to understand what people are saying and respond to it.

- Make organizational culture and operations apparent to everyone inside and outside the organization. Leadership is straightforward when talking to various audiences, and employees are accessible to reinforce the public view of the organization and help people when appropriate.

- Communicate results, both good and bad.

- Share knowledge products, insights, and processes to help build their networks.

- Admit their mistakes on social media channels or elsewhere.

THE BENEFITS OF TRANSPARENCY

Transparency benefits an organization by engaging its audiences and speeding up the processes of learning and growing, and it encourages programs and effectiveness to improve in ways they might not otherwise. Learning in public makes organizations smarter faster because they are engaging in conversations to improve results, and they are not hiding their mistakes or lack of knowledge.

Two of transparency's readily measurable benefits are increased efficiency and increases in the relationship components of trust, commitment, and satisfaction:

- *Increased efficiency.* Transparency makes organizations more efficient because it removes the gatekeeping function, which not only takes extra time but can be an exhausting way to work. When organizations are working transparently, problems are easier to solve, questions are easier to answer, and stakeholders' needs are met more quickly.

- *Increased trust, satisfaction, and commitment.* Rawlins's research has demonstrated that increased organizational transparency is directly tied to increases in trust, credibility, and satisfaction among the organization's stakeholders. He sees a key benefit of transparency as "enhancing the ethical nature of organizations in two ways: first, it holds organizations accountable for their actions and policies; and second, it respects the autonomy and reasoning ability of individuals who deserve to have access to information that might affect their position."[5] The more transparent an organization is, the more it is trusted. In organizations where trust is low, greater transparency has been shown to be the single most important "cure" for mistrust.[6] In Chapter Ten we discussed how important the elements of commitment and satisfaction are to your organization's relationships with its stakeholders. Transparency is one way to improve both satisfaction and commitment, since people who believe you are transparent are more likely to commit and be satisfied with what you are doing.[7]

Packard's "See-Through Filing Cabinet" Demonstrates Transparency's Benefits

Stephanie McAuliffe, who was director of organizational effectiveness (OE) and human resources at the Packard Foundation until her November 2011 retirement, was tired of hearing people say, "Foundations aren't transparent."[8]

And she realized that her OE program was sitting on a gold mine of resources inside its filing cabinets and hard drives:

- Helpful capacity-building tools and articles
- Insights from across its grant making, research in progress, and even internal (but not confidential) documents
- Its theory of change
- Its social media guidelines

She knew that making these documents available could be invaluable to grantees, foundations, and other stakeholders. So she and her OE team created a wiki to share this material, which was the beginning of Packard's "see-through filing cabinet" experiment in transparency. Foundation senior management was remarkably open-minded from the start regarding this project and continues to take pride in it.

The first steps were simple and easy; they set up the wiki and added content so others could have access to it. But working transparently is more than simply dumping documents on a wiki. Says OE director Kathy Reich, "It's the fact that we talk about it, we can follow up with a wealth of information, and we're asking for an open exchange." Staff members also regularly responded to questions on Twitter by pointing to documents on the wiki.

The OE program has also experimented with sharing the progress of a program evaluation, "The Goldmine Project," that looks at the results of OE grants from the past decade.[9] Typically when a foundation hires an evaluator to assess a program, that evaluator collects lots of information from a range of stakeholders, analyzes the data, writes a report, and discusses it with the funder. Then an abridged final report is shared with the field—maybe.

The OE program turned this traditional process on its head by sharing the insights from the report while it was in progress. They could have simply left it at sharing their program's evaluation data. If they had just put it on their wiki, that would be merely a form of disclosure—and faux transparency. But they went the extra step to engage in public learning. The OE team compiled existing grantee records and survey data, then facilitated a process through which evaluators shared their findings and solicited feedback. A section of the wiki was devoted to findings and feedback. Conversations also took place on Twitter, blogs, conference calls, and face-to-face meetings with specific stakeholder groups.[10]

OE team member Jeff Jackson reflects on the benefits of working this way:

> The first year was about making sure the work and processes most meaningful and useful to us were shared with the field, and that perhaps some people would engage enough to let us know we were not just being transparent to ourselves. While initially we weren't quite sure how to measure this, we now have more third party comments about our transparency than we know what to do with, including praise from *The Chronicle of Philanthropy*, which has said, "Packard is leading the way in working transparently."[11]

Efficiency became the earliest and most visible benefit of transparency. Foundation staff no longer have to answer individual requests for information by attaching this report or that tool to an e-mail. Their see-through filing cabinet is available for all to access and engage around. Says McAuliffe, "Based on tracking our time, I don't think of the wiki as taking time because it is a utility, and it saves time."

Jackson concurs about the efficiency gains: "We can easily point ourselves and others in the right direction faster and better than we did before with our disjointed filing cabinets." Reich points out that working this way has helped bust the myth of perfection for foundation program officers: "I feel empowered to be able to talk candidly about the work—all of its flaws and not just everything that is working well. It has made me a better listener and more open-minded. Program officers are hired to be content experts. I [used to] feel a lot of pressure to always be an expert in the room. Now I feel more comfortable saying, 'I don't know.' The more that I'm open to saying I don't have all the answers, the more people seem to respect and value what I have to say." He continues, "We're also learning that once we set our measures, the definition and scope of the term *our* changes. At the same time, we still believe that without measures or targets for distinct parts of the wiki (Goldmine for instance), we might not progress or know we are progressing."

MEASURING TRANSPARENCY

The Packard Foundation OE team was able to do some basic measurement of increases in efficiency and other benefits of increased transparency. Other more formal measurement techniques are now starting to be developed and used.

Transparency is like any other measurement challenge: you first need to be clear about what you are measuring. In this section, we look at two very different types of measurement. The first is assessing the impact of a change in transparency on your organization by measuring the change in the benefits of that transparency. The second is a self-evaluation to determine how transparent your organization is.

Measuring the Benefits of Transparency

How to Measure Improvements in Efficiency To measure efficiency, you need to have a chat with your accounting and operations departments to figure out what your leadership team is already tracking for efficiency metrics. If they aren't already doing it, then chances are that someone in one of those departments knows how to do it and can help you. Typical efficiency metrics include these:

- The percentage reduction in response time from inquiry to satisfied resolution

- The percentage reduction in staff hours responding to queries

- The percentage increase in satisfaction and knowledge of employees

The benefits of increased transparency can also be quantified by a relationship survey (see Chapter Ten).

How to Measure Improvements in Trust Several studies have shown that the more transparent people perceive an organization to be, the more likely they are to trust it.[12] The more the organization provides honest, open, and occasionally vulnerable communications, the more people trust the institution. Amazingly, the ability to be open and transparent was found to be more influential than competence in terms of willingness to trust. In other words, people care more about your willingness to be open and transparent than whether you are competent enough to do what you say you are going to do.[13] (Measuring trust is a component of relationship measurement that we discussed in Chapter Ten.)

How to Measure Your Own Transparency

While the field of transparency measurement is relatively nascent, thanks to the work of Rawlins and others there are established techniques to quantify it in your own organization. There are two elements to measuring your transparency: "How do I know just how transparent we are?" and "Do our stakeholders perceive us as transparent? And, consequently, do they trust us?"

Measurement of transparency examines four separate but equal components:

- *Participation.* The organization asks for feedback, involves others, takes the time to listen, and is prompt in responding to requests for information.

- *Substantial.* The organization provides information that is truthful, complete, easy to understand, and reliable.

- *Accountable.* The organization is forthcoming with bad news, admits mistakes, and provides both sides of a controversy.

- *Absence of secrecy.* The organization doesn't leave out important but potentially damaging details, doesn't obfuscate its data with jargon or confusion. It is not slow to provide data and does not disclose data only when required.

The following questionnaire developed by Brad Rawlins can be used by your organization to audit its own transparency.[14] Typically a survey like this is administered as a group discussion or a written survey followed by a group discussion of the results.

Is Your Organization Participative?

1. Do we involve stakeholders to help identify the information we need?

2. Do we ask the opinions of stakeholders before making decisions?

3. Do we take the time with stakeholders so they understand who we are and what we need?

Do We Provide Substantial Information?

1. Do we provide detailed information to stakeholders?

2. Do we make it easy to find the information stakeholders need?

3. Are we prompt when responding to requests for information from stakeholders?

4. Are we forthcoming with information that might be damaging to the organization?

5. Do we provide information that can be compared to industry standards?

6. Do we present more than one side of controversial issues?

Are We Accountable ?

1. Do we provide information in a timely fashion to stakeholders?

2. Do we provide information that is relevant to stakeholders?

3. Do we provide information that could be verified by an outside source, such as an auditor or GuideStar?

4. Do we provide information that can be compared to previous performance?

5. Do we provide information that is complete?

6. Do we provide information that is easy for stakeholders to understand?

7. Do we provide accurate information to stakeholders?

8. Do we provide information that is reliable?

9. Do we present information in language that is clear?

10. Are we open to criticism ?

11. Do we freely admit when we make mistakes?

Secrecy

1. Do we provide only part of the story to stakeholders?

2. Do we leave out important details in the information we provide to stakeholders?

3. Do we provide information that is full of jargon and technical language that is confusing to people?

4. Do we blame outside factors that may have contributed to the outcome when reporting bad news?

5. Do we provide information that is intentionally written in a way to make it difficult to understand?

6. Are we slow to provide information to stakeholders?

7. Do we disclose information only when it is required?

8. Do we disclose only "good" news?

The second part of transparency measurement is assessing whether your stakeholders perceive you as transparent. Since transparency leads to trust and trust is essential for any nonprofit, it is crucial to your success to be perceived as transparent.

THE SUSAN G. KOMEN FOUNDATION, TRANSPARENCY, AND TRUST

In early 2012, the Susan G. Komen Foundation announced that it would cease to fund grants to Planned Parenthood for breast cancer screening. This decision was widely assumed to be a result of political pressure by antiabortion groups.

Outrage and protests ensued, yet Komen's social media channels were silent and external communication was limited to a highly choreographed video and a single press release. The organization's chapters, volunteers, and supporters had no window into its decision making. As a result, the organization was portrayed as secretive, and much of the conversation deemed Komen no longer trustworthy.

After less than a week Komen reversed its decision, yet doubts and questions continued about the extent to which the foundation's policy might be influenced by politics. In the three months following the crisis, Komen suffered significant drops in reputation score, event participation, and donations.[15] The lack of confidence in Komen during and after this crisis was widely perceived to have its root cause in the organization's lack of transparency. Note that two hallmarks of networked nonprofits—the use of social media and an agile culture that can make rapid decisions—were not characteristic of Komen during this crisis.

To measure whether your supporters and stakeholders perceive you as transparent, you need to ask them whether they agree or disagree with the following statements:

1. The organization wants to understand how its decisions affect people like me.

2. The organization provides information that is useful to people like me for making informed decisions.

3. I think it is important to watch this organization closely so that it does not take advantage of people like me.

4. The organization wants to be accountable to people like me for its actions.

5. The organization wants people like me to know what it is doing and why it is doing it.

6. This organization asks for feedback from people like me about the quality of its information.

7. This organization involves people like me to help identify the information I need.

8. This organization provides detailed information to people like me.

9. This organization makes it easy to find the information people like me need.

10. This organization asks the opinions of people like me before making decisions.

KATIE'S KAT SHELTER MEASURES AND IMPROVES ITS TRANSPARENCY

Let's put Katie's Kat Shelter (KKS), our hypothetical nonprofit, to the transparency test. Beth, KKS's data geek, has been at a number of conferences where the term *learning in public* has come up, and she has noticed a few blog posts on the topic. She knows that after a number of nonprofit accounting scandals, transparency is attracting the attention of board members and her executive director. Moreover, she is aware of a systemic fear of looking bad in her organization, so most of what is disclosed to the public is standard feel-good news, and then only after a complicated approval process.

She has a meeting with Katie, her executive director, to share what she has been hearing about transparency. Katie has just returned from a national leadership conference where measurement, learning, failure, and transparency were big topics on the agenda. There was even a presentation about how certain cat shelters in California have collaborated on openly sharing cat adoption statistics, to their joint benefit. Katie is thrilled that Beth has taken the initiative on transparency.

Katie immediately agrees that Beth should set up a quick transparency survey of internal stakeholders. Fifteen minutes later, Beth had the survey ready to go in SurveyMonkey, and Katie sent it out to several board members and the communications team. Beth compiled the results and met with Katie. They both quickly realize they have a long way to go to improve KKS's transparency.

Katie asks Beth to put together a plan to begin to share information with other animal shelters online, and the initiative gets a half-hearted nod from the board. Beth compiles some basic information about the size and character of the KKS cat population, cat adoption rate, membership data, annual fundraising results, and the number of calls and traffic to its Web site and posts it to the KKS Web site.

Since the roof doesn't come tumbling down and the only feedback she got was expressions of gratitude from her peers in other shelters, Beth is confident enough to try to take transparency to the next level. Katie is fully behind the idea, and together they put together a presentation for the board to try to turn the half-hearted nod into full approval. The board was already beginning a conversation about surveying the external stakeholders on a number of other issues, so Beth and Katie convince them to add several questions to the survey to test perceptions of KKS's transparency.

The results tell KKS that they were not perceived as transparent at all and that this lack of transparency was in fact having a negative impact on their relationships with the community. They decide to hold a staff meeting to brainstorm ways to be more transparent and identify incremental improvements. They take a hard look at KKS's policies and work flows. They agree that their annual report isn't sufficient and begin posting monthly results. Beth then organizes an open LinkedIn group to share information with other cat shelters and posts a wiki on its Web site.

These efforts to improve transparency are soon rewarded improvements. A follow-up stakeholder relationship survey shows dramatic improvement on trust, commitment, and satisfaction scores.

Cathy Cat Lover III, one of the wealthiest and most influential cat lovers in the KKS community, was one of the first visitors to the shared wiki and one of the first to join the LinkedIn group. Cathy was someone Katie had been trying to cultivate for years. Cathy noticed that membership revenue was down for all of the area shelters, and while the number of cat adoptions was up, the overall cat population had increased significantly. She invited all the area cat shelter executive directors to lunch, where she broached her idea for a major gift that would support a cat adoption public awareness campaign in the community.

CONCLUSION

Jonathan Greenblatt, director of the Office of Social Innovation at the White House, said at the 2011 Social Innovation Summit in Palo Alto, California,

"The ability to be transparent and show progress is critical to success, especially in difficult financial times." The transition to transparency may be discomforting, but the benefits of inviting people in and sharing in an organization's development far outweigh the potential downsides. Imagine how much stronger the network's reactions, input, and suggestions will make your organization and how exciting it will feel to share your great work with more people. And with a measurement strategy in place, you can know that your effort has paid off and that your organization is changing from the inside out.

REFLECTION QUESTIONS

1. Does your organization know the line between transparency and confidentiality?

2. Do you have an opportunity to leverage the benefits of public learning by making your performance data or evaluations public and engaging in dialogue with your network?

3. What internal processes or information or works in progress would be appropriate to share for feedback and engagement at an earlier stage than you are sharing now? Think about whether sharing could help you improve or work more efficiently. What are the potential drawbacks about not being transparent about a particular process or program? What are the benefits?

4. How do people inside your organization view its level of transparency?

5. Do you know if your audience views your organization as transparent or not?

6. What is a small, low-risk pilot of working transparently that you can implement along with a measurement strategy?

Measuring the Impact of the Crowd

You really think "pitchfork count" is the
best metric for measuring crowdsourcing?

In 2006, Sameer Bhatia, a Stanford University undergraduate-turned-entrepreneur of South Asian heritage, was diagnosed with leukemia.[1] Leukemia is cancer of the blood or bone marrow, and for some individuals, the only form of treatment is a bone marrow transplant. In order to get a transplant, a patient must find someone whose tissue type matches his or her own as closely as possible. Thirty percent of patients in search of a bone marrow donor find a match within their immediate family. But for the other 70 percent, the only option is to turn to bone marrow registries.

All that is required to register as a potential bone marrow donor is a swab of one cheek, but there are extreme shortages of donors from ethnically diverse communities. After not finding a match within his family, Bhatia's chances of finding a potential donor were minuscule: 1 in 20,000.

100,000 CHEEKS: THE POWER OF HARNESSING THE CROWD

After hearing of his diagnosis, Bhatia's friends at Stanford University, led by Vineet Singal, were inspired to start a student-run organization they called 100K Cheeks. The inspiration behind the genesis of 100K Cheeks came from the story of Sameer's hyper-connected friends. Lead by Sameer's best friend Robert Chatwani, these determined individuals were able to utilize their online and offline social networks to generate a large-scale bone-marrow registration drive. 100K Cheeks is dedicated to recruiting 100,000 new registrants into the National Marrow Donor Program using social media and on-the-ground off-line tactics. By increasing the availability of donors, this project can potentially save thousands of lives.

Bhatia passed away in 2008, but the campaign was not in vain. In eleven weeks, his supporters recruited 24,611 South Asians into the bone marrow registry and found a match for him and Vinay, another South Asian diagnosed with leukemia. The 7,500 people who registered in the San Francisco Bay Area, where Bhatia and Vinay lived, yielded eighty matches for other leukemia patients, an unintended but celebrated consequence. Overall, of the 24,611 new people who registered, 266 were matches for patients in the first year.

This effort prompted Vineet Singal, Stanford professor Jennifer Aaker, and a team of students to join forces with Stanford's Haas Center for Public Service and other partners to implement a large-scale bone marrow registration drive that harnessed the power of social media and crowdsourcing by making an open call for ideas and assistance.

Says Singal, "Our hope is to solve the burning problem of a lack of donors (especially from South Asian and other ethnicities) in the bone marrow registry in the United States and even in countries like India and Indonesia. We also hope to educate people about how, thanks to new technologies, bone marrow donation is not dissimilar to blood donation."[2]

And they've gotten results. By 2011, they had inspired 100,000 people to swab their cheek and register as potential donors in the National Bone Marrow Registry. They did this by running a crowdsourcing campaign on OpenIDEO, an online platform that engages creative and passionate problem solvers from around the world.

290 Ideas from People in 175 Countries

In March 2011, the OpenIDEO platform encouraged everyone to participate in contributing ideas for 100K Cheeks.[3] The 100K Cheeks team and their partners reached out to their networks using social media and the mainstream press to encourage participation. Individuals were invited to contribute in a variety of ways, from inspirational observations, photos, and sketches of ideas to business models and snippets of code. Some contributions came in the form of comments, while others built off a previous contributor's work.

As Singal notes, "We learned that there are barriers to bone marrow donation, including people's fear of needles and a misunderstanding of the donation process, and we used crowdsourcing to overcome those barriers."

100K Cheeks is also assisting individual patient campaigns, including the recent "Amit Gupta Needs You" social media campaign to locate a bone marrow donor for Amit Gupta. And it is collaborating with DoSomething.org on the "Give a Spit About Cancer" Campaign to inspire college students on campuses around the country to act.

100K Cheeks Measures the Crowd

The 100K Cheeks team met their goal of adding 100,000 potential donors to the National Marrow Donor Program. But their ultimate impact will be the number of lives saved by transplants found by matches in the registry.

Could they have done it without crowdsourcing? Although it's difficult to prove exactly how many of those 100,000 were recruited thanks to the crowdsourcing, there is no doubt that the technique provided tangible value.

100K Cheeks received 290 ideas from people in 175 countries. From these, the team synthesized the best concepts into 10 ideas that they have used to guide their strategy. The benefits of crowdsourcing have been twofold: they've gotten ideas on how to reach their goals and have begun to build a global movement around this important issue.

Through the power of crowdsourcing, 100K Cheeks was able to save on the costs of hiring outside consultants to generate ideas, do research, and provide strategy suggestions. One invaluable yet difficult-to-value innovation that emerged from the OpenIDEO challenge was "swab parties," swab-testing events to which individuals invited their friends to get tested and register.[4] Previously calls to action had been made to inspire individuals to register, but these Tupperware-style swab parties dramatically increased the effectiveness of the project by registering groups of people at one time.

THE POWER OF CROWDSOURCING

The crowdsourcing concept—many individuals collecting ideas, taking action, or doing small tasks to achieve a goal—was being used long before OpenIdeo or even Wikipedia. The National Audubon Socicty has been organizing people to do an annual count of all the birds in the Western Hemisphere since Christmas Day 1900. Online crowdsourcing powered by social media is a recent phenomenon, but the efficiencies it brings to communicating within a large group make it tremendously useful in many ways.

Online crowdsourcing is not that different from the participatory processes nonprofits have used for years, particularly those working in the development sector. Participatory program planning and evaluation efforts are popular ways of incorporating more voices. Crowdsourcing online builds on these concepts by adding the power of social media, inexpensively extending and deepening participation over longer periods of time. The crowd votes, rates, or gives feedback and tips on ideas, products, places, and even people. Internet platforms like Yelp, eBay, and Amazon make it easy for crowds to vote, rate, and provide feedback.

Innovation is often a valuable by-product of listening and engaging with your network. Nonprofits that are listening to their stakeholders take ideas from social media comments, suggestions, and conversations and then identify program needs, campaign messaging, or other opportunities. In this sense, networked nonprofits can be said to be constantly crowdsourcing.

There are a growing number of examples of nonprofits getting the crowd to provide information toward the greater good, such as Ushahidi's platform, which makes it easier for rescue organizations to aggregate information from citizens during a crisis, and GlobalVoices, which assembles on-the-ground reports from citizen journalists about protests happening around the world.

In his definitive book on crowdsourcing, *Why the Power of the Crowd Is Driving the Future of Business*, Jeff Howe describes four models of crowdsourcing activities: wisdom, creation, voting, and funding.[5] There isn't one best way to do it, and many organizations use a combination of these models to meet their objectives.

Social media tools for engaging and capturing the work of crowds include custom platforms or Web sites that facilitate voting, rating, giving feedback, adding content, funding, and wikis. Typically social media tools such as Twitter, Facebook, and blogs are used to support engaging crowds to participate in the activity.

Aliza Sherman, author of *The Complete Idiot's Guide to Crowdsourcing*, suggests that you need to understand the different types of results that crowdsourcing generates so you know what you're measuring[6]:

- Doing the work
- Getting ideas
- Taking action

Sherman says that "each type of crowdsourcing dictates a different process and therefore requires different approaches to measuring and improving."

MEASURING THE ADVANTAGES OF THE CROWD

Formal measurement of crowdsourcing is still in its infancy, yet as the technique becomes more popular and refined, it will continue to develop rapidly. Measurement of crowdsourced programs may be more important than for other programs because crowdsourcing can create discomfort for nonprofit staffers who feel they have a tried-and-true methodology for implementing campaigns. After all, organizations often hire staffers for their expertise, which means they have a very good idea of what strategies work for which projects. Rather than silo this knowledge, however, staff should share those strategies with the crowd and show they are open to suggestions of how to improve.

If you are considering incorporating crowdsourcing processes into your programs or communications strategies, you should also be thinking about how you'll measure the results of your crowdsourcing efforts. The first step, as with other measurement approaches, is setting measurable goals and objectives.

Then you need to determine the value of these new ideas or efforts. Did they lead to better results in your strategy? Did getting people to help with the work save you time? Did getting people to take action create a tangible result, like more ticket sales, fundraising dollars, or conference registrations?

As with any other aspect of social media, the metrics you use are heavily dependent on the goals you have set. It may seem incongruous that an organization needs to develop clear goals while at the same time opening itself up to the crowd's wisdom and guidance. But if you are going to evaluate the effectiveness of crowdsourcing, you need defined objectives by which success can be measured. Clear goals and outcomes give the crowd (and the organization) a framework to work within as they share ideas or implement tasks. In this way, an organization spreads out the responsibility and increases the public buy-in.

Certain elements of crowdsourcing lend themselves to unique ways of quantifying results.

The Value of an Idea

Generating answers to questions, or ideas and feedback for campaigns, as 100K Cheeks did, is a common and valuable use of crowdsourcing. Crowdsourcing in this way has been dubbed "the new focus group."

An important question to ask is: "How innovative or valuable are the ideas as a result of crowdsourcing?" We often take the value of an idea for granted. The traditional approach to coming up with new ideas has been to gather people in a room to brainstorm. The session probably lasts a couple of hours and includes half a dozen people. If you're lucky, you come up with a dozen ideas, of which a third are usable.

Today, if you conduct the same sort of exercise using crowdsourcing, you are likely to involve thousands of people and come up with hundreds of ideas. For instance, Dell's IdeaStorm project generated two thousand usable product ideas and improvements in its first six months. In conversation Richard Binhammer, a senior manager at Dell, estimated that it would cost close to $100 million to hire consultants to come up with as many usable ideas—not a bad return for a reported investment of around $1 million.

While we understand that similar returns, never mind investments, are not possible for most nonprofits, the concept still applies. Every idea that a nonprofit generates from crowdsourcing that gets put to use has a value. Perhaps it is the cost savings, or perhaps it's a better approach to a problem. Either way, it's worth something. So one way to measure the impact of crowdsourcing is to count the ideas and track the ratio of usable to not usable ideas.

The Value of Costs Avoided

Says Sherman, "For nonprofits, crowdsourcing work can be a cost-effective way of taking care of repetitive tasks through sites like Crowdflower, Castingwords, and Clickworker. You might also tap into online communities of people willing to provide services through a site such as Sparked.com, where professionals volunteer time and talent to help nonprofits and causes with marketing and design needs."

Crowdsourcing repetitive tasks always sounds like a great idea, but it is often not as straightforward as it seems at first. If speed is a goal, crowdsourcing may not be your best option. And hidden costs make it a good example of why measuring return on investment in its truest sense is important.

To help ensure that there are some quality standards in place for work rendered, you are better off using a work-specific crowdsourcing site than trying to assemble an online crowd and manage them in an ad hoc way. Many crowdsourcing work sites provide some kind of rating system, meaning that the better, more accurate workers can rise to the top.

Whatever system you use, you are going to pay something for the work that is completed. That cost is typically justified by a reduction in internal costs. However, it is important to take into account the true investment, specifically account management of the project and, more important, the internal cost of quality assurance.

When evaluating work, it will help to start with a clear outline of the task at hand. Know what work you need done and the quality of work you'd like to receive. To avoid redoing work and other problems, be as specific as you can when outlining the task. Test the instructions on everyone from your mother to a ten-year-old.

As long as the quality and production meet your organizational standards, saving money and freeing up staff time can be reasonable measures of success, Work completion is clearly a goal, as is accuracy.

The Value of a Solution

A far more common way to value the impact of crowdsourcing is to look at the revenue saved or the potential revenue earned from a crowdsourced solution to a problem. When Paul Levy was the CEO of Beth Israel Hospital, he was faced with the prospect of laying off two thousand employees to reduce costs.

He crowdsourced the problem to his followers on Facebook and readers of his blog, many of whom were his own employees. He received so many good suggestions on how to reduce other costs that in the end, he had to lay off only a tenth as many employees. The obvious measure of success here is in achieving the required cost savings. Of greater value, but more difficult to quantify, are the health and happiness of the eighteen hundred people who escaped the axe.

The Value of Participation

Everyone appreciates being appreciated, and if you can help out a good cause at the same time, that's even better. This is why participating in crowdsourcing solutions is good for relationships; invariably, the crowd becomes part of your network. In effect, participation is a form of engagement and can be measured as such. (See Chapter Six for how to measure engagement.)

In recent years there has been an explosion of "vote for me" fundraising contests. At their best, they spread the awareness of a commercial brand and provide an opportunity for small nonprofits that don't typically receive large amounts of funding to win dollars. At their worst, they have inspired cause fatigue. But they do raise awareness and increase the sense of participation by an audience.

The Value of Decision Making

Crowdsourced philanthropy does not typically select the best idea or project to fund by popular vote. Many foundations have taken a hybrid approach by using a mix of openness and expert decision making to address a wicked problem or spur innovation. A hybrid design might include a sequence of:

1. Open call for submissions
2. Public vote or commenting
3. Group expertise to select the finalists

or:

1. Open call for submissions
2. Selection of a smaller group of finalists by experts
3. Public vote or commenting to select the winners

How to structure crowdsourced philanthropy based on voting or feedback depends on the intended outcomes of the project and a theory of change.

The Knight Foundation's News Challenge, Case Foundation's Make It Your Own awards, and Island Collaboration's Fund are examples of the hybrid process and are linked to a clear theory of change. Key to implementation is being clear and transparent about how funding decisions will be awarded.

Voting, rating, and feedback crowdsourcing projects have applications and value beyond philanthropy and marketing. They can help organizations make a traditionally closed process more transparent and ultimately improve the level of feedback. Conferences have taken this approach to shaping their agendas. NTEN used a hybrid crowdsourcing approach to solicit panel proposals for its NTC 2011, similar in design and approach to the method SXSW has used.[7]

The now-closed Craigslist Foundation did a crowdsourcing experiment to shape the agenda for its annual nonprofit boot camp. Its goals were to broaden the diversity of topics from previous years, incorporating new ideas and speakers. The team held a brainstorming session to identify topics and ideas that had been highly rated at past conferences. They took this initial list of ninety-eight ideas and used AllOurIdeas, an online crowdsourcing platform, to get feedback and additional ideas from the crowd. The result was more than three thousand votes, cast by more than four hundred people. An additional fifty-five session topics and twenty-five speakers were suggested.

KITTY KAT KROWDSOURCING

Formal measurement of crowdsourcing is only just beginning, so very few case studies are available. For an instructive hypothetical example, here is how Katie's Kat Shelter (KKS, our own hypothetical nonprofit introduced in previous chapters) might measure the impact of crowdsourcing.

With the publicity surrounding its Celebrity Cat Show and capital campaign, KKS had achieved an unprecedented level of awareness and prominence in the community. All of a sudden it was the go-to place for everything from cat sniffles to cat snowsuits. Everyone whose precious "Boots" had gone missing immediately called KKS to see if their pet could be located. KKS needed another staff member just to answer the calls and try to match the descriptions to their current resident population of cats.

Realizing that asking for an additional staff member at this point wasn't feasible, they posted the problem to their Facebook page and were quickly referred to a number of crowdsourcing pet finder sites where people who find strays and people who have lost their pets can connect. They went back to their fans and supporters for advice on picking the best one that was specific to their region.

Once an appropriate site had been identified, KKS asked for volunteers to help post pictures and descriptions of their strays to the site. Within a week, they had every lost pet posted and were able to post the referral information to their Web site and Facebook page. And thanks to an idea submitted by a friend on Facebook, they added a new option and message on their phone system for people trying to find lost pets. Here's how the measurement went:

Cost of staff time: $300

Direct costs: $0

Net staff savings: $20,000

Reconnecting fifteen kitties with their owners: Priceless

CONCLUSION

Crowdsourcing is a useful technique for generating ideas, encouraging people in your network to take action, and helping to get work done. If you are considering incorporating crowdsourcing processes into your programs or communications strategies, think about how you'll measure the results. While measuring the impact of the crowd is still an experimental technique, you can estimate the value of ideas, of costs avoided, and the benefits of increased participation by your network.

REFLECTION QUESTIONS

1. What are some opportunities for your nonprofit to get structured feedback and ideas from your network?

2. If you have generated ideas through crowdsourcing, how can you estimate their value? What is the value of the time it took you to collect and shift through them?

3. If you have used crowdsourcing, how would you estimate the costs that you avoided?

EPILOGUE: WITH MEASUREMENT AND LEARNING, NETWORKED NONPROFITS CAN CHANGE THE WORLD

We wrote this book for you. If you work for or with a networked nonprofit, then you are most likely driven by a deeply rooted desire to change the world, whether it is reducing climate change or fighting global poverty or helping the homeless in your community. You bring selflessness to that quest. It doesn't matter if you are nonprofit staff, a board member, a free agent activist, a volunteer, or a donor. Your passion for making the world a better place fuels your vision and keeps you from being discouraged.

We know that the world's problems are complex. And we also know that passion alone is not enough. Working as an isolated institution is not enough. We don't want to you to waste your most precious resources: your energy, hope, and optimism. And we want your organization to achieve amazing success.

Measurement is a path to your mission. We've said that measurement is the secret sauce for success, and you hold the recipe in your hand. You now have a methodology to better understand your networks, determine the value of your campaigns, and understand cause and effect. You have metrics to assess the building blocks of social change: connections with people, engagement, volunteers, and donations. You have the tools and tips to calculate without collywobbles and, better yet, to get actionable information to make better decisions that will accomplish social change. Becoming a measurement maven is a star well within your grasp.

When you put the advice in this book into action, your organization will experience many wins. Your successes will come one win at a time. Some will be dramatic and others incremental. Measurement and learning will help you understand how to replicate them.

But everyone stumbles, and you will no doubt suffer a few failures. With measurement, you'll learn why; you'll learn how to get back on your feet, and you'll move on to bigger and better successes.

Nonprofits work on a multitude of different issues and programs, but they share a single passion: to make the world a better place. For nonprofits, social change is the only bottom line.

Networked nonprofits effortlessly dance between the intersection of social change and social media. They know that social media isn't just another shiny new technology; rather, it is a tool for social change. And if social media is a tool *for* social change, then measurement is a tool *of* change—the process of focusing, channeling, and directing change. Nonprofits want to change the world, and measurement is how they know they are doing it.

The survey questionnaire statements in this appendix are from "Guidelines for Measuring Relationships in Public Relations" by Linda Childers Hon and James E. Grunig (1999, Institute for Public Relations). This paper is relatively short and available at no cost from the Institute for Public Relations Web site (www.insti tuteforpr.org/topics/measuring-relationships/). It presents a bracing argument "that the fundamental goal of public relations is building relationships with an organization's key constituencies." It discusses the underlying dimensions of relationships (trust, control mutuality, commitment, satisfaction, communal, and exchange) and provides a straightforward tool to measure them in the form of the questionnaire that follows. (The dimension of control mutuality, which refers to the degree to which parties agree on which has the rightful power to influence the other, is the topic of some controversy of late, and so it has been omitted here.)

We discuss the use of this questionnaire in Chapter Ten. We are including it to encourage your interest and demonstrate the relative simplicity of the technique rather than as an actual working reference. If you use these statements to measure relationships, you must refer to the paper for the correct procedure and helpful tips. (For instance, you do not need to use all the questions.) For more detail on administering the survey, see this follow-up paper by Jim Grunig, "Qualitative Methods for Assessing Relationships Between Organizations and Publics" (www.instituteforpr.org/topics/organizations-publics-relationships/).

GRUNIG RELATIONSHIP SURVEY

The following are agree/disagree statements. Frame each one in this way: "On a scale of 1 to 5, with 1 being do not agree at all and 5 being total agreement, do you agree or disagree with this statement?" If you are testing all six components of relationships, you need to include at least two, and ideally, three or four, of the statements for each component.

Tally the totals for each component, and average them for your score on each. Then average all of them if you want a final relationship health score. Note that the statements marked "(Reversed)" present the relationship in a negative rather than positive light. For these, reverse the numbers: 1 is good and 5 is bad.

To Measure the Component of Trust

1. This organization treats people like me fairly and justly.

2. Whenever this organization makes an important decision, I know it will be concerned about people like me.

3. This organization can be relied on to keep its promises.

4. I believe that this organization takes the opinions of people like me into account when making decisions.

5. I feel very confident about this organization's skills.

6. This organization has the ability to accomplish what it says it will do.

7. Sound principles seem to guide this organization's behavior.

8. This organization does not mislead people like me.

9. I am very willing to let this organization make decisions for people like me.

10. I think it is important to watch this organization closely so that it does not take advantage of people like me. (Reversed)

11. This organization is known to be successful at the things it tries to do.

To Measure the Component of Commitment

1. I feel that this organization is trying to maintain a long-term commitment to people like me.

2. I can see that this organization wants to maintain a relationship with people like me.

3. There is a long-lasting bond between this organization and people like me.

4. Compared to other organizations, I value my relationship with this organization more.

5. I would rather work together with this organization than not.

6. I have no desire to have a relationship with this organization. (Reversed)

7. I feel a sense of loyalty to this organization.

8. I could not care less about this organization. (Reversed)

To Measure the Component of Satisfaction

1. I am happy with this organization.

2. Both the organization and people like me benefit from the relationship.

3. Most people like me are happy in their interactions with this organization.

4. Generally speaking, I am pleased with the relationship this organization has established with people like me.

5. Most people enjoy dealing with this organization.

6. The organization fails to satisfy the needs of people like me. (Reversed)

7. I feel people like me are important to this organization.

8. In general, I believe that nothing of value has been accomplished between this organization and people like me. (Reversed)

To Measure the Component of Communal Relationships

1. This organization does not especially enjoy giving others aid. (Reversed)

2. This organization is very concerned about the welfare of people like me.

3. I feel that this organization takes advantage of people who are vulnerable. (Reversed)

4. I think that this organization succeeds by stepping on other people. (Reversed)

5. This organization helps people like me without expecting anything in return.

6. I don't consider this to be a particularly helpful organization. (Reversed)

7. I feel that this organization tries to get the upper hand. (Reversed)

To Measure the Component of Exchange Relationships

1. Whenever this organization gives or offers something to people like me, it generally expects something in return.

2. Even though people like me have had a relationship with this organization for a long time, it still expects something in return whenever it offers us a favor.

3. This organization will compromise with people like me when it knows that it will gain something.

4. This organization takes care of people who are likely to reward the organization.

APPENDIX B: CRAWL, WALK, RUN, FLY ASSESSMENT TOOL FOR NETWORKED NONPROFITS

This assessment tool lists the ideal best practices for networked nonprofits. Review each practice and self-assess whether you are crawling, walking, running, or flying. See the discussion of crawl, walk, run, fly in Chapter Two. Where could you improve current practice?

This assessment tool builds on and adapts the work of Ash Shepherd, who created an integrated communications audit and, with Beth Kanter's encouragement, set up a wiki to share the documents and encourage people to "remix it."[1]

Table B.1
Crawl, Walk, Run, Fly Assessment Tool

Practice	Indicator	CWRF Rating
Strategy		
Identified goals and measurable objectives	Identifies the most important overall results and creates measurable objectives based on those.	

Practice	Indicator	CWRF Rating
Identified specific target audience	Identifies specific audience target groups, including key stakeholders and influencers.	
Identifies success and value	Identifies what success looks like and the value it brings to the organization.	
Networked mind-set	Management understands and supports social media and networked approaches as part of the overall communications or program plan.	
Social media policy	Has formally identified appropriate personal and organizational use.	
Listening and influencer research	Has done research to learn what other organizations are doing and what the conversations are. Has done research to identify influencers and free agents.	
Allocates sufficient resources	Understands the capacity to implement by hiring staff or having social media tasks in job description or recruits volunteers. Tracks investment of time against results.	
Implementation		
Tool selection	Uses best practices on a selective number of social media tools that match audience and capacity to implement.	
Engagement	Takes steps to foster online engagement and conversations related to strategic objectives. Has a formal ladder of engagement and uses it to guide strategy and measurement.	
Transparency	Works in a transparent way and has measured trust and other factors.	
Content	Has an editorial calendar and strategy for linking, producing, and distributing content across social media and other channels.	

Practice	Indicator	CWRF Rating
Network building	Takes steps to foster online community or networked effects, with linkages to other organizations and free agents.	
Crowdsourcing	Gets feedback from network on ideas and strategies as appropriate and has a process to measure the value of feedback.	
Job description and training	Provides appropriate training to those responsible for implementation.	
Involves all staff	Social media are not isolated function. Most, if not all, staff or volunteers have some knowledge or participate as appropriate.	
Build valuable partnerships	Relationships have been made with stakeholders and other organizations to achieve goals. Measures relationships on a regular basis.	
Measure, monitor, evaluate	Activities are monitored, measured, and evaluated for improvement. A formal process for reflecting on data and improving is in place.	
Integration		
Web site	Strategic linkages and integration between social media and Web site include link, content, and distribution.	
Other social channels	Strategic cross-promotion and integration among social channels.	
Print materials	Strategic links between social media and printed materials.	
E-mail marketing	Strategic links between social media and e-mailed newsletters.	
Mobile	Strategic links between social media and mobile.	
Offline	Strategic links between offline activities and social media channels.	

APPENDIX C: SOCIAL MEDIA MEASUREMENT CHECKLIST

Define Your Measures of Success, Key Performance Indicators, and Dashboard

- ❏ Make a list of who influences your budget and sets your priorities.

- ❏ Set up a meeting of all those people to define your measures of success.

- ❏ Set the agenda for the meeting:

    - ❏ A definition of all key stakeholders

    - ❏ Prioritizing those audiences

    - ❏ Definition of measurable and tangible goals

    - ❏ Defining what or who you will be benchmarking your results against

    - ❏ Define the key performance indicators (KPIs) that they want to see

- ❏ Summarize the meeting in a document that includes the KPIs that you will be reporting on and the dashboard of charts or table that you will need to show.

- ❏ Get sign-off on those KPIs and the dashboard.

- ❏ Based on the KPIs, make a list of the data you will need to report on them.

Select a Listening or Monitoring Tool

- ❏ Make a list of the search terms (the companies, benchmarks, subjects, topics, issues, or peer institutions) you need to know about.

- ❏ Decide if your program is domestic, international, or some combination of the two.

❐ Make a list of the traditional media you need to monitor (determine for the first three whether you need actual tapes or whether transcripts will do):

❐ Network TV

❐ Cable TV

❐ Radio

❐ Newspapers

❐ Magazines

❐ Trade publications

❐ Analyst reports

❐ Make a list of the online media you need to monitor:

❐ Online versions of traditional media

❐ Online-only publications

❐ Make a list of the social media you need to monitor:

❐ Institutional blogs (ones that originate within your organizations)

❐ External blogs

❐ Pinterest

❐ Quora

❐ Consumer review sites such as Amazon, TripAdvisor, Yelp

❐ Google Plus

❐ YouTube

❐ Flickr

❐ Twitter

❐ Facebook

❐ MySpace

❐ LinkedIn

❐ Social bookmarking sites (Digg, Delicious)

❐ Virtual reality sites (Second Life)

- ❏ Listservs
- ❏ Forums

Make a List of the Quantitative Data You Will Need
- ❏ Number of mentions
- ❏ Number of comments
- ❏ Length of Facebook thread
- ❏ Number of YouTube or Flickr views or comments or votes
- ❏ Number of Twitter followers
- ❏ Opportunities to see (also known as impressions)
- ❏ Google rank
- ❏ Other rankings
  - ❏ Twitter authority
  - ❏ Technorati authority
  - ❏ Industry authority

Make a List of the Qualitative Data You Will Need
- ❏ Tonality: positive, neutral, balanced, or negative
- ❏ Spokesperson quote
- ❏ Affiliation of spokesperson
- ❏ Message content: Amplified, full, partial, incorrect, negative, or none
- ❏ Individual messages communicated
- ❏ Issues discussed
- ❏ Subjects mentioned
- ❏ Lines of business mentioned
- ❏ Dominance of mention
- ❏ Prominence of mention
- ❏ Recommendations or reviews

- ❏ Brand benefits mentioned
- ❏ Accuracy of mention

- ❏ Estimate volume of mentions using Google News or Technorati.
- ❏ Decide if you need an automated system, random sampling, or manual review.
- ❏ Decide whether you will be doing this work in house or will need measurement partners.
- ❏ Create a request for proposals that allows you to accurately compare vendors. Include your best guess as to the volume of mentions and a full list of what you need to track.

Select a Web Analytic or Customer Relationship Management Tool

- ❏ Create one or more unique URLs and landing pages so you can directly tie activities to results.
- ❏ Make a list of the engagement data you will need:
  - ❏ Unique visitors
  - ❏ Repeat visitors
  - ❏ Length of time on site
  - ❏ Click-throughs
  - ❏ Registrations
  - ❏ Conversions
- ❏ Make a list of the membership/conversion data you will need:
  - ❏ Number of registrations
  - ❏ Number of new donors
  - ❏ Number of repeat donors
  - ❏ Number of conversions
  - ❏ Market share
  - ❏ Value of member
  - ❏ Cost of social media program

- [ ] Talk to whomever within your organization manages the Web site and collects Web data to determine what data is missing.
- [ ] Decide if you need any additional tool.
- [ ] Create a request for proposal for web data collection and analysis.

Select a Survey Tool

- [ ] Make a list of audiences you need to survey.
- [ ] Determine if there is a list available in house or whether you need to purchase a list.
- [ ] Make a list of any perception data you will need:
  - [ ] Awareness
  - [ ] Perception
  - [ ] Preference
  - [ ] Consideration
  - [ ] Trust level
  - [ ] Commitment level
  - [ ] Satisfaction level
  - [ ] Exchange or communal relationship level
  - [ ] Control mutuality level
- [ ] Draft a list of questions to which you need answers.
- [ ] Identify a professional expert, academic, or internal or external partner to create and test your survey instrument.
- [ ] Provide your list of questions to the expert.
- [ ] Review the proposed instruments.
- [ ] Test the proposed instruments.
- [ ] Field the survey.
- [ ] Review the cross-tabulations to make sure you have the data you need.
- [ ] Analyze the results, and draw conclusions.

Analyze and Report Results

❏ Put all relevant data into a KPI table.

❏ Look for significant failures—where a program did not deliver.

❏ Look for exceptional successes.

❏ Drill down into the data to determine cause and effect.

❏ Pull most relevant charts and data into a PowerPoint presentation.

❏ Report results and make recommendations.

APPENDIX D: A CHECKLIST FOR MONITORING SERVICES

You will use this checklist only if you have already decided to use content analysis as a measurement methodology. (See Chapter Eight.) Since the number of measurement and monitoring vendors is growing in direct proportion to the size of the social media space—there's one new measurement tool announced for every 1 million Tweets or Facebook posts published—this checklist will not try to match capabilities and options to any specific vendors. What it will do is to outline some of the decisions any new customer for one of these tools will need to answer.

DAILY ALERTS SETUP

These are the ubiquitous alerts that arrive on your Blackberry or iPhone by a certain time each morning that are either an unedited stream of partially relevant data or a carefully screened, limited report of what people are saying about your brand today. Before you begin a daily alert feed, you will need to answer these questions:

Question 1: Search the universe? _____ Search key publications only? _____.

This question requires that you state a preference for what might be called a full body cavity search or just a mild pat-down. In other words, do you want to see everything from everywhere, or just a limited stream of news from key sources?

Question 2: What search terms are you looking for? Your company name _____ Your brand _____ Competitors' brands _____.

In the industry, these terms are commonly referred to as search strings, and you will need to put together a list of relevant search terms before any monitoring can begin. But even before you get into the specifics of the terminology by which people might be referring to you (and don't forget acronyms, abbreviations, ticker symbols, and slang) you need to decide how big a universe you want to search. We typically recommend searching for whatever your customers and your marketplace considers interesting and relevant to your business.

Question 3: By what time do you need your alert delivered? _____ a.m. EST _____ p.m. EST.

Most news services can deliver the prior day's report by 9:00 a.m. Some are as late as 10:00 a.m. If you need an alert delivered sooner, be prepared to miss some items that appear very early in the morning on the U.S East Coast or very late in the day in Europe.

Question 4: What format do you want your alert to take? PDF _____ Word _____ Blog _____ HTML _____ Text _____

Most monitoring tools will send an e-mail to whomever you specify. Agencies use private blogs so that anyone you have authorized can access it from any device.

Question 5: Vomitous river of data? _____ or human selected and screened? _____.

Given that some brands are receiving many thousands of posts a day, you almost always will need some level of screening. This can be done badly by machines or much better by humans who understand your goals and priorities.

MONITORING SYSTEM SETUP

Some of the more mundane parts of putting brand or corporate monitoring in place will already have been answered if you opt for daily alerts—the search string and competitors, for example, will have already been defined. However, there are still some additional questions you will need to answer:

Question 1: Is one news source sufficient? _____ I need to make sure I get *everything* _____

In reality, even Google doesn't get everything. You may want to set up Google Alerts to supplement and check the completeness of other feeds such as Factiva, Twitter search, Boardreader, Nexis, MyMediaQ, and others. You need to set expectations and decide how comprehensive your search needs to be.

Question 2: I'm going to monitor _____ (number of) competitive companies _____.

Depending on the size of the competitor, its market share, and its projected growth rate, you can assume that you will spend as much to measure a competitor as you do measuring yourself. Certainly a lot of mentions will contain two or more brands, but in general, the overlap isn't more than about 20 percent. So for budgeting purposes, if you are spending $20,000 a year on your own monitoring budget, then plan on $40,000 for two competitors, $60,000 for three, and you should be fine.

Question 3: I want all my data available every day _____ once a week _____ once a month _____.

Most media channels and monitoring companies do not deliver data in real time. We find anywhere from a twenty-four-hour to two-week lag for some services. If real-time data delivery is important, make sure you get it in writing from your provider.

MEASUREMENT SETUP

Given the torrent of Tweets and other social mentions that must be part of any measurement system in today's media environment, you need to ask these questions:

Question 1: Do I get sufficient volume to warrant automated coding? Yes _____ No _____

Computers do a really good job of putting words into buckets. In most cases (unless you are Visa or Sun or GE or SAS or have some other unfortunately ubiquitous brand name), computers can go through the torrent and pull out mentions of your brand and put them into a database complete with the date of the mention, the source, the author, and the title. A really good system can accurately determine if you are the focal point of the story, if your thought leaders are quoted, and what the primary subject of the article or post is.

This is generally the extent to which you should be comfortable relying on computer-aided analysis. Beyond that, for analysis of sentiment, messaging, positioning, and so on, rely on humans. The most sophisticated computer-aided systems, like SAS and Cymfony, can be "taught" key messages, specific definitions of positive or negative, and some general concepts. However, it takes time and testing to set up such a system. So chances are that if you are getting fewer than fifteen hundred mentions a month, it's probably cheaper and more efficient to use humans. They learn faster, can adapt to changes more rapidly, and get the sense of a story without explicit mentions of key words. If you want your qualitative metrics done right, use a human.

Question 2: Do I need to random sample? Yes _____ No _____

For brands that receive more than two thousand mentions a month, you can trust an automated system to get sentiment and subjects right about 60 percent of the time. If you are comfortable with those odds, use a computer. If not, you may need to select a random sample of all mentions for a human to code.

We recommend random sampling at least 10 percent of each channel of news that you receive. So, that's 10 percent of Twitter, 10 percent of Facebook, and 10 percent of YouTube.

Question 4: How will you define positive? 4-point scale _____ 6-point scale _____

Typical categories of sentiment are: Positive (leaves the reader *more* likely to do business with the company, Negative (leaves the reader *less* likely to do business with the company), Neutral (contains no sentiment at all), and Balanced (contains equal levels of positive and negative comments). Some prefer a more nuanced scale, which would include these categories: very positive, somewhat positive, neutral, somewhat negative, very negative, and balanced.

Question 5: Do you have messages to convey to your publics? Yes _____ No _____

Key messages are the daily bread and butter of most communications departments, and even in the uncontrolled environment of social media, you will want to track them. We apply the following scale: $+3$ = amplified key message, $+2$ = full key message, $+1$ = partial key message, 0 = no message, -2 = incorrect or wrong message.

Question 6: Do you care how you are positioned in the conversation? Yes _____ No _____

Frequently, whether you planned it or not, the social media conversation is likely to position you favorably or unfavorably on a number of key issues, such as sustainability, social responsibility, or leadership. Positioning is similar to messaging but not specific to your brand. You can apply positioning statements to your own brand or just as effectively to any of your competitors.

Question 7: Are different audiences more important than some others? Yes _____ No _____

If the answer is yes, then you will need to specify which audiences are more or less important and how you define each audience.

Question 8: Is the visibility of your coverage important? Yes _____ No _____

Studies have shown that the more visible your brand is, the more likely people will be to remember it. The same is true for your messages. You need to define what "visibility" means. Typically it is defined as "mentioning your brand in a headline or the top 20 percent of an article." Another factor is dominance, the extent to which a story, mention, thread, or Tweet is about your brand or mentions other brands. We define three categories for dominance:

- All about you

- Mostly about you but mentions other brands

- Mentions you only in passing

Question 9: Is there anything else you need tracked? Yes _____ No _____

If you have initiatives, analysts, key battles, programs, or anything else that you are spending an exceptional amount of time on in the next six to twelve months, now is the time to bring it up to ensure that any references to it are captured.

Question 10: Do you need to know if a link back to your Web site or blog is included in the story?

Links are key to tracking marketing effectiveness, so if it is important to know if a link has appeared, you need to account for that in your report.

REPORTING SETUP

Most communicators pay attention to their measurement programs only when the results are reported. The details are mundane and frequently tedious to work out. But to get your reports right requires just as much attention to detail. With the widespread use of interactive dashboards, you can pretty much dream up your own, totally personalized reporting mechanism. In order to make the right choice, you need to answer some fundamental questions:

Question 1: Style: I want to create my own reports _____ I want someone else to prepare them for me _____.

Many organizations today expect their PR agencies to prepare their monthly reports, complete with insights, advice, and recommendations. Others would rather leave it to a third-party firm that can take a totally unbiased approach to analyzing the data. Still others prefer the do-it-yourself approach and want to go to a desktop application themselves and pull down and analyze the data. How you answer this question will have a large bearing on what solution you choose. Most monitoring companies are essentially software providers and do not have the expertise to analyze and interpret the data in a way that is relevant to your specific goals.

Question 2: I want to see results reported in: PowerPoint _____ HTML/ Online _____ Blog _____ Word _____ Excel _____ Other _____.

The real question is whether you are comfortable with reporting online with links or cutting and copying data from your dashboard into PowerPoint.

Question 3: I want to receive reports: weekly _____ monthly _____ every six months _____ annually _____.

Not only do you need to decide frequency but you need to plan delivery backward from when you need to make decisions. If you do your budgeting and planning in January, you need to have fresh and current data available in December. That means that your annual report will include data from October of one year to October of the next year. Ideally you will look at data over a thirteen-month cycle to make sure you account for any seasonality in the results.

Question 4: I prefer trend charts _____ period charts _____ both _____.

When you are reporting first-quarter results, you will need to show the results from that period. You should also compare and contrast those numbers with prior periods.

Question 5: I prefer reporting results: week-to-week _____ month-to-month _____ quarter-to-quarter _____.

There are pluses and minuses for both approaches. Quarterly results show big trends; monthly or weekly reporting enables you to pinpoint specific activities and correlate those activities to results. Monthly enables you to point to a specific program that took place in a month and see the results. Weekly or daily reporting is best when correlating to Web traffic and web analytic data.

Question 6: I need to report on specific key performance indicators. Yes _____ No _____.

If you have established key performance indicators for your department and report on them regularly, you need to let your vendors know so they can program that number into the dashboard, or at the very least provide it on a regular basis.

Question 7: I need a top ten list for: Reporters _____ Publications _____ Bloggers _____ Stories/headlines _____ Popular links _____.

It is frequently useful to see a top ten list of reporters, authors, stories, or publications that can easily be referred back to. We recommend no more than ten, but some clients prefer a top 1,000 list.

FOREWORD

1. Hope Consulting study, "Money for Good," http://www.hopeconsulting.us/money-for-good.

2. B. Kanter and A. Fine, *The Networked Nonprofit* (San Francisco: Jossey-Bass, 2010).

PREFACE

1. B. Kanter and A. Fine, *The Networked Nonprofit* (San Francisco: Jossey-Bass, 2010).

CHAPTER ONE

1. B. Kanter, "When Is One Million Fans on Facebook Worth More Than a Million Bucks?" *Beth's Blog*, Nov. 2011, http://www.bethkanter.org/million-fans/.

2. C. Newmark, "Who Rules Social Media: A Look at Social Media Impact by Nonprofits," Nov. 2011, http://craigconnects.org/2011/11/who-rules-social-media-a-look-at-social-media-impact-by-nonprofit-issues.html.

3. C. Lewis, e-mail correspondence with B. Kanter, Oct. 2011.

CHAPTER TWO

1. B. Kanter and A. Fine, *The Networked Nonprofit* (San Francisco: Jossey-Bass, 2010).

2. W. Harman, e-mail conversation with Beth Kanter, Jan. 2011.

3. "Mobile Accord's mGive Platform Raises More Than $41 Million for Red Cross to Help Earthquake Victims in Haiti," *Mobile Accord*, Jan. 2010, http://mobileaccord.wordpress.com/2010/01/19/mobile-accords-mgive-platform-raises-more-than-22-million-for-red-cross-to-help-earthquake-victims-in-haiti/.

4. Herndon Alliance, "Quick Guide: Post-Passage Message," Oct. 13, 2010, http://herndonalliance.org/resources/what-s-new/quick-guide-post-passage-message.html.

5. K. Rowe-Finkbeiner, e-mail correspondence with B. Kanter, July 2011.

6. B. Kanter, "The Knowledge is in The Room: How to Let it Out," *Beth's Blog*, Feb. 2011, http://www.bethkanter.org/knowledge//.

7. International Institute for Education, "E-Mediat Program," Jan. 2011, http://www.emediat.org/.

CHAPTER THREE

1. E. Peterson, "The Myth of Data Driven Business," *Eric Peterson's Blog at Web Analytics Demystified*, Sept. 6, 2011. http://blog.webanalyticsdemystified.com/weblog/2011/09/the-myth-of-the-data-driven-business.html/.

2. B. Kanter, "Data-Driven or Data Informed?" conversation on Google, Sept. 2011, https://plus.google.com/107965826228461029730/posts/VKwsH1kpVxe.

3. M. Morino, *Leap of Reason* (Washington, D.C.: Venture Philanthropy Partners, 2011), http://www.vppartners.org/leapofreason/getit.

4. Kanter, *op. cit.*

5. N. Lublin, e-mail and telephone interview with B. Kanter, Sept. 2011.

6. G. Weiner, e-mail and telephone interview with B. Kanter, Sept. 2011.

7. B. Filbin, e-mail with B. Kanter, Aug. 2011.

8. J. Lovett, *Social Media Metrics Secrets* (Hoboken, N.J.: Wiley, 2011).

9. Sara Thomas, conference call peer learning group with David and Lucile Packard Foundation grantees with Beth Kanter, Sept. 2011.

CHAPTER FOUR

1. L. Leong, private e-mail interview with B. Kanter, Oct. 2011.

2. A. Fine, e-mail to B. Kanter, Nov. 2011.

3. T. Witherington, e-mail interview with B. Kanter, Oct. 2011.

4. These steps are discussed more completely, and with emphasis on for-profit businesses, in K. Paine, *Measure What Matters: Online Tools for Understanding Customers, Social Media, Engagement, and Key Relationships* (Hoboken, N.J.: Wiley, 2011).

5. B. Kanter, "25 SMART Social Media Objectives," *Beth's Blog*, May 2011, http://www.bethkanter.org/25-smart/.

6. P. Houa Moua, e-mail correspondence with B. Kanter, Sept. 2011.

7. A. Weldon, e-mail correspondence with B. Kanter, Sept. 2011.

8. V. McMurchie, e-mail correspondence with B. Kanter, Sept. 2011.

9. A. Samuel, "Scoring with Social Media," *HBR Blog Network*, Sept. 21, 2009, http://blogs.hbr.org/cs/2009/09/scoring_with_social_media_6_ti.html.

10. C. Lindberg, e-mail correspondence with B. Kanter, Sept. 2011.

CHAPTER FIVE

1. B. Kanter, "Greater Washington Give to the Max Day Training Event," *Beth's Blog*, Oct. 2011, http://www.bethkanter.org/give-to-max-dc/.

2. K. Reich, e-mail correspondence with B. Kanter, Oct. 2011.

3. D. Yates, e-mail correspondence with B. Kanter, Nov. 2011.

4. T. Kelly, e-mail with Beth Kanter, Nov. 2011.

CHAPTER SIX

1. Wikipedia, "AIDA," http://en.wikipedia.org/wiki/AIDA_(marketing).

2. C. Giller, interview with B. Kanter, Sept. 2011.

3. B. Kanter, "Living Case Studies," *Beth's Blog*, July 2011, http://www.bethkanter.org/living-case-study/.

4. J. Zimmerman, "Farming Is the New Hipster Occupation of Choice," *Grist*, Mar. 7, 2011, http://www.grist.org/sustainable-farming/2011–03–07-farming-is-the-new-hipster-occupation-of-choice.

5. Grist, "Photos of Devastation from East Coast Earthquake," Aug. 23, 2011, http://grist.org/list/2011–08–23-photos-of-devastation-from-the-east-coast-earthquake/.

6. J. Nielsen, "Participation Inequality," *Jakob Nielsen's Alertbox*, Oct. 9. 2006, http://www.useit.com/alertbox/participation_inequality.html.

7. V. McMurchie, e-mail correspondence with B. Kanter, Sept. 2011.

8. D. J. Neff and C. M. Perrone, e-mail correspondence with B. Kanter, Nov. 2011.

CHAPTER SEVEN

1. "New Report: 2011 Nonprofit Social Network Benchmark Report," *NTEN*, Mar. 2011, http://www.nten.org/blog/2011/03/18/new-report-2011-non profit-social-network-benchmark-report.

2. Ibid.

3. "Quarterly Digital Giving Index," *Network for Good*, June 2011, http://www.onlinegivingstudy.org/quarterlyindex.

4. F. Barry, "The Power of Social Fundraisng and Friends Asking Friends," *NetWits Think Tank*, June 2011, http://www.netwitsthinktank.com/friends-asking-friends/the-power-of-social-fundraising-and-friends-asking-friends-infographic.htm.

5. Case Foundation, "The Giving Challenge 2009: Assessment and Reflection Report," June 2010, http://www.casefoundation.org/case-studies/giving-chal lenge-2009.

6. D. Nelson, e-mail correspondence with B. Kanter, Sept. 2011.

7. P. Young, e-mail correspondence with B. Kanter, Aug. 2011.

8. Autism Speaks, "Light It Up Blue Campaign," press release, June 2011, http://www.autismspeaks.org/about-us/press-releases/over-1000-build ings-join-autism-speaks-light-it-blue-campaign-celebrate-worl.

9. M. Sirkin, e-mail correspondence with B. Kanter, June 2011.

10. K. Andresen, "The 7 Signs You Are Doing Things Right Across Channels," *Katya's Non-Profit Marketing Blog*, Aug. 15, 2011, http://www.nonprofitmar ketingblog.com/comments/the_7_signs_you_are_doing_things_right_across_ channels/.

11. L. Shaw, e-mail correspondence with B. Kanter, Oct. 2011.

12. S. Gordon, e-mail correspondence with B. Kanter, Oct. 2011.

13. Ibid.

14. G. Livingston, e-mail correspondence with B. Kanter, Oct. 2011.

CHAPTER EIGHT

1. M. Trudel, R. MacPherson, and J. Sen, "How Strong Is Your Social Network?" *Trudel MacPherson*, Nov. 2011, http://www.trudelmacpherson.com/how-strong-is-your-social-net-2011-results/.

2. M. Trudel, e-mail correspondence with B. Kanter, Nov. 2011.

3. S. Burke, e-mail interview, Oct. 2011

4. H. Ross, e-mail correspondence with B. Kanter, Nov. 2011.

5. B. Kanter, "Are You Using the Best Ever Social Media Analytics Tool?," *Beth's Blog*, July 2011, http://www.bethkanter.org/survey/.

6. "2011 Nonprofit Social Networking Benchmark Report," Nov. 2011, http://www.surveymonkey.com/s/NTENChange1

7. D. Stacks, "Dictionary of Public Relations Measurement and Research" (Gainesville, Fla.: Institute for Public Relations, 2006), http://www.instituteforpr.org/wp-content/uploads/PRMR_Dictionary.pdf.

8. NTEN, "2011 Nonprofit Social Network Benchmark Report," Mar. 2011, http://www.nten.org/research/2011-nonprofit-social-networking-benchmark-report.

9. "Survey Reveals More Than Half of Minorities in Connecticut Feel They've Experienced Healthcare Inequality," *PRWeb*, Nov. 16, 2010, http://www.healthjusticect.org/wp-content/uploads/2011/07/HJCT-Press-Release_Survey-Reveals-11.16.10.pdf.

10. http://www.qualtrics.com/.

11. K. D. Paine, "How to Set Benchmarks in Social Media: Exploratory Research for Social Media, Lessons Learned," in Y. Koichi (ed.), *Research That Matters to the Practice: Twelfth Annual International Public Relations Research Conference* (Mar. 2009), p. 442, http://www.iprrc.org/docs/IPRRC_12_Proceedings.pdf.

12. J. Johnson, e-mail correspondence with B. Kanter, July 2011.

13. A. Kapin, e-mail interview with B. Kanter, Nov. 2011.

14. A. McCrehan, e-mail correspondence with B. Kanter and K. D. Paine, Nov. 2011.

15. D. Ford-Scriba, e-mail correspondence with B. Kanter, Oct. 2011.

16. For papers on measurement, go to http://www.instituteforpr.org/topic/measurement-and-evaluation/.

CHAPTER NINE

1. Independent Federal Reserve, "The Drawing Board," Mar. 10, 2010, http://www.youtube.com/watch?v=Kj9-kRv0e6s&feature=related

2. A. Boyd, e-mail correspondence with B. Kanter, Nov. 2011.

3. B. Kanter, "Social Media Dashboard Design Tips from the Smithsonian Institution Archives," *Beth's Blog*, Aug. 2011, http://www.bethkanter.org/dashboard-tips/.

4. D. Smith, e-mail correspondence with B. Kanter, Sept. 2011.

5. B. Kanter, "Bench Learning: Zoos and Aquariums Social Media," *Beth's Blog*, Aug. 2011, http://www.bethkanter.org/benchlearning/.

6. H. Kam, e-mail interview with B. Kanter, Oct. 2011.

CHAPTER TEN

1. K. Huyse, "Case Study: ROI of Social Media Campaign for SeaWorld San Antonio: A Year Later," *Communication Overtones*, Apr. 18, 2008, http://overtonecomm.blogspot.com/2008/04/case-study-roi-of-social-media-campaign.html.

2. W. Harman, e-mail correspondence with B. Kanter, Feb. 2011.

3. A. Ostrow, "Rep. Weiner Meant to Send Lewd Photo as Direct Message," *Mashable Social Media*, June 6, 2011, http://mashable.com/2011/06/06/anthony-weiner-direct-message/. "More Face Wal-Mart Blogs, Edelman Fesses Up," *Marketing Vox*, Oct. 20, 2006, http://www.marketingvox.com/more_fake_walmart_blogs_edelman_fesses_up-022878/. Beth Kanter, "What Was Your Biggest Social Media Mistake? What Did You Learn?," *Beth's Blog*, Feb. 2011, http://www.bethkanter.org/mistake/.

4. American Red Cross, "Twitter Faux Pas," Feb. 2011, *American Red Cross Blog*, http://redcrosschat.org/2011/02/16/twitter-faux-pas/.

5. L. C. Hon and J. E. Grunig, "Guidelines for Measuring Relationships in Public Relations" (Gainesville, Fla.: Institute for Public Relations, 1999), http://www.instituteforpr.org/topics/measuring-relationships/.

6. H. Kang, K. J. Garciaruano, and Y.-H. Lin, "Factors Affecting E-Mail Rumor Belief and Activity: The Effects of Type of Rumor and Organization-Public Relationships, in *The Proceedings of the Eleventh International Public Relations Research Conference* (Gainesville, Fla.: Institute for Public Relations, 2008), http://www.instituteforpr.org/wp-content/uploads/IPRRC_11_Proceedings_4.pdf.

7. H. F. Sisco and T. McCorkindale, "Communicating 'Pink': An Analysis of the Communication Strategies, Transparency, and Credibility of Breast Cancer Social Media Sites," in *The Proceedings of the Fourteenth International Public Relations Research Conference* (Gainesville, Fla.: Institute for Public Relations, 2011).

8. S. Burke, private correspondence with K. D. Paine, Nov. 2011.

9. B. Kanter and A. Fine, *The Networked Nonprofit* (San Francisco: Jossey-Bass, 2010).

10. M. Kelly and D. W. Supa, "How the Nation's Largest Insurer Leverages Social Media," in *Proceedings of the Fourteenth International Public Relations Research Conference* (Gainesville, Fla.: Institute for Public Relations, 2011), p. 411, http://www.instituteforpr.org/wp-content/uploads/14th-IPRRC-Proceedings.pdf

CHAPTER ELEVEN

1. B. Kanter and A. Fine, *The Networked Nonprofit* (San Francisco: Jossey-Bass, 2010). J. Holley, *Network Weaver Handbook* (N.p., 2011). GEO, "Conference Resources," Oct. 2011, http://www.geofunders.org/conferences/networks-conference-2011/resources.

2. B. Kanter, "The Story of Stuff," *Beth's Blog*, Feb. 2011, http://www.bethkanter.org/storyofstuff/.

3. A. Leonard, e-mail correspondence with B. Kanter, Feb. 2011.

4. D. L. Hansen, B. Shneiderman, and M. A. Smith, *Analyzing Social Media Networks with NodeXL: Insights from a Connected World* (San Francisco: Morgan Kaufmann, 2011).

5. M. Garlinghouse, e-mail correspondence with B. Kanter, Nov. 2011.

6. D. Scearce, "Catalyzing Networks for Social Change: A Funder's Guide" (Washington, D.C., and San Francisco: Grandmakers for Effective Organizations and Monitor Institute, 2011), p. 22, http://www.geofunders.org/storage/documents/Catalyzing_Networks_for_Social_Change_2011.pdf .

7. S. Tenby, e-mail correspondence with B. Kanter, Oct. 2011.

CHAPTER TWELVE

1. B. Kanter, "Blog Action Day: "Blog Action Day: Can One Person Make A Difference? Challenging Poverty With Social Media," *Beth's Blog*, Oct. 2008, http://beth.typepad.com/beths_blog/2008/10/blog-action-day-can-one-person-make-a-difference-challenging-poverty-with-social-media.html.

2. P. Sheldrake, *The Business of Influence* (Hoboken, N.J.: Wiley, 2011), offers a deeper discussion of influence. B. Solis, *Engage: The Complete Guide for Brands and Business to Build, Cultivate, and Measure Success in the New Web* ((Hoboken, N.J.: Wiley, 2010).

3. E. Roper wrote *Personal Influence* in 1955. His work inspired E. Keller and J. Berry, *The Influentials* (New York: Free Press, 2003). D. Crosbie, "Winning Friends and Influencing People in the Digital Age," *Gfktrendtalk*, Nov. 3, 2011, http://www.gfkroperpulse.co.uk/tag/influentials/.

4. "Influentials Market Analysis 2.0," GfK Custom Research, North America, n.d., http://www.gfkamerica.com/practice_areas/roper_consulting/roper_influentials/index.en.html.

5. M. Gladwell, *The Tipping Point* (Boston: Back Bay Books, 2002).

6. B. Kanter, "Good News for Giving 2.0: Round Up of Research Studies," *Beth's Blog*, Nov. 2011, http://www.bethkanter.org/good-news/.

7. E. Bakshy, J. M. Hofman, W. A. Mason, and D. J. Watts "Everyone's an Influencer: Quantifying Influence on Twitter," in *Proceedings of the Fourth*

International Conference on Web Search and Data Mining (New York: ACM, 2011).

8. M. Horvath, e-mail to B. Kanter, Oct. 2011.

9. S. Burke, private e-mail conversation, Oct. 2011.

10. Blue Key Campaign, "Blue Key Campaign: Become a Champion," *The Blue Key Blog*, May 2011, http://bluekeyblog.org/become-a-blue-key-champion.

11. S. Burke, "Want to Identify Online Influencers?" *Waxing Lyrical*, June 2011, http://www.waxingunlyrical.com/2011/06/07/want-to-identify-online-influencers-try-traackr/.

12. S. Burke, e-mail correspondence with B. Kanter, June 2011.

13. "Exploring and Defining Influence: A New Study," @BrianSolis, Sept. 29, 2010, http://www.briansolis.com/2010/09/exploring-and-defining-influence-a-new-study/

14. N. Castañeda, e-mail correspondence with B. Kanter, Sept. 2011.

CHAPTER THIRTEEN

1. P. Ni, private e-mail correspondence with B. Kanter, Dec. 2011.

2. J. Harold, comment made on a conference panel at the Center for Effective Philanthropy Conference, Boston, May 2011.

3. B. Rawlins, "Measuring the Relationship Between Organizational Transparency and Employee Trust," *Public Relations Journal*, 2008, 2(2), 1–21, http://www.prsa.org/searchresults/view/6d-020202/0/measuring_the_relationship_between_organizational.

4. J. Harold, tweet at a conference at the Center for Effective Philanthropy, Boston, May 12, 2011.

5. B. Rawlins, "Measuring the Relationship Between Organizational Transparency and Employee Trust," *Public Relations Journal*, 2008, 2, (2), 1–2.

6. K. D. Paine, "Greater Transparency Is the Key to Building Greater Trust," Sept. 2007, http://kdpaine.blogs.com/themeasurementstandard/2007/09/greater-transpa.html.

7. Rawlins, *op. cit.*

8. D. Scearce, "The Wiki Workplace and a Network Mindset—Part 1," Sept. 2011, *Transparency Talk*, http://blog.glasspockets.org/2011/09/scearce_2011 0926.html.

9. P. Connolly, "The Glass Filing Cabinet: What the Packard Foundation Is Learning About Public Learning," *Philantopic*, July 11, 2011, http://pnd blog.typepad.com/pndblog/2011/07/the-glass-filing-cabinet-what-the-packard-foundation-is-learning-about-learning-in-public.html.

10. Packard Foundation, "Engagement with the Goldmine," *Packard Foundation-OE*, Nov. 2011, http://packard-foundation-oe.wikispaces.com/Engagement+with+the+Goldmine.

11. D. Scearce, "The Wiki Workplace and a Network Mindset, Part 2," *Transparency Talk*, Oct. 5, 2011, http://blog.glasspockets.org/2011/10/scearce_20111005.html

12. Paine, "Greater Transparency Is the Key to Building Greater Trust."

13. Rawlins, *op. cit.*

14. Ibid.

15. "Scandal Rocks America's Support for Susan G. Komen for the Cure, According to Twenty-Third Annual Harris Poll EquiTrend Study," *Harris Interactive*, n.d., http://www.harrisinteractive.com/NewsRoom/PressReleases/tabid/446/ctl/ReadCustom%20Default/mid/1506/ArticleId/994/Default .aspx. N. Singer, "With Support Off as Events Begin, Komen Works to Revive Its Image," *The New York Times*, Apr. 27, 2012, http://www.nytimes.com/2012/04/28/us/with-komen-image-hurt-support-for-affiliates-lags.html? pagewanted=al.

CHAPTER FOURTEEN

1. J. Aaker and A. Smith, "The Story of Sameer and Vinay," *The Dragonfly Effect*, Sept. 2010, http://www.dragonflyeffect.com/blog/dragonfly-in-action/case-studies/the-story-of-sameer-and-vinay/.

2. J. Aaker and S. Veneet, e-mail correspondence with B. Kanter, Oct. 2011.

3. OpenIdeo, "Challenge Brief," Dec. 2011, http://www.openideo.com/open/how-might-we-increase-the-number-of-bone-marrow-donors-to-help-save-more-lives/brief.html.

4. OpenIdeo, "Swab Parties (on the Basis of Tupperware Parties)," n.d., http://www.openideo.com/open/how-might-we-increase-the-number-of-bone-marrow-donors-to-help-save-more-lives/winners-announced/swab-parties-on-the-basis-of-tupperware-parties/.

5. J. Howe, *Crowdsourcing: Why the Power of the Crowd Is Driving the Future of Business* (New York: Crown, 2008).

6. A. Sherman, "Measuring Your Crowdsourcing Efforts by Aliza Sherman," *Beth's Blog*, July 2011, http://www.bethkanter.org/measure-crowd/. A. Sherman, *The Complete Idiot's Guide to Crowdsourcing* (New York: Penguin, 2011).

7. NTEN, "Help Shape the NTC Agenda," Sept. 13, 2010, http://www.nten.org/blog/2010/09/13/help-shape-2011-ntc-agenda-session-proposal-voting-now-open. "SXSW Panel Picker 2012," Aug. 2011, http://panelpicker.sxsw.com/.

APPENDIX B

1. "Nonprofit Social Media Audit," http://nonprofitsocialmediaaudit.wikispaces.com/.

GLOSSARY

Advertising value equivalent (AVE)   An unproven and discredited measure of public relations value based on calculating the column inches of a story and determining the equivalent cost of buying the same size advertising space in the same publication.

Baseline or benchmark   An initial measurement against which subsequent measures are compared.

Benchmarking or benchmark study   A measurement technique that involves having an organization learn something about its own practices or the practices of selected others (or both) and then compare these practices. Research that establishes a benchmark.

Causal relationship   A relationship between variables in which a change in one variable forces, produces, or brings about a change in another one.

Census   A collection of data from every person or object in a population.

Circulation   Number of copies of a publication as distributed. Not usually the same as the number actually read, but as a practical matter, synonymous with *opportunities to see*, *impressions*, and *reach*.

Column inches   The total length of a printed article if it were all one column, measured in inches.

Communications audit   A systematic review and analysis of how effectively an organization communicates with all of its major internal and external audiences.

Content analysis   An informal research methodology and measurement tool that systematically tracks messages (written, spoken, broadcast) and translates them into quantifiable form by defining message categories and specified units of analysis.

Correlation   A statistical test that examines the relationships between variables.

Cost per message communicated (CPMC)   Similar to cost per thousand, but adjusted for the number of messages that actually appeared in the media coverage.

Cost per thousand (CPM)   Cost per impression or cost per person reached. As used in advertising, it is the cost of advertising for each one thousand homes reached.

Dashboard   A technique for simplifying data reporting by displaying a small number of important summary measures together in one location. Like an automotive dashboard, a public relations dashboard includes only the measures most critical for assessing the progress or health of a program or company.

Demographic analysis   The analysis of a population in terms of social, political, economic, and geographic subgroups (for example, age, sex, income level, race, educational level, place of residence, occupation).

Demographic data   Data that differentiate groups of people by social, political, economic, and geographic characteristics.

Editorial or earned media   (1) The content of a publication written by a journalist, as distinct from advertising content, which is determined by an advertiser. (2) An article expressing the editorial policy of a publication on a matter of interest (also known as a *leader* or *leading article*). (3) Space in a publication bought by an advertiser that includes journalistic copy intended to make the reader think it originates from an independent source (also known as an *advertorial*).

Focus group methodology   An informal research technique that uses a group discussion approach to gain an in-depth understanding of a client, object, or product; not generalizable to other focus groups or populations.

Frequency   A descriptive statistic that represents the number of objects being counted (for example, number of advertisements, number of people who attend an event, number of media release pickups).

Gross rating points (GRP) A measure most broadcast advertisers use to determine the extent to which their advertising messages have penetrated a specific audience. The GRP of a show or ad represents the percentage of the total audience who viewed it.

Impressions A measure of the number of potential people exposed to a story or message. Also referred to as *opportunities to see.* (*See* reach)

Key message A specific statement or concept that an organization is trying to communicate about itself. A common general goal of PR is to get key messages into media coverage. A key message ought to be unique to an organization, and it must be something that a journalist is likely to print—for example, "Company X provides the best customer service in the industry," or, "Company Y's product is of the highest quality."

Message content (1) The verbal, visual, and audio elements of a message. (2) The material from which content analyses are conducted. (3) A trend analysis factor that measures what planned messages are actually contained in the media.

Message content analysis Analysis of media coverage of a client, product, or topic on key issues.

Message strength How strongly a message about a client, product, or topic was communicated.

Objectives A clearly defined set of goals that are in line with overall strategic marketing, sales, and corporate objectives.

Omnibus survey An all-purpose national consumer poll usually conducted on a regular schedule (once a week or every other week) by major market research firms; also called a *piggyback* or *shared-cost* survey.

Opportunities to see (OTS) A number equal to the total audited circulation of a publication. *Opportunities to see, circulation, impressions*, and *reach* are synonymous.

Outcomes Quantifiable changes in attitudes, behaviors, or opinions that occur as end results of a public relations program.

Outputs The physical products of a public relations program; anything that is published or directly produced by the public relations team. Outputs can be articles, white papers, speaking engagements, the number of times a spokesperson is quoted, specific messages communicated, specific positioning on an important issue, or any number of quantifiable items.

Outtakes   What members of a target audience take away from a program—the messages, perceptions, and understandings that a program has generated. The perceptions generated by outputs.

Poll   (1) A form of survey research that focuses more on immediate behavior than attitudes. (2) A short survey-like method using a questionnaire that asks only short and closed-ended questions.

Positioning   How an organization is perceived on broad industry characteristics such as leadership, innovation, employer of choice, and neighbor of choice.

Program or campaign   The planning, execution, and evaluation of a public relations plan of action aimed at solving a problem.

Psychographic research   Research focusing on nondemographic traits and characteristics such as personality type, lifestyle, social roles, values, attitudes, and beliefs.

Public   (1) A group of people whose behavior may have consequences for an organization or who are affected by the consequences of organizational decisions. (2) A group of people from which a public relations campaign or program selects specific targeted audiences in an attempt to influence behavior or attitudes regarding a company, product, issue, or individual.

Qualitative research   Studies that are somewhat to totally subjective but nevertheless in depth, using a probing, open-ended response format.

Quantitative research   Studies that are highly objective and projectable, using closed-ended, forced-choice questionnaires; research that relies heavily on statistics and numerical measures.

Questionnaire   A measurement instrument that uses questions to collect data for the analysis of some aspect of a group. May be employed through the mail, Internet, in person, or by telephone. May be both closed ended and open ended, but typically employs more closed-ended questions. A questionnaire is the instrument used in a *survey*.

Reach   The scope or range of distribution and thus coverage that a given communication product has in a targeted audience group. The total audited circulation of a publication. In broadcasting, the net unduplicated (also called *deduplicated*) radio or TV audience for programs. Actual reach is very hard to determine in social media due to a lack of audited readership data that make it easier to assess with traditional media. In reality, most of what we can measure in social media is actually opportunities to reach or potential reach, since there is in fact no guarantee that a message has actually reached a person or has made an impression. Opportunities to reach or potential reach can be calculated by counting unique blog visits, number of Facebook fans, or Twitter followers, LinkedIn page views, community or forum size, and so on. Multipliers should not be used to calculate reach in social media (or traditional media, for that matter, unless validated by audited readership data). In fact, we recommend using dividers for most social channels. On any given channel, only a small percentage of people are likely reached by any given piece of content. On Facebook, for example, there is some evidence that only a small percentage of the people who "like" a page or brand will actually see the content published to that brand page, as the Facebook algorithm shows pages only to people who have demonstrated recent or frequent engagement with the brand content. On Twitter, an average follower sees less than 10 percent of posts. This means Twitter reach should not include second-level followers. Comments on a blog post should not be ascribed the same reach as the initial post. Although it can be assumed that every visitor may read the initial post, a decreasing number of visitors will see each subsequent comment.

Reach demographics   Reach into specific demographic segments, determined using data from one of the generally accepted sources such as SRDS or Simmons.

Response rate   The number of respondents who complete an interview or reply to some request, usually expressed as a percentage of all those who received the interview or request.

Sample   A group of people or objects chosen from a larger population.

Share of ink (SOI)   The percentage of total press coverage or opportunities to see devoted to a particular client or product.

Share of voice (SOV)   The percentage of total radio or television coverage or opportunities to see devoted to a particular client or product; also known as *share of coverage.*

Survey   The process of gathering data from a sample of a population. The instrument used in a survey is called a *questionnaire*.

Target audience   A specific subset of a total audience, differentiated by some characteristic or attribute (for example, sports fishermen) that is the specific focus of a marketing or public relations effort.

Targeted gross rating points (TGRP)   *Gross rating points* (GRP) with respect to a particular group or target audience.

Tone   Trend and content analysis factor that measures how a target audience feels about the client, product, or topic; typically defined as positive, neutral or balanced, or negative.

Trend analysis   Tracking of performance over the course of a public relations campaign or program. A survey method whereby a topic or subject is examined over a period of time through repeated surveys of independently selected samples.

RESOURCES FOR TOOLS, TUTORIALS, AND ASSISTANCE

Beth's Blog: http://www.bethkanter.org

Beth Kanter's Resource Wikis: http://bethkanter.wikispaces.com

Beth Kanter's Social Media Measurement and Nonprofits Curated Resources: http://www.scoop.it/t/social-media-and-nonprofits-measurement

Eric Peterson's Blog at Web Analytics Demystified: http://blog.webanalyticsdemystified.com/

Guidelines for Market Research, Advertising Research Foundation, 2003: http://robertoigarza.files.wordpress.com/2008/09/gui-guidelines-for-market-research-arf-2003.pdf

Institute for Public Relations: www.instituteforpr.org

KDPaine's Measurement Blog: http://kdpaine.blogs.com

Measurement Standard: www.themeasurementstandard.com

Measuring the Networked Nonprofit Book Site: http://www.measurenetworkednonprofit.net

Networked Nonprofit Wiki: http://networkednonprofit.wikispaces.com

Occam's Razor by Avinash Kaushik: http://www.kaushik.net/avinash/

Society for New Communications Research: www.sncr.org

INDEX

A

Aaker, J., 236, 237

Aha! moments, 152–153

Ahmed, S., 208

AIDA concept/marketing funnel, 78

Alexa, 211

Alignment, 53–56

American Leadership Forum—Silicon Valley (ALF), 147

American Red Cross, 14–15, 62, 175, 176, 208; adoption of social media, 15; Twitter faux pas, 176–177

Analysis Exchange, 30, 37, 147–148

Andresen, K., 107

Annie E. Casey Foundation, 74–75

AOL, Cause Module, 103

Appinions, 216

ASPCA (American Society for the Prevention of Cruelty to Animals), 179; Aha! moment for relationship studies, 183

Audiences, defining, 47–48

Authority, 134–135

Autism Speaks, 104–107; customized asks, 106–107; e-mail segmentation, 106–107; ladder of engagement, 105–106; Light It Up Blue campaign, 104–107

Automated content analysis, 133

Average mentions, 136

Average path length, networks, 195

Awareness, 138; measuring, 123

B

Bakshy, E., 206

Balanced tone, 135

Barry, F., 100

Benchmarks, defining, 48–49

Bernholz, L., 164

Best Friends Animal Society, 87–90; Dog Wall, 90; e-mail messaging, 88; Invisible Dogs campaign, 87–88; Invisible Dogs Pledge Form, 89; #invisibleDogs hashtag, 88; National Shelter Check-in Day project, 88; nationwide Invisible Dogs events, 88–90

Bhatia, S., 236

Binhammer, R., 240

Birmingham Museums, 123

Blades, J., 7–8

Blogs, and crowdsourcing, 239

Blue Key Campaign, 208–215, 210; data in context, 213; experience, learning from, 214–215; and Google Analytics, 213; influencers, finding to recruit as champions, 210–211; keywords used to identify influencers, 210; and measurement, 209–210; results, tracking, 211–212; Tweetathon, 211–212

Boyd, A., 155

Breslaw, M., 209

Brigham Young University, 224

Brigida, D., 199

Brown, A., 164

Burke, S., 121, 179, 209–215, 210, 211

Business of Influence, The (Sheldrake), 204–205

C

Case Foundation, 101; Make It Your Own awards, 243

Castañeda, N., 219

Castingwords site, 241

Causes (social fundraising platform), 101

Causes.com, 109

Challenge for Children, University of California, San Francisco (UCSF), 108–109

charity:water, 102–104; as data-informed organization, 103–104; fifth anniversary celebration, 103; metrics, use of, 104; mycharitywater.org, launch of, 102; online measurement tools, 104; September Campaign strategy, 103–104

Chase, C. D., 161–162

Chu, D., 199–200

Clickworker site, 241

"Closing the triangle" (network weaving technique, 200

Clusters, 192

Commitment in relationships, 180

Communal relationships, 180

Community Catalyst, 53–56; as grass-tops advocacy organization, 53; key performance indicators (KPIs), 55; and social media, 54; social media measurement pilot, 54–56

Community engagement, 109–110

Complete Idiot's Guide to Crowdsourcing (Sherman), 239

Conclusionary headlines, 159

Connolly, P., 226

Constant Contact, 130, 183

Constant experimentation, importance of, 33

Content analysis tools, 120

Control mutuality, 180

Convio, 183

Core, 191

Correlations, 156–158

Costs, defining, 56–57

Craigslist Foundation, crowdsourcing experiment, 243

Crawl stage, 22–23; data-informed culture, 34

Crawl, walk, run, fly (CWRF) hierarchy, 20–24

Cremonini, R., 194

Crowdflower site, 241

Crowdrise, 101

Crowdsourcing, 237–239; Craigslist Foundation experiment, 243; decision making, 242; ideas, value of, 240–241; Katie's Kat Shelter (KKS), 243–244; measurement of, 239–243; online, 238; participation in, 242; power of, 238–239; of repetitive tasks, 241; solution, value of, 241–242

Croxton, E., 81–82

Curator of metrics, defined, 37

Customized research, syndicated research vs., 145

D

Dashboards, 151, 158–159; sharing, 163–165; Smithsonian Institute Archives (SIA), 161–162

Data: accuracy of, 158; fresh, 156; presenting, 159; sharing, 158–159; telling stories with, 160; without insight, 159

Data analysts, siloing, 33–34

Data collection, 56, 151; charity:water, 103–104; data reflection vs., 33; and measurement tools, 121; project, 37–38; tools, selecting, 51–53

Data-driven culture, defined, 30

Data-informed culture: consultants, 36–37; crawl stage, 34; creating, 29–39; curator of metrics, 37; data collection project, 37–38; defined, 7; disagreements, 36; expectations, managing, 36; experiments, use

of, 37; fly stage, 35–36; HiPPO, 32; information-based introspection, use of term, 31; and internal conversations, 36–38; and leadership, 32; learning from results, 38; and nonprofit/public sector practitioners, 31; run stage, 35; walk stage, 35

Data/results, telling stories with, 151

Data review, 151

David and Lucile Packard Foundation, 21–22, 70

DC Give to the Max Day event (Nov. 2011), 110

Disclosure, 223

Dogfish Head, 176–177

Dominance, 135

Dominant mentions, 135

Donations, and social media, 70

DoSomething.org, 30–34, 237, *See also* Data-informed culture; data analysts, siloing of, 33–34; data collection vs. data reflection, 33; data-informed culture creating, 32–34, 237; data mining, 32; fail-fest meetings, 33; key performance indicators (KPIs), 31–32; purpose of, 30; sharing small wins, 34; staff resistance, overcoming, 34

Dr. Don Stacks' Primer of Public Relations Research, 126

Dubner, S. J., 160

E

Earned revenue, and social media, 70

eCairn, 216

Edge/periphery, 192

Effect, and influence, 205

Efficiency: as benefit of transparency, 227; measuring improvements, 228; metrics, 228

Engage (Solis), 205

Engagement: behaviors, 90–91; metrics, 195; relationships revealed by, 181–182

Excel (Microsoft), 131, 168

Exchange relationships, 180, 182

Exclusive mentions, 135

External stakeholders, sharing dashboards/reports with, 164–165

F

Facebook, 139, 148, 206, 216; and crowdsourcing, 239; and Our Daily Bread (ODB), 61–62; posting needs on, 71; stories vs. statistics, 20

Fail-fest meetings, DoSomething.org, 33

Federal Reserve Bank of Cleveland, Aha! moment, 153

Feeding America, 132; conversions, measurement of, 140–141; Facebook tracking, 141

Filbin, R., 33–34

Fine, A., 14–15, 44, 180, 188

Fly stage, 25; data-informed culture, 35–36

Focus groups, 129

Food Movement Rising campaign, Roots of Change, 144

Ford-Scriba, D., 147

Foundation for Early Learning, 21

Foundation transparency, 224

Freakomonics (Levitt/Dubner), 160

Free agent fundraisers, 204

Free agents, 102; effectiveness/impact of, 217; influence of, 206–208; Mark Horvath, 207–208; passion of, 207; Shawn Ahmed, 208

Frequency, influencers, 216

Fresh data, 156

"Funder's Guide to Networks: Growing Social Impact in a Networked World, A," 188

Fundly (social fundraising platform), 101

Fussell-Sisaco, H., 178

G

Garciaruno, K. J., 178

Garlinghouse, M., 193–194

gfkamerica.com, 205

Giller, C., 79, 82–84

GiveMN, 109

Gladwell, M., 205

Goals, defining, 46–47

Goldmine Project, 226–227

Goodwill Industries International, 143–144

Google Alert, 64, 134

Google Analytics, 83, 103, 120, 122, 139, 140, 142, 211, 213, 216; and Blue Key Campaign, 212–213

Google Forms, 123

Google Keyword finder, 216

Gordon, S., 108, 109

Government 2.0, 30

Grantmakers for Effective Organizations, 72–73; theory of change of, 73

Grantmakers in Film and Electronic Media, 223–224

Greater Pittsburgh Nonprofit
    Partnership, 222–223
GreatNonprofits, 222–223
Greenblatt, J., 233–234
Grist: content, 83–84; coverage on food,
    81; editorial mission, 79; engagement,
    82–84; engagement, as measure,
    81; "Farming Is the New Hipster
    Occupation of Choice" (article), 82;
    footprint, as measure, 81; indexes,
    82–84; individual behavior change, as
    measure, 81; key measures, 81; ladder
    of engagement, 80–81, 84–87; societal
    change, as measure, 81;
    societal influence, challenge of
    measuring, 84; surveys, 82, 84; Twitter
    hashtags, move to climate hawks,
    81–82; use of measurement to deepen
    relationships, 79–80
Grunig, J., 178, 182
Grunig, J. E., 178
Grunig, L., 178, 182
Grunig Relationship Survey, 125, 130,
    178, 181, 184
"Guidelines for Market Research"
    (Advertising Research
    Foundation), 124
Gupta, A., 237

H

Habitat for Humanity, 110
Haiti earthquake (2010), 14–15
Hansen, D. L., 192
Hard results, See Tangibles
Harman, W., 14–15, 62, 176
Harold, J., 224

harrisinteractive.com, 231
Harrison, S., 102
"Heads in beds" metric, 70
HelpAttack, 101
Herndon Alliance, 19
Hewlett Foundation, Philanthropy
    Program at, 224
High-level engagement
    behaviors, 91
Hill, D., 61
HiPPO, use of, 32
Hoffman, R., 32
Hofman, J. M., 206
Holley, J., 188
Hon, L. C., 178
Horvath, M., 207–208
Hosseini, K., 213
Hosseini, R., 211
Houa Moua, P., 49
Howard, A., 30
Howe, J., 239
Hubs, 192
Hulu, 103
Humane Society of the United States
    (HSUS), 4–5, 37, 164; fans of, 5;
    infographic to report results, 164–165;
    Million Fan campaign
    Facebook page, 6
Huyse, K., 175

I

Idealware, 148
IdeaStorm (Dell), 240
Impact, measuring, 140
Independent Federal Reserve, 153
Indianapolis Art Museum, 164–165

Influence, 102, 204–206; action, 216–217; identifying data already available, 215; measurement of, 215–219; and popularity, 205; search terms/key words used to find your site, 215–216; trust, 216–217

Influence score, calculating, 218

Influencers, 102, 192, 205

Influentials, use of term, 205

InMap, 193–194, 198

Innovation, 238

Institute for Public Relations, 148

instituteforpr.org, 148

Intangibles, 70–71

Integrated campaigns, *See* Multichannel integrated campaigns

Integrated, defined, 107

International Institute for Education, 22

InvisiblePeople.TV, 207–208

Island Collaboration's Fund, 243

J

Jackson, J., 227

Johnson, J., 139

K

Kam, H., 164

Kang, H., 178

Kang, S., 178

Kanter, B., 14, 21, 44, 101, 123, 148, 161, 164, 166, 176, 180, 188, 189, 198, 204, 205; on crawl, walk, run, fly (CWRF) hierarchy, 21–22; Devil's Tower, insight from, 167; Facebook Insights dashboard, 166–167; on mapping her LinkedIn network, 198

Kapin, A., 142

Kapoor, R., 32

Katie's Kat Shelter (KKS), 91–97, 128, 182; audiences, defined, 92; benchmarks, defined, 93; board of trustees, presentation of results to, 168; capital campaign, measurement of, 115–117; Cathy Cat Lover III, 233; data collection, selecting the right tool for, 96–97; donations, 95; high-level engagement metrics, 94–95; history of, 91; investment, defined, 92; kitten placement, 95; ladder of engagement, 91–97; low-level engagement metrics, 93–94; metrics, defined, 93; midlevel engagement metrics, 93–94; organizational goal, 92; possible influencers, 216; satisfaction/long-term engagement, measuring, 95–96; SMART objective, 92; transparency of, 232–233

kdpaine.blogs.com, 148

Kearny Street Workshop (KSW), 42–44; experiments with social media, 42–43; goals/metrics, 43; measurement efforts of, 43–44

Kelly, M., 180

Kelly, T., 74–75

Key performance indicators (KPIs), 31–32, 49–50, 209; priorities/goals, 50; Smithsonian Institute Archives (SIA), 161–162

Klout, 218

Knight Foundation, News Challenge, 243

Kred, 218

L

Ladder of engagement, 79; autism Speaks, 105–106; grist, 80–81, 84–87; Katie's Kat Shelter (KKS), 91–97; Surfrider Foundation, 85–86

Leadership, and data-informed culture, 32

Leadership Learning Community, 219

Learning in public, 224–225

Leonard, A., 188–191, 190

Leong, L., 42–43

Levit, S. D., 160

Levy, P., 241–242

Lewis, C., 4–5, 37; consultations, 6–7; as curator of social media metrics, 5–6; on participatory campaigns, 5–6

Lewis, E. St. E., 78

Lilly, J., 32

Lin, Y-H., 178

Lindberg, C., 54–55

LinkedIn, InMap, 193–194, 198

Livingston, G., 110

Logic model, 72–73

London National Theatre, 176–177

London Symphony Orchestra, use of social media data, 139

Longitudinal survey, 125

Lovett, J., 37

Low-level engagement behaviors, 90

Lublin, N., 32–33; on constant experimentation, 33

M

Macpherson, R., 120

Maddow, R., 160

Manual content analysis, 133

Market research lab, University of New Hampshire, 146

Mason, W. A., 206

Matching grants, 102, 104

McAuliffe, S., 225–226

McCorkindale, T., 178

McCrehan, A., 143–144

McMurchie, V., 49–50, 85, 86–87

Measure What Matters (Paine), 46

Measurement: and the Aha! moment, 151–169; correlations, 156–158; cost of, 144–147; defined, 7, 31; determining context of results, 182; fresh data, 156; getting started in, 56–57; iterative nature of, 159; pie charts, 161; power of, 41–57; as a process, 44–45; of relationships, 173–201; "So what?", use of, 155–156; tips for getting started in, 56–57; uses of, 31; using words/charts, 161

Measurement tools, 120–149; awareness, measuring, 123; content analysis tools, 120; and data collection, 121; educating yourself about, 148; longitudinal survey, 125; matching with objectives, 52; media content analysis, 131–138; omnibus survey, 126; polls, 125; preference, increasing, 125; relationships, improving, 125; selecting, 122; snapshot survey, 125; spreadsheets, 121, 147; survey tools, 120; surveys, conducting, 126–131; types of, 51; Web and social analytics/behavioral metrics, 139–143; Web and social analytics tools, 120

Media content analysis, 122, 131–138; Analysis Exchange, 147–148; authority, 134–135; conversation type, 136–137; elements coded for, 134; manual vs. automated, 133–134; media, selecting, 134–135; messages communicated, 136; selecting a monitor tool, 134; sources mentioned/quoted, 136; for USO, 138; visibility, 136

Meebo, 103

Melley, K., 54

Metrics: defining, 49–50; social fundraising, 110, 114–115

Michel, D., 132

Midlevel engagement behaviors, 90–91

Minimal mentions, 136

Minnesota's "Give to the Max Day," as largest online giving event, 101

Mobile applications/strategies, 141–144; measuring mobile, 142–143

MomsRising, 7–11; benchmarks, use of, 155; data used to refine strategic tactics, 10; decision making, 9; failure, measuring, 10; good measurement as good governance, 9; growth of, 7; incremental success, 10; letters to Congress, 19–20; measurement, 8–11; "Metrics Monday" staff meeting, 10, 156; operation of, 155; planning for success, with measurement, 9; policymakers, grabbing the attention of, 8; as poster child for networked nonprofits/nonprofit measurement, 7; rapid-response campaigns, 19; reports of social media results, 9; social change, used to define successes, 8; stories vs. statistics, 19–20; using data for effectiveness/efficiency, 9; value of measurement at every level of functioning, 11

Monterey Bay Aquarium, 164

Morino, M., 31

Mothers Against Drunk Driving (MADD), Aha! moment, 153

Mozilla, 32

Multichannel, defined, 107

Multichannel integrated campaigns, 107–115

Murphy, P., 105

Museum of History and Industry (MOHAI), 21

N

Name collection, cost of, 145

National Marrow Donor Program, 237

National Wildlife Federation, 207; network mapping, use of, 193; sticky notes/markers, use of, 199–201;

Neff, D. J., 87, 88–90

Negative tone, 135

Nelson, D., 101

Network Weaver Handbook (Holley), 188

Networked For Good, 100, 101, 107

Networked Nonprofit, The (Kanter/Fine), 14, 15, 17, 44, 188, 198

Networked nonprofits: alignment, 53–56; audiences, defining, 47–48; being and doing, 18; benchmarks, defining, 48–49; characteristics of, 17–19; crawl, walk, run, fly (CWRF) hierarchy, 20–25; data collection tools, selecting, 51–53; data-informed cultures, 17;

defined, 7, 15; experimentation/
experience, 17; goals, defining, 46–47;
inspiration, 17; leadership/roles/
structures, 18; levels of social media
practice:, 20; as masters of social media,
19; measurement, getting started in,
56–57; and measurement programs,
8–11; measurement steps for, 46–53;
metrics, defining, 49–50; and missions,
174; recognition of organization as part
of larger ecosystem of organizations/
individuals, 17; rise of, 13–25; social
culture, 18; social impact, 67–71; and
social media, 246; social networking
analysis (SNA), 188; time and costs,
defining, 50–51; transparency, 18; and
transparency, 221–234

Networks, 187–201; average path length,
195; clusters, 192; core, 191; ebb and
flow of, 15; edge/periphery, 192; hubs,
192; measuring the value of, 194–195

Neutral tone, 135

Newmark, C., 5

Ni, P., 222–223

Nielsen, J., 85

Nodes, 191

Nonprofits: balance of overreliance
on passion and over-fetishization
of data/analysis, 31; and informal
measurements, 7; keys to success, 7;
and social media, 19; and social media-
enabled networking, 7

Norris, S., 177

NTEN, 100, 121, 126, 243; *Change*
journal, 123; omnibus survey, 126;
Webinars, 148

O

Ocean Conservancy, 38

OE (organizational effectiveness)
grants, 225–226

Office of Social Innovation at the White
House, 233–234

Omnibus survey, 126

Omniture, 122, 140

100K Cheeks, 236–237; contribution of
ideas for, 237; crowdsourcing, 237–238;
"Give a Spit About Cancer" campaign,
237; measurement of the crowd,
237–238

Online measurement tools, 104

OpenIdeo, 237, 238

Optimizely, 104

O'Reilly Media, 30

Organizational culture, changing, 36

Organizational goals: expressing results
in terms of, 59–75; expressing value of
social media in terms of, 67

Ostrow, A., 176

Our Daily Bread (ODB), 61–62

P

Packard Foundation, 225–227

Paine, K. D., 137, 138, 146, 225, 227; Aha!
moment, 153–154; Aha! moment for
ASPCA relationship studies, 183; on
measurement, 160; measurement
steps for networked nonprofits, 46–53

Participation statistics, 195

Peer organizations, sharing dashboards
with, 163–164

Perception metrics, 218

Perrone, C. M., 87–88

Petersen, E., 30

Philanthropy and Social Investing Blueprint, 164

Philanthropy Program, at Hewlett Foundation, 224

Phone surveys, 126

Pie charts, 161

Piggyback survey, 126

Polls, 125, 129

Positive tone, 135

Preference, increasing, 125

Process outcomes, 70

Prominence, 135

PRWeb, 128

Q

Qualitative vs. quantitative research, 129

Qualtrics, 130, 183

Questionnaire, surveys, 145

R

Radian 6 tool, 132

Rawlins, B., 224–225, 228, 229

Razoo, 101

Redmond, S., 163

Reflection, 38

Reich, K., 70, 226

Relationships, 173–185; commitment, 180; communal, 180; components of, measuring, 180–183; control mutuality, 180; exchange, 180, 182; Grunig Relationship Survey, 178; improving, 125; measurement of, 183–184; and nonprofits, 174; revealed by engagement, 181–182; satisfaction, 180; and social media, 181; trust, 180; value of, 174–177

Relevance, influencers, 216

Reports: getting to the point, 160; use of, 151

Resonance, influencers, 217

Resource planning, 53

Return on investment (ROI), 50; defined, 62–63; expressed as percentage, 63; how to use, 62–67; improper use of term, 65–66; using to compare return on social media efforts, 63–65; "What's the ROI?" roadblock, 66

Roots of Change, 144

Roper, E., 205

Rose, A., 207

Ross, H., 121

Rowe-Finkbeiner, K., 7–8

Run stage, 24–25; data-informed culture, 35

S

Sachs, J., 208

Samuel, A., 51

San Francisco Gay Men 's Chorus, 44

Sanchez, M., 30

SAS, 183

Satisfying relationships, 180

Save the Children, 208

Scearce, D., 194, 225, 227

Scriba, D. F., 147

Seacoast Concert for a Cure, 63

SEARAC, 49

SeaWorld, relationships and crisis, 175

Self-selecting survey groups, 145

Sen, J., 120

Shared-cost survey, 126

Shaw, L., 108–109

Sheldrake, P., 204–205

Sherman, A., 239

Shneiderman, B., 192

Shue, A., 30

Singal, V., 236–237

Sirkin, M., 105–107

Sisco, H. F., 178

SMART objectives, 47, 49, 56, 148; setting, 111–112

Smith, A., 236

Smith, D., 163–164, 164

Smith, M. A., 192

Smithsonian Institute Archives (SIA), 161–162

Snapshot survey, 125

Snowball sample, defined, 128

Social change, 62

Social fundraising, 99–118; Autism Speaks, 104–107; benchmark, establishing, 113; big ask, defined, 110–111; campaigns, steps to, 111–115; charity:water (organization), 102–104; continuous ongoing metrics, sue of, 110–111; data supply, auditing, 113–114; defined, 99; measuring the contribution of specific tactics, 115; metrics, 110, 114–115; Minnesota's "Give to the Max Day" as largest online giving event, 101; Networked For Good, 101, 107; number of nonprofits using, 99; online platforms, 101; as part of multichannel integrated campaigns, 107–115; prioritizing stakeholders, 112–113; SMART objectives, setting, 111–112; steps to a well-measured campaign, 110; tools/techniques, 101–102; used with other fundraising activities, 111; value to a nonprofit, 100

Social impact, 67–71

Social media: alignment with organization program/communications goals, 62; investments in, 60; measuring influence on, 217–218; planning the values of, 68–69; thinking strategically about value of, 67; as valuable communication channel during natural disaster, 15

Social media measurement, 44, 54

Social Media Metrics Secrets (Lovett), 37

Social network mapping tools, 196–200; NodeXL (Excel plug-in), 196; TechSoup Global, 196–198

Social network, ties, 191; visualizations, 193

Social networking analysis (SNA), 188, 192–193; and strategy, 195

Social networks: basics of, 191–192; nodes, 191

Society for New Communications Research, 148

Soft results, See Intangibles

Solis, B., 205, 219

Solomon R. Guggenheim Museum, 163

Spelling, A., 30

Spreadsheets, 121, 147, 152–153

SPSS, 131, 183

Stacks, D., 125

Stakeholders, measuring who influences, 208–215

Stehle, V., 223–224

Story of Broke (film), 191

Story of Stuff project, 189–191; and feedback, 190

Stupa, D. W., 180

Success, measurement of, 60

Surfrider Foundation, 49; content, tracking, 87; ladder of engagement, 85–86; and measurement, 87; mission, 85

Survey tools, 120

SurveyMonkey, 122, 123, 130, 183

Surveys, 122, 183–184; analyzing results, 131; basic steps in conducting, 127–131; comparison of tools, 126; conducting, 126–131; controlling the cost of, 145; desired answers, defining, 129–130; fielding, 130–131; instrument, creating, 130; mail, 126–127; objectives for research, defining, 128; online, 126–127; phone, 126–127; questionnaire, 145; response to, 145; testing survey questions, 130; universe for survey, defining, 128–129; using to learn about audience content preference, 123

Susan G. Komen Foundation, and fund grants to Planned Parenthood, 231

T

Tangibles, 70

Target audience behavior, changes in, 139

Technorati, 122, 135, 211

TechSoup Global: mapping of its network, 196–198; social network analysis map of, 197

Tenby, S., 196–198

themeasurementstandard.com, 148

Theory of change, 71, 72–75; defined, 72; developing, 74; SMART objectives, articulation of, 72

Thomas, S., 38

Thorp, I., 31

Time and costs, defining, 50–51

Tipping a market, 205

Tipping Point (Gladwell), 205

Tone, categories of, 135

Traackr, 216; keywords used to identify influencers in, 210

Transparency, 221–234; accountability, 229–230; assessing, 229–232; benefits of, 225–228; and commitment, 225; compared to other measurement challenges, 228; defined, 223–224; disclosure, 223; and efficiency, 225; efficiency, measuring improvements in, 228; and exposure of an organization's weaknesses, 224; GreatNonprofits, 222–223; learning in public, 224–225; measurement components, 229; measuring benefits of, 228–232; mistrust, 225; and participation, 229; questionnaire, 229–230; and satisfaction, 225; secrecy, 229–230; substantial information, provision of, 229; transition to, 234; and trust, 225; trust, measuring improvements in, 228

Trudel, M., 120

Trudel MacPherson and Sen Associates, 120

Trust, 180; and influence,
216–217
Trust, measuring improvements, 228
TweetDeck, 64–65
Tweetlevel, 218
Twitalzyer, 135, 218
Twitter, 102, 135, 139, 148, 206, 216;
and crowdsourcing, 239; stories vs.
statistics, 20
TypePad, 122

U

Uncultured Project, 208
UNICEF, 31
United Nations High Commissioner for
Refugees (UNHCR), 208–209
University of California, San Francisco
(UCSF) Challenge for Children,
108–109
University of New Hampshire, market
research lab, 146
USA for UNHCR, 209;
after-action review, 214;
campaign activities, 213
USO, Aha! moment, 153

V

Veneet, S., 237
Vicks, M., 179
Visibility, 135–136

W

Walk stage, 23–24; data-informed
culture, 35
Washington, D.C., Give to the Max Day
event (November 2011), 110
Watts, D., 206
WeAreVisible (Web site), 208
Web and social analytics tools, 120
Web Trends, 140
Webtrends, 122
Weiner, A., 176
Weiner, G., 32
Weldon, A., 49
Why the Power of the Crowd Is Driving the
Future of Business (Howe), 239
Wicked problems, defined, 207
Wikipedia, 78
WinCross, 131, 183
Witherington, T., 44
WordTracker, 216

Y

Yates, D., 72–73
Young, P., 102–104
YouTube, 148

Z

Zimmerman, J., 82
Zoomerang, 130
19